Social Security Law in Bulgaria

Social Security Law in Bulgaria

Vassil Mrachkov

This book was originally published as a monograph in the International Encyclopaedia of Laws/Social Security Law.

Founding Editor: Roger Blanpain
General Editor: Frank Hendrickx
Volume Editor: Willy van Eeckhoutte

Wolters Kluwer

Published by:
Kluwer Law International B.V.
PO Box 316
2400 AH Alphen aan den Rijn
The Netherlands
E-mail: lrs-sales@wolterskluwer.com
Website: www.wolterskluwer.com/en/solutions/kluwerlawinternational

Sold and distributed by:
Wolters Kluwer Legal & Regulatory U.S.
7201 McKinney Circle
Frederick, MD 21704
United States of America
E-mail: customer.service@wolterskluwer.com

ISBN 978-94-035-0756-9

e-Book: ISBN 978-94-035-0936-5
web-PDF: ISBN 978-94-035-0946-4

The Author

Professor Vassil Mrachkov was born in 1934 in Brachlian, Bourgas district, Bulgaria. He studied Law at the 'Saint Kliment Ohridski' University, Sofia from 1952 to 1957, receiving his Master's in Law in 1957 and a PhD in Law (Sofia) in 1963. Prof. Mrachkov received his *agrégé* in Higher Education in 1969. He was a research associate and Associate Professor in Labour Law in the Institute of Legal Sciences at the Bulgarian Academy of Sciences from 1962 to 1973 and Director of the Institute from 1982 to 1989, and has been a professor since 1980. He became a Doctor of Sciences in 1985. He has been a professor of Labour Law and Social Security Law at the 'Saint Kliment Ohridski' University, Sofia, since 1981. Since 2000, he has been teaching Labour Law and Social Security Law at the 'Paisii Hilendarski' University, Plovdiv. He is Doctor honoris causa of Sofia University 'St. Kliment Ohridski'.

From 1995 to 1997 and 2001 to 2005 he has been a Chairman of the Consultative Legislative Council by the National Assembly. He is Honorary President of the Bulgarian National Society of Labour Law and Social Security Law.

Prof. Mrachkov has also been actively involved in international matters. He was an International Civil Servant with the International Labour Organization, Geneva from 1973 to 1979. From 1986 to 1992, he has been a Member of the United Nations (UN) Committee on Economic, Social and Cultural Rights. He is former president of the Bulgarian National Association of Labour Law and Social Security Law and member of the Executive Committee of the International Society of Labour Law and Social Security. In 1993, he was a visiting professor at the Catholic University of Leuven, Belgium.

Prof. Mrachkov has written numerous books in Bulgarian, as well as numerous essays and articles in Bulgarian, French, English, Russian, German and Spanish for Bulgarian and international journals.

His national monograph on Bulgarian Labour Law was first published in 1979, and updated since in 1995, 2001, 2011, 2014 and 2017, and his national monograph on Bulgarian Social Security Law – in 1999, 2006, 2011, 2014 and 2017 by Kluwer Law International.

The Author

Table of Contents

List of Abbreviations

APC	Administrative Procedure Code
BSP	Bulgarian Socialist Party
BGN	Bulgarian Lev
CD	Civil Department
CEDB	Citizens for European Development of Bulgaria
CIS	Commonwealth of Independent States
CITUB	Confederation of Independent Trade Unions in Bulgaria
CL	'Podkrepa' Confederation of Labour
CMC	Consultative Medical Commission
D	Decision
DPSC	Decree of the Plenum of the Supreme Court
EA	Employment Agency
EPL	Employment Promotion Law
EU	European Union
FSC	Financial Supervision Commission
HIL	Health Insurance Law
HL	Health Law
IC	Insurance Code
ILO	International Labour Organization
LC	Labour Code of 1986, as amended
LSSSB	Law on State Social Security Budget
Lv.	Leva (Bulgarian currency)
LC of 1951	Labour Code of 1951, repealed
MP	Member of Parliament
NATO	North Atlantic Treaty Organization
NFC	National Frame Contract
NHIPCDO	National Health Insurance Pay Cash Desk Office
NII	National Insurance Institute
NMEC	National Medical Expert Commission
OJ	Official Journal

List of Abbreviations

PSC	Plenum of the Supreme Court
RHIPCDO	Regional Health Insurance Pay Cash Desk Office
SBL	State Budget Law
TFEU	Treaty on the Functioning of the European Union
SIC	Social Insurance Code
TMEC	Territorial Medical Expert Commission
UDF	Union of Democratic Forces
UF	Unemployment Fund
UNESCO	United Nations Educational, Scientific and Cultural Organization
USD	US Dollar

General Introduction

§1. Social and Economic Background

1. The Republic of Bulgaria is situated in the south-east of Europe, on the Balkan Peninsula. It has a territory of 111,000 km^2. In 2021, from 7 September until 10 October, the National Statistical Institute took a census of the country's population. The official data of the census will be announced at the end of 2021. As at 31 December 2020, the total number of the population is 6,916,548, out of them 3,349,715 being men, and 3,566,833 being women.[1] To the east, Bulgaria borders the Black Sea; to the north, Romania; to the west, Serbia and Macedonia; and to the south, Greece and Turkey.

2. The political system was established by the New Constitution of 12 July 1991. Bulgaria is a unitary State with local self-government. No autonomous territorial formations are admitted (Article 2 of the Constitution). The functions and the parameters of the State bodies are defined on the basis of the principle of separation of powers (Article 8 of the Constitution). Article 1, paragraph 1 of the Constitution establishes a parliamentarian republic as the form of the State.

3. After the collapse of the totalitarian regime on 10 November 1989, the country started its slow and painful transition from totalitarian to democratic social system and from centralized planned economy, based on State property, towards market economy based exclusively on private property. As a whole, this process ended in late 2004. This transition was characterized by two particularities. One of them was common for all the former socialist countries of Central and Eastern Europe. It consisted of the unique complexity of the transition. Such a complex transition, which was both a political and economic one, had neither never been made so far – a transition from totalitarianism to democratic organization of society and from centralized, wholly nationalized planned economy to market economy – not there was any historical experience in carrying out this transition. There was another particularity, which was characteristic of Bulgaria. The transition was carried out in a situation of severe political, economic, social and moral crisis of society. This slowed down the realization of the transition, brought about greater difficulties in conducting it and gave a specific hue to the country's social and economic background. These were its major points.

1. Statisticheski Spravochnik na Republika Bulgaria [*Republic of Bulgaria – Statistical Reference Book*] 21 (National Statistical Institute 2021).

4. Over the past thirty-two years, the country has undergone profound economic, social and political changes.

5. Since the beginning of 1990 output has dropped sharply. Gross domestic product has decreased by approximately 50% in the first eight years. The former market relations broke up with the collapse of the Comecon system, traditional markets were lost, but no new ones were created. The national economy turned out to be highly dependent on the former Soviet Union. The two basic branches of national economy – industry and agriculture[2] – were severely affected.

6. The change of ownership and the transformation of State property into private property were in delay. Although the Privatization Law was passed as early as the beginning of 1992 (promulgated in the OJ, No. 38 of 1992), its numerous amendments were to follow while the actual steps in privatization were few. Privatization gathered speed in the summer of 1997. However, in 1998 it was slow again.[3]

7. Since the beginning of 1999 privatization has gathered speed again. Its rapid development continued until the end of the legislature of the 38th National Assembly in June 2001, under the rule of the Union of Democratic Forces (UDF), as well as after the parliamentary elections for the 39th National Assembly in June 2001, under the rule of 'Simeon the Second' National Movement (July 2001–July 2005), on the grounds of the new Privatization and Post-privatization Supervision Law (promulgated in the OJ, No. 28 of 19 March 2002, amended). As a result of the accelerated development of privatization throughout the period 1999–2005, over 80% of the State-owned property was privatized by September 2005. This pushed forward the process of economic reforms and the introduction of market economy in the country, and as a result thereof in late 2003 the European Union (EU) recognized Bulgaria as a country with functioning market economy. However, along with its positive aspects, the speedy conduct of a large part of the 1999–2005 privatization had its negative aspects as well: the absence of sufficient transparency in conducting it, the sale of several major State-owned objects at prices which were unfavourable to Bulgarian State, and so on.

8. In 1996, a severe crisis occurred in the financial and banking system. In the period 1991–1995, dozens of private banks were hastily set up without sufficient control by the Central Bank. Citizens deposited their savings at a temptingly high interest, and later they could not withdraw their savings because it turned out that the banks did not have enough cash. This brought about the bankruptcy of fifteen banks and the property interests of hundreds of thousands of people were injured. Citizens lost confidence in the national banking system. The whole financial system

---

2. *Human Development Report Bulgaria 1997* 8 (UNDP 1997); 'Statisticheski Spravochnik na Republika Bulgaria' [*Republic of Bulgaria – Statistical Reference Book*] 89, 114–126 (National Statistical Institute 1997).
3. A. Baklova, *We Sell Factories for One Lev*, *Sega* [*Now*] *Newspaper*, 15 May 1998.

of the country collapsed. The currency reserve of the country fell to the critical threshold of US Dollars (USD) 518 million.[4]

9. In these years, the country was taken up by high inflation. It reached 3,000% over the past eight years and in 1997 alone it was 579%. In December 1996–January 1997, the whole country underwent the shock of hyperinflation. There was a sharp devaluation of the national currency and at the end of January 1997 it reached extreme values: USD 1 was exchanged for Bulgarian Lev (BGN) 3,000.

10. The severe economic crisis was accompanied by a sharp rise in the social tension and political destabilization. This led to the dissolution of the National Assembly, and early parliamentary elections for the National Assembly (38th legislature) were held on 19 April 1997. The former opposition – the United Democratic Forces – won an impressive victory while the ruling Democratic Left suffered a serious defeat.[5]

11. In this serious economic and political situation in the country, the relations with the international financial institutions – the International Monetary Fund and the World Bank – became more complicated as well, these being institutions whose credits and help Bulgaria has been relying on since 1990. After long negotiations, which began as early as 1996, in the new economic and political situation, a radical decision was reached: on 1 July 1997, the Currency Board was introduced. Bulgarian national currency (the leva) was tied to the German mark in the ratio of DM 1 to BGN 1,000. Later on, when Euro was introduced in the EU on 1 January 2001, the Bulgarian Lev turned out to be tied to it as it was the currency which replaced the German mark. The ratio of the national currency to the Euro has remained almost unchanged (as at 28 February 2014, EUR 1 was BGN 1.95).

12. The former regime – the one before 10 November 1989 – was characterized by full employment of the active population. By the way, this is one of the points that even now some strata of the population feel social nostalgia for. This has to be evaluated sensibly with the benefit of hindsight.

The cardinal tenet of employment policy after the Second World War was a commitment to full employment. This was achieved – if the absolute number of employed persons in 1946 was 629,204; in 1985, it was 4,588,530 – that is about seven times more than forty years before. It is true that this full employment had some very important particularities: it was neither sufficiently free (because of the existing limitations in the free movement of working people from one enterprise to another) nor productive because of the general low-level of labour productivity.

But, all people were able to work, had their jobs, remuneration and standard of living even if it was modest in comparison with European standards. In this sense, the existing full employment was more social than effective.

4. *Human Development Report Bulgaria 1997* 9 (UNDP, 1997).
5. Decision No. 25 of the Central Election Commission dated 23 Apr. 1997 for announcing the results of the elections of 19 Apr. 1997 for the National Assembly – OJ, No. 34 of 1997.

Since 1990, a significant deterioration in employment and a sharp spurt of unemployment has taken place because of the massive fall in economic output. The number of unemployed persons in 1991 was 419,123 (12%), in 1992 – 576,893 (14%), in 1993 – 720,348 (17%), in March 1998 – 540,000 (14%),[6, 7] in March 2001 – 725,000 (21.2%). Since that time the situation has improved considerably: in December 2002 the number of the unemployed decreased to 530,000 (16.3%), in 2003 – to 500,000 (13.5%), in December 2004 – to 450,000 (12.2%), in November 2005 – to 334,000 (10%),[8] in December 2010 – to 342,000 (9.2%),[9] in January 2011 – to 9.7%,[10] in September 2013 – to 12.4%,[11] and in October 2016 – to 270,000 (7.8%).[12]

13. Healthcare is also going through a severe crisis. The free public healthcare that has existed since 1951 – for fifty-five years – pursuant to Article 52, paragraph 1 of the new Constitution was replaced by the citizens' right to health insurance that guarantees accessible medical care and free medical services under the terms and in the due course stipulated by the law. However, the problem is that the transition to the health insurance system has been underway for the last fifteen years. Unfortunately, up to the present, this transition has only destroyed the old system of free health services, brought about a serious crisis in healthcare and deranged the system that existed in the past without the new system of healthcare having been established. And it is the ordinary citizens who need medical care that suffer most of all from that.

14. In recent years, there was a sharp drop in the standard of living of most strata of society. About 50% of the population has great difficulty in satisfying everyday needs of food, clothing, heating, lighting and other similar bare necessities of life. Apart from that, poverty takes clearly expressed regional and ethnic dimensions. It is greater in the villages than in the towns and greater among the Turkish and Gypsy population than among the Bulgarian one.[13]

15. Since late 2002 there has been a general upsurge in economy. The amount of foreign investments increased, and as at 31 December 2009 it exceeded USD 25 billion.[14] In 2008 the increase of the gross domestic product of the country was 6% but – after the 2009 crisis – in 2013 it is expected to be only 0.2%.[15] In September

6. Statisticheski Godishnik na Republika Bulgaria [*Statistical Yearbook of the Republic of Bulgaria*] 72 (Science and Art Publishing House 1989).
7. Statisticheski Spravochnik 1997, 38–50; *Troud* [*Labour*] *Newspaper*, 20 Apr. 1998.
8. Statisticheski Spravochnik 2010, 47.
9. *Troud [Labour] Newspaper*, 14 Feb. 2011.
10. *Troud [Labour] Newspaper*, 30 Dec. 2010.
11. *Pressa Newspaper*, 5 Oct. 2015.
12. *Troud [Labour] Newspaper*, 28 Oct. 2016.
13. *Human Development Report Bulgaria* 204, 34–45.
14. Statisticheski Spravochnik 2010, 108–112.
15. Statisticheski Spravochnik 2013, 16.

2005, Bulgaria was included for the first time in the UN list of the fifty-seven most intensively developing countries in the world, although it takes the 52nd position in this classification.[16]

16. Foreign investments, which used to play a significant role in the provision of the country's ascending economic development in the preceding years (*see supra* paragraph 15), suffered a slump in 2009, when the crisis came on the country. At the end of 2009, these investments amounted to USD 3 billion, in 2010 and 2011 – USD 1 billion, in 2012 – USD 800 million only, and in the first half of 2013 – only about USD 500 million. The economic growth slowed down as well: from 6% in 2008, it was only 0.2% in 2012, and in 2013 it is expected to be about 0.9%. The country has not gotten out of the crisis yet.[17]

17. The political situation in the country was stabilized. After the pre-term parliamentary elections were held in April 1997 (*see supra* paragraph 10), in the following twelve years the three legislatures of the 38th (1997–2001), 39th (2001–2005) and 40th (2005–2009) National Assembly completed their full mandates of four years each. In view of the multiparty system existing in the country, the change of the ruling majority through free, democratic, and fair parliamentary elections is something normal. In 1997–2001, the period of the 38th National Assembly, the majority belonged to the UDF; while in the period 2001–2005, the 39th National Assembly, it belonged to the 'Simeon the Second' National Movement in coalition with the Movement for Rights and Freedoms; in the period 2005–2009, the 40th National Assembly, it belonged to the three-party (trilateral) coalition, namely the Bulgarian Socialist Party (BSP), the 'Simeon the Second' National Movement and the Movement for Rights and Freedoms; and in the period since the end of July 2009, the 41st National Assembly, it belongs to the Political Party 'Citizens for European Development of Bulgaria' (CEDB) supported in the beginning by the Blue Coalition (the UDF and Democrats for Strong Bulgaria) and by the Political Party 'Ataka' ('Assault') during the first two years of the 41st legislature. The 41st National Assembly, which was elected at the parliamentary elections in July 2009, was unable to complete its four-year mandate in July 2013. Due to the large-scale protests and the demonstrations of discontent, the government of the CEDB political party, chosen by this legislature, filed its resignation at the end of February 2013 and, owing thereto, early parliamentary elections for the 42nd National Assembly were scheduled and held on 12 May 2013 (*see infra* paragraph 18).

18. On 12 May 2013, the parliamentary elections for the 42nd National Assembly were held in the country. The Assembly was made up of 240 MPs from the following political parties and coalitions: CEDB – 97; Coalition for Bulgaria – 84;

16. *Troud* [*Labour*] *Newspaper*, 5 Sep. 2005.
17. Statisticheski Spravochnik 2016, 126.

Movement for Rights and Freedoms – 36; Assault (Ataka) – 23.[18] On 29 May 2013, the 42nd National Assembly elected a coalition government, consisting of representatives of the Coalition for Bulgaria and the Movement for Rights and Freedoms. The 42nd National Assembly was unable to finish its mandate. Some of its decisions, for instance, the election of a President of the State Agency for National Security, have drawn wide social disapproval and protests. Difficulties have also arisen in ensuring quorum for holding the regular parliamentary meetings, this being due to the opposition parties' refusal to attend the meetings of the Parliament. In August 2014, the coalition partner 'Movement for Rights and Freedoms' left the governing two-party coalition, and this necessitated the dissolution of the National Assembly and the holding of early parliamentary elections. They were held on 5 October 2014. The newly elected 43rd National Assembly has a mandate of four years and is currently acting. It consists of 240 deputies from the following political parties having the mentioned number of deputies: Political Party 'CEDB' – 84; BSP 'Left Bulgaria' (a coalition) – 39; Movement for Rights and Freedoms – 38; Reformative Block (a coalition) – 23; Patriotic Front (a coalition) – 19; 'Bulgaria without Censorship' (a coalition) – 15; 'Assault' ('Ataka') – 11; 'Alternative for Bulgarian Revival' – 11. A coalition government was formed with the participation of four political parties: the CEDB, the Reformative Block, the Patriotic Front and the 'Alternative for Bulgarian Revival'. The 'Alternative for Bulgarian Revival' party left the coalition government in May 2016; however, the government composed of the other three parties continues its mandate.

19. In recent years, Bulgaria has entered the European and Euro-Atlantic structures and organizations. Along with its membership in a number of world organizations – UN (1955), International Labour Organization (ILO) (1920), United Nations Educational, Scientific and Cultural Organization (UNESCO) (1948), World Health Organization (1948) and other specialized organizations of the UN, Bulgaria is also a member of the Council of Europe (1992), since 1 May 2004 it has been a member of North Atlantic Treaty Organization (NATO), and since 1 January 2007, Bulgaria has been a member of the EU.

(a) The period 2018–2021, and especially its second half (2020–2021) – the political party CEDB having ruled continuously for twelve consecutive years – is characterized by growing discontent among numerous social strata as a result of poverty, acute deficit of democracy, the feeling of corruption on the high levels of power and the like. Since the beginning of the year 2020, the discontent has been finding its expression in spontaneous mass manifestations of citizens in the centre of the capital city Sofia, in front of the buildings of the Council of Ministers and the Parliament, with chants 'Resignation! Resignation of the government!', 'Mafia! Mafia!' and the like, and with the participation of tens of thousands of citizens. There were such manifestations in all the district towns of the country, as well. Since June, a lot of young people have taken part in these

18. These data are quoted from: Central Electoral Commission, 'Bulletin for the results of the elections for MPs on 12 May 2013' (Central Electoral Commission 2013), 9; Central Electoral Commission, 'Resolution No. 220 of 2013' (Central Electoral Commission 2013), 14.

manifestations, mainly European university students and thousands of Bulgarian citizens working abroad – in Germany, France, Italy, Spain, Holland, Greece – who came back to spend their vacation in the Motherland. There were severe clashes between protesters and policemen; the force used by the police exceeded the limits allowed and permitted by law, as evidenced by the records made by hidden cameras on the square and 'under the columns' of the Council of Ministers. These records were shown on television during the first caretaker government and were followed by investigation activities – disciplinary and criminal proceedings were instigated against policemen, and some of them were dismissed. On 4 April 2021, parliamentary elections for the 45th National Assembly were held, and CEDB won again the greatest number of seats, yet highly insufficient to form a government, and none of the other five parliamentary parties was willing to enter into a coalition with CEDB. Consequently, after two months of unsuccessful negotiations on the formation of a coalition government, and one month of sittings of the new 45th National Assembly, the latter was dissolved by the President of the Republic and new elections were scheduled for the 46th National Assembly. These elections took place on 15 July 2021. This time the newly formed party 'There is Such a People' won the greatest number of seats; however, after lengthy negotiations, this party did not manage to form a coalition government, and, due to that, new parliamentary elections were scheduled to be held on 14 November for the 47th National Assembly, and presidential elections on 14 November 2021 (first round) and 21 November 2021 (second round in case of a run-off).

The results of the parliamentary elections held for the 47th National Assembly and the distribution of seats are: seven parties enter the Parliament, and the seats therein are distributed as follows: Political party 'We Continue the Change' – 67; Coalition CEDB-UDF – 59; Movement for Rights and Freedoms – 34; BSP – 26; 'There is Such a People' – 25; Democratic Bulgaria – 16; and Party 'Vazrazhdane' ('Revival') – 13. Negotiations for the formation of a coalition government are forthcoming. As for the presidential elections – for President and Vice President for the next five years – two couples competed: the team of the acting President and Vice President Rumen Radev and Iliana Yotova, nominated by an initiative committee and supported by the party 'We Continue the Change', BSP, 'There is Such a People', and the team of Anastas Gerdzhikov and Nevena Mateva, nominated by an initiative committee and supported by the coalition CEDB-UDF. The run-off on 21 November 2021 was won by the team of Rumen Radev and Iliana Yotova with 66.7% against the team of Anastas Gerdzhikov with 31.8%.[19]

(b) The Covid-19 pandemic, which hit the world, took hold of Bulgaria at the beginning of March 2020. State of emergency was declared in the country through a Law of the National Assembly under Article 84, item 12 of the Constitution, and the state of emergency continued until 12 May 2020. The amendments and supplements to Article 63 of the Health Law of 13 May, which took effect on 14 May 2020 (promulgated in the OJ, No. 44 of 2020), laid down a

19. *24 Hours Newspaper*, 23 Nov. 2021.

new regulation which is still effective during the periodic waves. The new regulation introduced the so-called emergency pandemic situation in the event that an immediate danger is posed to the citizens' life and health as a result of epidemic spread of any of thirteen contagious diseases including Covid-19 that are listed exhaustively. This 'situation' is a specific one and represents a milder form when compared to the state of emergency. The said regulation provides for bearable restrictions: mandatory wearing of masks indoors (shops, cinemas, theatres, restaurants, buses and other means of public transport and the like), mandatory distancing of 1.5 m between people, sharp rise in mass performance of online activities, such as training given by educational institutions, steep increase in work from home on the part of workers, employees and civil servants wherever possible, depending on the scope of activities of enterprises and organizations, introduction of alternate periods of duty time with one or two employees working at their workplaces, and the like.

Actually, an emergency pandemic situation is not a state of emergency within the meaning of Article 84, item 12 of the Constitution, as the latter is declared through a Law of the National Assembly at the proposal of the President or the Council of Ministers. This position was also taken by the Constitutional Court in its D. No. 10 of 23 July 2020 on constitutional case No. 7 of 2020. The state of emergency presupposes a higher percentage of infected people and deaths and a more severe condition of the country's internal situation. When a state of emergency is imposed, the restrictions on citizens' rights under Article 57, paragraph 3 of the Constitution are greater and stricter and might result in complete closure of the activities of enterprises, institutions and organizations, the imposition of a curfew and the like. The restrictions in a declared emergency epidemic situation are more moderate ones. In mid-September 2021, when the country's epidemic situation deteriorated considerably, emergency epidemic situation was declared by the executive power bodies – the health authorities and the administrative ones – in three steps: 1) the epidemic situation evaluation made by the Chief State Health Inspector; 2) proposal made by the Chief State Health Inspector to the Minister of Health; 3) proposal made by the Minister of Health to the Council of Ministers, the latter being the competent State body that is entitled to declare an emergency epidemic situation in the country. Such situation was declared in May 2020, and, after the deterioration in mid-September 2021, more severe requirements were imposed, namely wearing masks, transition to online training in elementary and secondary schools with rotation of classes and, at the discretion of the academic boards, online training in higher-education institutions, depending on the epidemic situation both in the country as a whole and in the town in which the higher school (university, institute, etc.) is located.

(c) In the period 2018–2021, numerous amendments and supplements were made to the Social Security Code: twenty-eight during the preceding four years, or an average of seven per year. In the year 2021, they are four, which is fewer because during the predominant part of the year 2021 the country was ruled by two caretaker governments appointed by the President of the Republic, and the legislative body – the National Assembly – was dissolved, and there was no parliamentary legislative activity taking place. After the parliamentary elections of

14 November 2021, the parliamentary political parties are expected to be able to form a regular government, and the National Assembly is supposed to resume its traditional legislative activity and to exercise parliamentary supervision over the activity of the newly formed government.

§2. Historical Background

20. The Bulgarian State was formed in 681 and based on the Proto-Bulgarian and Slav tribes that inhabited ancient Moesia. It existed as an independent State until 1018. At that time it came under Byzantine rule from which it freed itself in 1187; thereafter, Bulgaria continued its independent existence up to the end of the fourteenth century. In 1396 the country came under Ottoman domination. It was not liberated until 1878 as a result of the 1878 Russo-Turkish War, and then embarked on the road to free development.

21. On 1 March 1940, during the Second World War, the ruling Government of Bulgaria joined the Trilateral Treaty as an ally of Germany. It was a step with far-reaching consequences.

22. After the Second World War, on 9 September 1944, a socialist system with a proletarian dictatorship was established in Bulgaria. The country was placed under the direct political influence of the former Soviet Union. Radical changes were introduced into society. Political pluralism and parliamentary democracy were gradually abolished (1944–1946). Marxism-Leninism was adopted and proclaimed as the official State ideology. The leading force in the State and society was the Bulgarian Communist Party which enjoyed the monopoly of power. Private property was expropriated (1945–1947) and free private initiative was eliminated. A centrally planned and administered economy on the basis of State ownership was established. This was legally consolidated by the Constitution adopted on 4 December 1947, which was subsequently replaced by a new Constitution on 16 May 1971. The political foundations of both the Constitutions of 1947 and of 1971 were the political ideas and decisions of the Bulgarian Communist Party. This development of the country lasted until the ousting of T. Zhivkov – former General Secretary of the Central Committee of the Bulgarian Communist Party and former President of the State's Council – by reformers in the Communist Party on 10 November 1989.

23. A period of profound political changes leading to political pluralism and democratization began in the country on 10 November 1989. The UDF was created as an anti-communist coalition which rapidly grew to form the first political force opposing the Bulgarian Socialist (former Communist) Party (BSP). Since 1990 economic changes leading to market economy also started. However, their fulfilment ran slowly and painfully. In 1992 Bulgaria became a Member of the Council of Europe and since 1 February 1995 received the status of associated country to the EU.

24. The social security in Bulgaria begins after the Liberation of Bulgaria from Ottoman domination in 1878 (*see supra*). The first legislative Acts were connected with pension insurance of State employees. These Acts are based on Article 166 of the Tirnovo Constitution of 16 April 1879 according to which – 'The officials who hold their office by appointment of the government are entitled to acquire a pension, the basis and amount thereof being determined under specific laws.' Thus, in the period 1888–1915, several pension laws were consecutively adopted: the Teachers' Pension Law of 1957, as amended (PL) of 28 December 1888, the Civil Department Clerks' and Employees' PL of 15 December 1891, the Elective Institutions Employees' PL of 21 May 1915, and so on. These laws regulate the old-age pensions of the respective categories of civil servants as well as the terms under which the pensions are granted.[20]

25. In 1918 the first social security law on employees' insurance against accident and general sickness was adopted. The law is grounded on the Bismarckian approach to pension insurance. It introduces employees' mandatory insurance against industrial accident and general sickness. The law provides a legal definition of an industrial accident: any injury that has occurred as a result of doing work and has caused the employee's incapacity for work or his/her death. The law provides for the payment of temporary incapacity benefit for no more than twenty-six weeks of incapacity caused by an industrial accident or general sickness.[21]

26. The next major step was taken in the 1920s. In 1924 the social insurance law was adopted. It introduced mandatory insurance against accident, general sickness, maternity, disability or old age for all employees in public and private enterprises and establishments and created the Social Insurance General Fund. The law provided for payment of benefit in case of both temporary incapacity for work caused by the occurrence of social risks insured against (accident, illness, maternity) and temporary incapacity for work (disability, old age and death).

The adoption of the Law on Unemployment Insurance and Employment in 1925 was an important point in the development of social security law. This Law introduced mandatory insurance against unemployment for all employees, seamen, civil servants aged 15–60 (Articles 28–34'a'). It provided for payment of unemployment benefit for twenty-six weeks from the Unemployment Special Account of the Social Insurance Fund (Articles 35–42).[22]

27. In 1941 the Social Security Institute Law was passed. This is an organizational law, which regulated the administration and financial structure of social insurance in the country. The Law provided for the establishment of the Social Security Single National Fund. This fund had separate accounts for the various types of

20. Iv. Katzarov, *Social Security of Employees* 61 (Science and Art Publishing House 1957).
21. I. Zlatinchev, *The Struggle for Labour Legislation in Bulgaria 1878–1944* 173–182 (Profizdat, 1961).
22. L. Radoilski, *Labour Law. Historical Development* 192 (Science and Art Publishing House 1957).

insured social risks: general sickness, accident, maternity, disability, death, unemployment and the benefits in case of occurrence of the respective risk were paid out of these separate accounts.[23]

28. The Social Security Law of 1949 was an important stage in the development of social security after the Second World War. It systematized and codified in one law all the provisions of social security – both temporary and permanent (pension) ones. It regulated all the basic points of social security: administration, financing, scope of insured persons, mandatory nature of social insurance, various types of insurance – general sickness, maternity, industrial accident, disability, old age, death, different types of pensions, family allowances. The administration of the whole system of social security was realized by the Social Security Institute. This law was operative for a short time: it was repealed by the Labour Code of 9 November 1951.[24]

29. Along with labour relations, the Labour Code of 1951 dealt in its Part III with the employees' social insurance. It regulated both the general points of social security (the scope of insured persons, the insured social risks, the insurance contributions, etc.) and the types of insurance benefits: (a) the temporary incapacity benefit; (b) pensions – permanent incapacity pension; old-age pension; disability pension and survivors' pensions.[25]

30. In 1957 the pension provisions were taken out from the Labour Code and they were set as a separate law – the PL. It codified all the legal provisions concerning the old-age pensions, disability pensions, social pensions, special merits pensions and survivors' pensions. Its provisions concern the pensions of all individuals: employees, persons dealing with trade, freelance practitioners, and so on. It was operative until the end of 1999, when it was repealed and replaced by the Social Insurance Code (SIC) (*see infra* paragraph 42), which came into force on 1 January 2000 and is still operative now.[26]

31. The Labour Code of 1986 regulated only the labour relations, while the regulation of social security was left over to the Social Security Bill, which was under preparation at that time. Thus, the legislator expressed his/her basic notion of separating social security law from labour law and setting up social security law as a separate branch of the legal system.[27] Although no such law has been adopted so far since the mid-1980s social security law has developed as a separate branch of effective law and since the beginning of the 1990s it is taught as an obligatory legal discipline in the Faculties of Law.

---

23. *Ibid.*
24. L. Radoilski, *Labour Law: Historical Development*, 214–215; Iv. Katzarov, *Social Insurance of Employees*, 64–65.
25. L. Radoilski, *Labour Law of the People's Republic of Bulgaria* 628–723 (Science and Art Publishing House 1957).
26. V. Mrachkov, *Social Security Law* 69–71 (Sibi Publishing House 6th ed. 2013).
27. V. Mrachkov, *The Separation of Social Security as an Autonomous Branch of the Legal System*, Pravna Missal Rev. 1, 10 25 (1986).

32. The increase in the number of unemployed at the end of 1989 brought about specific provisions for unemployment as a separate social risk. In the beginning, the provisions were contained in Regulation No. 57 of the Council of Ministers dated 5 December 1989 (promulgated in the OJ, No. 96 of 1989), which underwent many amendments.[28] At the end of 1997, a separate Protection against Unemployment and Employment Promotion Law (EPL) was adopted (promulgated in the OJ, No. 120 of 1997). It regulated unemployment in detail as being a separate social risk. The Law took effect on 1 January 1998. At the end of 2001 it was repealed, and the regulation of the unemployment risk is now contained in Article 54'a'–54'h' of the SIC (*see infra* paragraph 42).

33. In May 1998, the Health Insurance Law (HIL) was adopted. This is the first autonomous law in this field. It regulates the health insurance of citizens as a part of their social insurance. It introduces mandatory and voluntary health insurance, specifies the scope of provided medical care, its financing and the due health insurance contributions, and so on. The Law was promulgated in the OJ, No. 70 of 19 June 1998 and became effective on 23 June 1998. The health insurance system introduced by this Law will be considered later (*see infra*, Part III).

34. In 2004 the Health Law (HL) was adopted. It regulates the organizational matters connected with the protection of citizens' health. This law established the national healthcare system, the health protection activities, and so on. It repealed the People's Health Law of 1973. The adoption of the Health Law completed the health legislation reform (*see infra* paragraph 42).

35. This brief review of the historical development of social security makes it possible to draw several conclusions.

36. First, Bulgarian social security legislation appeared along with the restoration of the Bulgarian State after the Liberation of the country from the Ottoman domination in 1878. Since that time it has developed as a part of our legal system. In the mid-1980s, it was separated from the labour law and was set up as an autonomous branch of law.

Second, social security law has developed historically as insuring against specific social risks, following the Bismarckian approach to social insurance – insuring only the employees at the very beginning, and later – insuring persons who deal with trade and freelance practitioners. This development shows the tendency towards enlargement of the scope of persons insured and of social risks insured.

Third, under the terms of transition to democratic organization of society and market economy, social security legislation has its further development. The major problems it faces are financial ones. However, the adoption of the new security and health legislation in 1999–2004 completed the outline of the reform thereof.

a) The summary of the above exposition (*see supra* paragraphs 4–19c, 32–36) for the last two years – 2020 and 2021 – takes us to today's disturbing period of time,

---

28. K. Sredkova, *Employment and Insurance Rights of the Unemployed* 117–188 (Sibi Publishing House 1995).

especially throughout the year 2021. These years are dominated by the extremely severe Covid-19 pandemic situation. In addition to the serious health crisis and the periodic 'pandemic waves', the current being the fourth one, the overloading of the health system for inpatient care and the wholehearted medical personnel – doctors, nurses, drivers and hospital attendants – the slowdown of the economic growth, a certain increase in unemployment and inflation rate, some decrease in the economic rate and the low quantitative parameters of the number of vaccinated persons, there is also a political crisis in the country and division in society. Because of the expiry of the mandate of supreme State bodies, both parliamentary and presidential elections were held on 14 November 2021 (*see supra* paragraphs 19a and 19c). Thus, within a year only – the year 2021 – it was necessary to hold three national parliamentary elections in the period from April until late November, namely in May, July and November. It was during the intervals between them that the legislative body – the National Assembly – was functional, though for a short time – about a month or two. This allowed for amending and updating and increasing the estimated State expenses under the budget laws – the Law on the State Budget and the Law on State Social Security Budget (LSSSB), which provided financial guarantee for the payments under these laws. Thus, in spite of the severe general situation in the country, a comparatively bumpless implementation of these budgets has been ensured. That was particularly necessary and important for both the overall State budget and the State social security budget, as well as for the budget of the National Health Insurance Pay Cash Desk Office (NHIPCDO) until the end of the year 2021.

§3. Sources of Social Security Law

I. General

37. Depending on their origin, the sources of social security law are divided into two major groups: internal and international ones. The sources that are internal by origin become part of the internal social security law on their coming into force (Article 5, paragraph 5 of the Constitution), while the international ones do so in the presence of conditions specified in Article 5, paragraph 4 of the Constitution: (a) the international treaties they are contained in have been ratified by Bulgaria through the constitutionally established procedure; (b) they have become effective for Bulgaria and (c) their texts have been promulgated in the Bulgarian language in the Official Journal (OJ).

38. Internal sources of law. Depending on the body that has issued them, they can be divided into three major groups: (a) State sources; (b) Non-statutory sources; (c) mixed sources.

II. Internal Sources

A. State Sources

39. The State internal sources of social security law are as follows: (1) The Constitution; (2) Laws; (3) Sublegal normative acts of the Council of Ministers; (4) Sublegal normative acts of the Ministers. The State internal sources of law are most widely applied in social security law.

40. The Constitution of 12 July 1991 is a source of social security law through its provisions relating to social insurance and social insurance rights of the citizens. They are contained in the Preamble, Chapter 1 'Basic Principles' and Chapter 2 'Citizens' Fundamental Rights and Obligations'. Here are the most important of them:

> The Constitution defines our State as a social one (the Preamble, paragraph 5). The social nature of our State has one of its most typical and impressive manifestations in social security and social security law.
>
> The Constitution also contains several more provisions that are directly related to the social security protection of citizens.
>
> Article 51 of the Constitution is of essential importance. It specified the constitutional ground of social security law in two directions. First, the citizens' right of social security is approved and recognized as a fundamental citizens' right (Article 51, paragraph 1 of the Constitution). The current social security legislation is the further development and realization of this citizens' constitutional right in its various forms. Second, it explicitly acknowledges unemployment as an insured social risk and the right to social insurance against unemployment arises from it (Article 51, paragraph 2 of the Constitution).

The constitutional canons of maternity protection and child protection are very important for the development of social security law. Pursuant to Article 14 of the Constitution, 'The family, maternity and children are under the protection of the State and society.' This fundamental idea has found its further development in Article 47, paragraph 2 of the Constitution, according to which 'The mother is entitled to the special protection of the State, which provides her a paid leave before and after the birth, free obstetric care, facilitation of labour and other social benefits.'

41. After its adoption on 12 July 1991, the Constitution has been amended five times: in 2003 (promulgated in the OJ, No. 85 of 2003), in February 2005 (promulgated in the OJ, No. 18 of 2005), in March 2006 (promulgated in the OJ, No. 27 of 2006), in February 2007 (promulgated in the OJ, No. 12 of 2007) and in December 2015 (promulgated in the OJ, No. 100 of 2015). Four of them were necessitated by the preparation of Bulgaria for its forthcoming membership in the EU, as well as by other domestic problems of constitutional importance. The first one of them (September 2003) concerns judiciary matters (Articles 129, 131 and 132), the second one (February 2005) concerns the participation of Bulgaria in the formation and development of the EU (Article 4, paragraph 3), the possibility of surrendering a Bulgarian citizen to another State or international court for the purpose of criminal prosecution where an international treaty provides for it, this treaty being ratified, promulgated and effective for the Republic of Bulgaria (Article 25, paragraph 4), the election of members of the European Parliament and the participation of citizens of the EU in the elections for local authorities (Article 42, paragraph 3), ratifying and denouncing, through a law, the international treaties which vest the EU with powers ensuing from the Constitution (Article 85, paragraph 1, item 9, paragraphs 2–4), the obligation of the Council of Ministers to inform the National Assembly about matters concerning the obligations of the Republic of Bulgaria arising from its membership in the EU, and the elaboration and adoption of acts of the EU (Article 105, paragraphs 3–4), the third (March 2006) and the fourth (February 2007) ones concern the judiciary, the Armed Forces and the budget of the Parliament. The last amendment (December 2015) concerns judiciary matters and, especially, the division of the Supreme Judicial Council into two colleges – the College of Judges and the College of Public Prosecutors.

42. The laws are the main source of social security law. The following insurance laws deserve being mentioned:

(a) The SIC (promulgated in the OJ, No. 110 of 1999, amended) is one of the main sources of social security law. It consists of three Parts and forty-one Chapters, in which its 417 Articles are distributed. Its regulation comprises the legal regulation which used to form part of the Mandatory Social Insurance Code of December 1999, effective since 1 January 2000, and, following the amendments of July 2003, it also contains the regulation of additional voluntary pension insurance, which was contained in the Additional Voluntary Pension Insurance Law of July 1999 (promulgated in the OJ, No. 65 of 1999, amended, repealed) and the regulation of mandatory and voluntary insurance against unemployment, which was contained in the Protection against Unemployment and EPL of December 1997 (promulgated in the OJ, No. 120 of 1997, amended, repealed). Owing to the enlarged scope thereof, in July 2003, its title was changed from Mandatory Social Insurance Code into SIC (promulgated in the OJ, No. 67 of 2003). In its three parts, it regulates three large groups of social relations: Part I (Articles 1 through 120), which regulates the basic mandatory social insurance against incapacity for work and unemployment, this insurance being carried out by the State and administered by the National Insurance Institute (NII); Part II (Articles 120'a' through 343), which regulates the additional insurance, this Part being composed of: (a) mandatory pension insurance, (b) voluntary pension insurance, and (c) voluntary insurance against unemployment, and Part III (Articles 344 through 355), which regulates the compulsory administrative measures and administrative sanction responsibility. All the insured social risks under the operative social security law have been covered.

(b) The SIC, in its wording of July 2003, was a continuation of the positive tendency in the development of modern security legislation – its codification and the formation of its three-pillar structure: basic, additional mandatory and additional voluntary insurance. This structure has been unevenly built up in the various fields of social insurance. It has been completely built up for pension insurance with the basic and additional (mandatory and voluntary) insurance. The unemployment insurance has been incompletely built up – basic mandatory and additional voluntary insurance. However, it has not been built up at all for temporary incapacity for work insurance. The basic mandatory State social insurance is the only one that exists for it.

(c) The SIC is a complex law. It contains structural, substantive law, procedure law and administrative law provisions. Along with the classical imperative and public law provisions of the State and social structures in accordance with the models of Bismarck and Beveridge, it also includes a number of private law provisions, the mechanisms of which are taken from commercial and insurance law, adapted to a large scope of insured persons.

(d) In the last twenty-two years (2000–2021) since it took effect, the SIC has undergone numerous changes. A part of them consists in supplementing it with new regulations, such as the 2002 one (Articles 260–316 of the SIC) changing its title of Mandatory Social Insurance Code (1999 version) into its today's title of SIC. The other part of changes, which is larger, consists of current amendments made in recent years. These amendments were usually made at the end of the respective calendar year – in December – when the Budget Law of the State Social Insurance was adopted. However, it often happened that the SIC was amended in the course of the calendar year as well. A large part of these 'current amendments' used to have and still have a conjuncture nature. For instance, such were the supplements made in December 2009 providing for an increase of the deceased spouse's pension received by the surviving spouse from 26.5% to 40% in the period 2011–2015, which were repealed at the end of 2011. The amendments to the SIC made in the late 2010 had a similar fate. They repealed Articles 89 and 90 of the SIC, which regulated the old-age social pension and the disability social pension, respectively, commencing on 1 January 2013. These pensions have been present in Bulgarian insurance legislation since 1975 and their application – especially in view of the population's growing poverty in the years of transition and, moreover, in the conditions of a crisis – was a step in a wrong direction. These amendments caused public discontent and, at the end of 2012, i.e., prior to the time their repeal should have taken effect, 'their repeal was repealed', and these regulations were restored *in extenso* in the texts of Article 89a and Article 90a of the SIC (promulgated in the OJ, No. 99 of 2012, effective since 1 January 2013). The amendments to the SIC regarding the extension on the age and insurance length of service for acquiring the right to pension for length of insurance and old age were inconsiderate as well. At the end of 2010 an age extension by six months per calendar year until reaching the age of 63 for women and 65 for men was approved, starting from 2011. And only a year later – at the end of 2011 – this legislative solution was abandoned, and a new one was adopted: starting from 1 January 2012, each year the insurance length of service of both women and men – 34 and 37 years, respectively – was to be extended by four months per year until reaching 37 and 40 years, respectively. It is with the same pace – four months a year – that the retirement age of both women and men – 60 and 63 years, respectively – was extended until reaching 63 for women and 65 for men. Thus, in 2015 the retirement age reached 60 years and 8 months for women and 63 years and 8 months for men, and the insurance length of service reached 34 years and 8 months for women and 37 years and 8 months for men. From 31 December 2016 onwards, the age will keep increasing from the first day of each calendar year as follows: the age for women will increase by 2 months each calendar year until 31 December 2029, and from 1 January 2030 by 3 months until reaching 65 years of age, while the age for men will increase each calendar year by 2 months until 31 December 2017 and by 1 month from 1 January 2018 onwards, until reaching 65 years of age. The idea is to have the age for men and women become the same after several years, reaching the age of 65. In 2016 it is 35 years and 2 months for women and 38 years and 2 months for men. From 31 December 2016 onwards, it will increase by 2 months each calendar year until reaching 37 years for women and 40 years for men. Thus, the difference of 3 years in the length of service of men and women will be present in the future as well.

The frequent changes in the SIC destabilize the social insurance legislation and make it impossible for a sustainable practice of its application to be established. Such changes have a conjuncture nature. Their soundness is not confirmed by practice and, whenever the conjuncture changes, the legislator either repeals them as hurriedly as he has adopted them or changes them anew. This brings about legal insecurity, which – in today's unfavourable conditions of a severe economic crisis in the country – is borne primarily by the large social strata of the poor and results in profound social discontent.

(e) The HIL (promulgated in the OJ, No. 70 of 1998, amended) is the next important source of insurance law, regulating the part of insurance law which deals with health insurance. The health insurance regulation it contains is new and has been unknown to the legal traditions existing so far. It has replaced the system of nationwide State free medical care, which has existed for decades (since 1949) and has been provided in State medical treatment institutions, by the system of health insurance. The HIL regulates two main forms of its realization: the basic mandatory health insurance (Chapters 1 and 2, Articles 3–80) and additional voluntary health insurance (Chapter 3, Articles 81, 82, 83, 85). The HIL is 'the Law' in the sense determined under Article 52, paragraphs 1 and 2 of the Constitution, which regulates the basic right of citizens to health insurance, and the realization of their constitutional right to health, as well as the procedure of its financing.

(f) Other health laws are also sources of health insurance: the Health Law (promulgated in the OJ, No. 70 of 2004, amended), the Law on Professional Organizations of Physicians and Dentists (promulgated in the OJ, No. 83 of 1998, amended), the Law on Professional Organizations of Nurses, Midwives and Associated Medical Specialists (promulgated in the OJ, No. 46 of 2005), the Law on Medical Treatment Institutions (promulgated in the OJ, No. 62 of 1999), the Law on Drugs and Pharmacies in Human Medicine (promulgated in the OJ, No. 10 of 2000, amended) and others, which regulate specific matters of health insurance.[29]

(g) Through the adoption of the HIL and the other health laws, health insurance has been established as a separate branch of social security law, symmetrical to social insurance.

(h) In establishing the financial independence of social and health insurance, the budget laws have their important place among the legal sources of insurance law: the Law on the State Social Security Budget (LSSSB) for 2021 and the Law on the NHIPCDO Budget for 2021. Taking into consideration the worsening pandemic situation in the country and the growth in the daily number of infected people (about 150–200 per day) and the increasing death rate of 120–150 persons per day and the creeping inflation, the LSSSB for the year 2021 (promulgated in the OJ, No. 103 of 4 December 2020, amended and supplemented in the OJ, No. 77 of 16 September 2021) increased the revenues and expenses of the State Social Security up to BGN 15,566,455 (about USD 9,235,312) for the year 2021. For the same reasons, the revenues and expenses under the Law on the Budget of the NHIPCDO were amended, supplemented and increased up to BGN 5,446,312 (about USD 3,231,312) for the year 2021.

(i) There is also a new Law on establishing the length of service and the insurance length of service through the court (promulgated in the OJ, No. 26 of 2011, effective since 2 April 2011). If a written initial document is available, according to this Law the person is entitled to establish through a court adversary procedure – through filing in an ascertainment claim – and to prove by witnesses that he/she has worked under an employment relationship and has been insured against all social risks for a period of time for which, due to reasons beyond his/her control, he/she does not have a Labour Record or an Insurance Record or another official document.

(j) After 13 March 2020, when the country's state of emergency was declared under Article 84, item 12 of the Constitution because of the outbreak of the Covid-19 pandemic, in view of the uncertainty and its possible recurrence, the legislator foresightedly created a new general legal provision – Article 3a of the SIC, namely 'Performance of Liabilities in a Declared State of Emergency' (promulgated in the OJ, No. 28 of 2020). It regulates the general limitations imposed in the field of social security when a state of emergency is declared. Para. 1 of the new provision lays down three 'general' limitations when a state of emergency is declared: 1) the legal timeframes set for insured persons and pensioners stop running, these being the timeframes related to the application of Part One, Chapters IV–VIII of the SIC. These are the provisions concerning the social security benefits due by the insurance body upon the occurrence of any social risks insured against in the State social security, and additional mandatory and additional voluntary pension insurance of the insured persons (Article 41–259 of the SIC); 2) statements, complaints and other documents connected

29. V. Mrachkov, *Social Security Law*, 71–73; K. Sredkova, *Social Security Law* 85 (Sibi Publishing House 5th ed. 2016).

with pecuniary compensations, benefits and pensions are filed either electronically or through a personal identification code; 3) an official's failure to render a timely decision on the granting and payment of unemployment benefits or pensions during a state of emergency is not regarded as a tacit refusal. All the three limitations specified above are necessitated by the state of emergency, which, because of its nature, obstructs the timely service in the course of social security implementation. Those documents which are filed by the insured persons within fourteen days after the state of emergency is over are regarded as filed in due time (Article 3a, paragraph 2). This provision is aimed at taking into account the inevitable difficulties when servicing the insured persons. This provision protects the insured persons' interests and rights.

43. Sublegal normative acts of the Council of Ministers. They continue having an important place in social insurance law. This is explained both by the nature of social relationships forming the subject matter of social security law regulation and their dynamic development and by the continuing drive for overdevelopment of the sublegal normative infrastructure including those matters which should be regulated by law. The sublegal normative acts issued by the Council of Ministers are the following ones: decrees, rules and regulations:

(a) Decrees of the Council of Ministers (Article 114, sentence 1 of the Constitution and Article 6, item 1 of the Normative Acts Law). Lately, they have been predominantly used for approving and repealing regulations and rules, and less often as sublegal normative acts containing primary direct legal infrastructure. In the field of social security law, such decrees are the following ones: the Decree of the Council of Ministers No. 263 dated 30 December 1999 on the adoption of the Regulation on those components of remuneration and income on the grounds of which the insurance contributions are made, and the pecuniary compensation for temporary incapacity for work, pregnancy and childbirth are calculated, the Regulation on establishing, examining and reporting industrial accidents, Decree No. 30 dated 10 March 2000 on the adoption of the Regulation on Pensions and Insurance Length of Service, the Regulation on Social Insurance of self-insured persons and Bulgarian citizens abroad, the Guidelines of 21 December 2012 on the provisions of the 2013 LSSSB, and so on.

(b) Rules (Article 114, sentence 2 of the Constitution, Article 6, item 1 and Article 7, paragraph 1 of the Normative Acts Law). They are issued both for the application of laws and for the regulation of matters connected with the organization and structure of administrative bodies and the like. The following are such Rules in the field of social security law: the Rules on the Structure and Activity of the NHIPCDO, and so on.

(c) Regulations. They are issued for the application of certain provisions or parts of laws (Article 114, sentence 2 of the Constitution, Article 6, item 1 and Article 7, paragraph 2 of the Normative Acts Law). Such regulations are the following ones: the Regulation on those components of remuneration and income on the grounds of which the insurance contributions are made, and the pecuniary compensation for temporary incapacity for work, pregnancy and childbirth are calculated, the Regulation on Pensions and Insurance Length of Service, the Regulation on Categorization of Labour upon Pensioning, the Regulation on the Access of persons with health insurance to the medical treatment institutions for inpatients and outpatients, and so on.

The above sublegal normative Acts have the same legal effect and have the same place in the hierarchy of sources of social security law. In case of discrepancies, they are construed and applied on the grounds of the time of their issue, and the relationship among them, in view of the nature of the created legal infrastructure – a general normative act, a special one, and so on.

44. Sublegal normative acts issued by Ministers (Article 115 of the Constitution, Article 7 of the Normative Acts Law). These acts are as follows: Rules, Regulations and Instructions. Most often, the Ministers vested with the power to issue such acts in the field of social security law are the Minister of Labour and Social Policy, the Minister of Health Care and the Minister of Finance.

The sublegal normative acts issued by the Ministers are departmental normative acts. They differ substantially from the sublegal normative acts – Rules and Regulations of the same title, issued by the Council of Ministers, by the fact that the latter have superior normative effect than the acts of the same title issued by the Ministers:

(a) Rules (Article 115 of the Constitution, Article 7, paragraph 1 of the Normative Acts Law). An example thereof is the Rules on the structure and activities of the regional healthcare centres, issued by the Minister of Health Care (promulgated in the OJ, No. 35 of 2001).
(b) Regulations (Article 115 of the Constitution, Article 7, paragraph 2 of the Normative Acts Law). An example of such a regulation is Regulation No. 7 of the Minister of Health Care specifying the basic package of healthcare activities (promulgated in the OJ, No. 106 of 1999).
(c) The Instruction is a specific sublegal normative act (Article 115 of the Constitution, Article 7, paragraph 3 of the Normative Acts Law). It is through the Instruction that the Minister gives directions to the subordinate bodies and departments concerning the application of a normative act in case the Minister either has issued it or has to ensure the enactment thereof. An example of such an act is Instruction No. 27 of the Minister of Health Care concerning the issue of documents by healthcare institutions for their being used abroad (promulgated in the OJ, No. 20 of 1982).

B. Non-statutory Sources

45. The non-statutory sources of social security law are the following ones: the collective labour contracts and the Statutes of commercial shareholding companies, which carry out additional mandatory and voluntary pension insurance, additional voluntary insurance against unemployment and additional voluntary health insurance:

(a) *Collective labour contracts*. The legal provisions relating to the collective labour contracts are contained in the Labour Code (Articles 50–60). The questions they post are dealt with by labour law.[30] Here, attention will be drawn only to those aspects of theirs, which characterize them as a source of social security law.
(b) The parties to the collective labour contracts are the trade union organizations and the employer or the employers' organizations (Article 51'a', paragraph 1, Article 51'b', paragraph 1, Article 51'c', paragraph 1 of the Labour Code (LC)). And, as it will be pointed out below, the social security relationships involve the insured persons, the insurers and the insurance body (*see infra*). By the way, the parties to the collective labour contract differ from the parties to the social security relationships. The latter do not involve trade union organizations, which are one of the two parties to the collective labour contract. And the collective labour contract does not involve the insurance body, which occupies a key position in social security relationships. Owing thereto, it is impossible for what has been agreed under the collective labour contract to be directly transferred to the plane of social security relationships, because of the risk for it to face the resistance, or at least the non-acceptance, on the part of a public (State) body, as the insurance body is, which has participated neither in the collective bargaining nor in the collective labour contract entered into. This greatly diminishes the possibility of settling social security relationships under collective labour contracts.
(c) Yet, there exist a certain number of matters of social security relationships which can be agreed in the collective labour contracts without engaging the insurance body. For example, making the payments from the enterprise's social funds, these being payments for additional sums to the short-term general sickness benefit, industrial disease benefit, industrial accident, pregnancy and childbirth, covering the expenses on medicines of insured employees, covering the expenses on treatment (medical treatment, medicines and the like) or a part thereof, and so on. In practice, such matters are settled in the collective labour contracts at the level of the enterprise.
(d) However, this question has another aspect as well. According to Article 50, paragraph 1 *in fine* LC, the collective labour contract may regulate only those matters of labour and social security relationships which are not regulated by the imperative provisions of law. And, because of the wide application of the authoritative imperative regulation of the social security relationships in the field of State social security, the 'free legal space' for contracting the social security relationships in the field of the State mandatory social and health insurance is limited. However, in return for it, there exist real possibilities for the spread of collective bargaining in additional mandatory and voluntary pension

30 V. Mrachkov, *Labour Law – Bulgaria, International Encyclopaedia of Laws* Suppl. 373, 226–244 (Kluwer Law International, 2011).

insurance. Articles 232 and 284 of the SIC explicitly provide for collective bargaining in additional voluntary pension insurance and additional voluntary insurance against unemployment. And, in spite of its not being explicitly provided for in the HIL, the admissibility of collective bargaining in additional voluntary health insurance ensues from the general rule of Article 50, paragraph 1 of the LC, according to which the social security relationships constitute a subject matter of collective bargaining inasmuch as the matters thereof are not regulated by the imperative norms of the law. Of course, in these cases the collective bargaining is applicable only where the insured persons are employees, that is, persons working under employment relationships.

(e) *Statutes of commercial companies*. The additional pension (mandatory and voluntary) insurance, the additional voluntary insurance against unemployment and the additional voluntary health insurance is carried out by the commercial shareholding companies (*see infra*). These companies are established under the Commercial Law. However, the SIC lays down a number of special rules regarding these companies, the said rules creating their image of a special type of commercial shareholding insurance companies which conduct only social security activities (additional mandatory and voluntary pension insurance and additional voluntary insurance against unemployment) and activities of additional voluntary health insurance (Articles 120–123‘i’ of the SIC). The Statutes of these companies regulate a number of specific matters connected with the additional insurance made by the respective commercial insurance company. It is through these rules of theirs that the Statutes are sources of the insurance made by the companies. The Statutes of the commercial shareholding insurance companies are not a general source of social insurance law, but rather a source of additional insurance only, the latter being carried out in accordance with the subject of insurance the law has assigned thereto.

C. *Mixed Sources*

46. Specific sources of social security law. There are only two acts belonging to this group – the National Frame Contracts (NFCs). They are not sources of the entire social security law, but rather sources of a part of it only – the mandatory health insurance (Article 53 of the HIL). Its issue and content are regulated by Articles 53–57 of the HIL. For this reason, the new statutory regulation and the legal nature thereof will be considered further on within the framework of mandatory health insurance (*see infra* Part III, Chapter 4, §1). Here they are identified only for the purpose of stating their existence as well as for the sake of completeness of the exposition.

III. International Sources

47. The international sources of social security law are the multilateral international treaties that refer to the security rights. They are adopted by international organizations within the scope of their competence. The following are such multilateral international treaties that contain provisions on security relations: Article 9 of the International Covenant on Economic, Social and Cultural Rights by virtue of which the Member States of the Covenant recognize each person's right to social security, including social insurance, and Article 10 of the Covenant, which provides for special protection of mothers for a reasonable period of time before and after the child is born, with payment of the respective social security benefits.

The social security conventions of the ILO are extremely important in the field under consideration. Those conventions of the ILO on social security that have been ratified by the Republic of Bulgaria in the due course stipulated by the Constitution have become effective for the country and they have been promulgated in the OJ. Due to that, according to Article 5, paragraph 4 of the Constitution, they form part of our internal sources of social security law.[31]

Bulgaria has ratified twenty conventions of the ILO on social security matters and the following are among them: Social Security (Minimum Standards) Convention, 1952 (No. 102), the conventions on industrial accident benefits (Convention Nos 12, 17 and 19), conventions relating to general sickness and occupational disease benefits (Convention Nos 18, 24, 25 and 42), conventions concerning old-age pensions, disability pensions and survivors' pensions (Convention Nos 35–40), and so on.

48. In 2000, through a law, Bulgaria ratified the European Social Charter in its revised version of 3 May 1996 (promulgated in the OJ, No. 43 of 2000). Articles 12 and 13 of the Charter are among those provisions which were adopted in the course of ratification, these provisions concerning the right to social insurance, as well as the right to social and medical care, and so on. The ratification of the Charter took effect for Bulgaria on 1 August 2000.

Since 1 January 2007, when Bulgaria became a member of the European Union, the social security law of the European Union has had its ever-wider application – regarding both its scope and significance – in the domestic legal order of the country. The EU social security law comprises the legal rules of the Union on the regulation of the social security relationships among the twenty-seven Member States when their citizens exercise their social security rights and move freely. These rules are contained in both the primary and the secondary EU law.

As for the primary law, these rules form part of the Original Treaties – the Treaty on European Union (Article 2), Article 45 and Article 46 of the Treaty on the Functioning of the European Union (TFEU) and Article 34 and Article 35 of the Charter of Fundamental Rights of the European Union, etc. As for the secondary EU law, there are two regulations and several directives. The regulations in the field of social security law are: Regulation No. 883 (EU) of the European Union and of the Council on the coordination of social security systems and Regulation No. 987/2009 of the European Parliament. Like all regulations, these ones also have their direct implementation in the national social security systems of the Member States and their content is strictly applied without any interference therein through amendments or supplements on the part of the competent State bodies of the Member State. There are also several directives adopted in the EU law: Directive No. 79/7/

31. La sécurité sociale et la primauté du droit, BIT, Genève, 2011, 5–132.

EEC on the equal treatment of men and women in matters of social security; Directive No. 2010/41/EU on the equal treatment of men and women engaged in an activity in a self-employed capacity, etc.

The legal rules of the European Union in the field of social security have their impact on the national social security law through the harmonization and coordination of the Member States' national social security systems. Harmonization is directed at the unification of the Member States' national social security systems and the introduction of common solutions regarding social security in all Member States. Coordination is necessary among the national social security systems for overcoming any inconsistencies and attaining the common goal, which consists in guaranteeing the social security rights of citizens and especially those of the most vulnerable strata – the disabled and elderly people, the migrants and their family members, the minorities, etc. The basic principles underpinning the realization of coordination are: equality of the treatment of citizens, creation of real opportunities for Member States citizens to move freely on the territories of other European countries, to exercise their social security rights on the territory of any other Member State regardless of the distance between the countries, to enjoy their social security rights without formalities or obstructions, regardless of their citizenship and irrespective of the country in which the social security rights have been acquired, such as the right to pension, health insurance and access to medical care, at the place where a citizen is at a given point in time when the need for such care arises, etc.[32]

49. The following is a hierarchical arrangement of the sources of social security law according to the legal force they have:

(1) The Constitution of the Republic of Bulgaria.
(2) Ratified international treaties that meet the requirements of Article 5, paragraph 4 of the Constitution, as well as Regulations of the EU (Article 288, §2 of the Treaty on Functioning of the EU and Article 15(2) of the Normative Acts Law).
(3) Laws.
(4) Ordinances, rules and regulations of the Council of Ministers.
(5) Rules, regulations and instructions of the Ministers.
(6) Collective labour contracts.

The legal effects of the hierarchy thus outlined of the sources of social security law are displayed in several directions:

(1) the position of the source determines its rank and legal force. This force is superior to the force of those normative acts that come after it in the hierarchical arrangement and is inferior to the force of those normative acts that come before it in this arrangement;
(2) the legal force of the sources of social security law, depending on the position they have in the hierarchy of sources, has the following effect: in the case of

32. K. Sredkova, *Social Security Law* 619–641 (Sibi Publishing House 5th ed. 2016).

contradiction between normative acts, the one that is superior in rank applies. This displays the dominant force of superior normative acts in relation to inferior ones. This is also legally set out under Article 15 of the Normative Acts Law, according to which if an act contradicts a superior normative act, then the higher-degree normative act applies, the latter having superior legal force;
(3) the Constitution is the supreme and fundamental law and all the other legal acts should comply with it;
(4) the international treaties that meet the requirements of Article 5, paragraph 4 of the Constitution have priority over any source of internal law with the exception of the Constitution. It is only the Constitution that has superior legal force compared with them.

50. It is necessary to draw several conclusions from the preceding exposition:

(1) The operative social security law has sources of various nature, origin and legal force. This fact shows both the abundance of legal provisions concerning social security relations and the large opportunities of the law for regulating the social security relations by choosing a normative act of a specific type and rank.
(2) In the recent sixteen years, a serious reform was made in social security legislation, which has totally changed its pattern. After the HIL was adopted in 1998 and the Mandatory Social Insurance Code was adopted in 1999 (renamed 'Social Insurance Code' in 2003, following the amendments thereto), two major parts were differentiated in Bulgarian social security law:
   (a) Social insurance, comprising the insurance in case of incapacity for work, resulting from general sickness, industrial accident and occupational disease, unemployment, increased expenses in connection with childbirth, which result in the decrease of the income for the maintenance of the insured persons and the members of their families.
   (b) Health insurance, providing accessible medical care for insured persons and the members of their families. The presentation which follows will be committed to them (*see infra* Parts II–X).
(3) Apart from the basic mandatory State social insurance, the reform of 1998–2003 also introduced additional – mandatory and voluntary – private insurance. It put the beginning of setting up the national insurance system upon the principle of its three-pillar structure: basic mandatory State social and health insurance, additional mandatory social insurance and additional voluntary insurance. This system is not applied in all the fields of social security law, but only in some of them; additional mandatory social insurance is applied only in the field of pension insurance, additional voluntary insurance is applied only in the field of pension insurance and in the field of social insurance against unemployment. On the other hand, while the basic mandatory social and health insurance is carried out and managed by the State with the participation of representatives of civil society (representatives of the representative organizations of employers and trade unions, etc.), it is the private initiative and capital that made their way into the additional (mandatory and voluntary) social and health insurance through the reform of 1999–2003.

(4) Social security law is in the process of constant development and enrichment. Its development does not end with the adoption of laws; it only starts with them. After the crisis which the country underwent in 1995–1997, the economic situation has stabilized and has been slowly improving. However, in spite of it, and due to the general poverty our country and its population live in, over the past twenty-five years, our insurance system has been in a state of constant financial hardship and strain. It can hardly provide the insured persons with the indispensable legal benefits in their over-modest amounts. Owing thereto, the most serious problems faced by the social security law in the country at the current stage of its development concern its financial provision with sufficient funds for having the insurance benefits regularly paid and their amount increased, this forming part of the efforts of the State for improving the standard of living of the insured persons, both employees and pensioners. The economic crisis, which has ridden the country since 2009, has still further deepened the poverty of the insured persons, who rely on the insurance benefits – pensions, indemnities for temporary incapacity for work and unemployment. The amounts of these benefits were modest even before the crisis, and yet, in the years of ascending economic development, they were increased each year, though slightly. While for the past six years, since the crisis hit the country, their amounts have been 'frozen' at the low levels which they had in 2008. And that has even further aggravated the social standing of an enormous portion of the insured persons, and particularly the pensioners, in view of the poverty they live in.

IV. Judicial Practice

51. According to Article 117 of the Constitution, the judiciary defends the rights and legal interests of the citizens, legal persons and the State. The task of the courts is to apply the law and not to create new legal norms (Article 8, paragraph 1 of the Law on the Judiciary, 2007). Their decisions reveal the content of effective legal provisions, and in concrete social insurance disputes, the 'law is pronounced' (*jurisdictio*). These disputes fall within the jurisdiction of the administrative courts and the Supreme Administrative Court. This also holds good for the interpretative resolutions of the Plenum of the Supreme Administrative Court (Articles 124 and 125 of the mentioned Law). These decisions and resolutions of the judicial administrative bodies reveal the content of the respective legal norms, enjoy great authority and possess a definite, though different, binding force. The interpretative decisions of the Plenum of the Supreme Administrative Court serve as guidance to the courts and special jurisdictions, and have to be followed by the courts, the special jurisdictions and the administrative organs whose acts are subject to judicial review (Article 130, paragraph 2 of the Law on the Judiciary). However, the binding force cannot make these resolutions acts of a legal character, because in spite of their binding force they are and remain interpretative (revealing the content of the legal norms) and not lawmaking acts.

V. Decisions of Tripartite Bodies

52. According to Article 3 of the Labour Code, the State performs the regulation of the insurance relationships in cooperation and consultations with the representative trade union organizations and employers' ones. In order for the cooperation and consultation to be carried out, on the grounds of Article 3'a' and 3'b' of the Labour Code, there were set up municipal, sector, branch and district councils for tripartite cooperation, as well as a National Council for Tripartite Cooperation (*see infra*). These bodies also take decisions regarding security relationships matters. The leading position among them belongs to the decisions of the National Council for Tripartite Cooperation.

53. The decisions taken by the National Council for Tripartite Cooperation as well as those taken by the other tripartite bodies, by industrial branches or by those created at local (municipality or district) level are not regarded as sources of Social Security Law. These decisions have the character only of commonly agreed proposals to the competent public organs such as the government, relevant minister, municipal council mayor, prefect, and so on. They are not of any legally binding character. Legally speaking, it depends upon the final decision of the competent public organ to accept or not to accept the solutions discussed, drafted and addressed to it. This basic idea is in principle embodied in Article 3, paragraph 1 of the Labour Code in providing that the State carries on the regulation of labour relations and social security as well as questions concerning the standard of living after consultations with the representative trade unions and employers' organizations. The stress is put on the prerogative of the State (and of its competent organs) to regulate labour relations with the sole duty to do it with the collaboration of and after having consulted the social partners. But, the final decision to adopt the relevant regulation belongs to the State. It does not mean, however, that the proposals made by the tripartite bodies do not have any value or authority. They do. Such value or authority consists in how well founded these proposals are, and in the moral engagement of the relevant State organs which have participated in their development and adoption by the competent public authority.

On the other hand, insurance relations are becoming essentially *power relations*, whereby the decision-making authority is challenged by the collective power the trade unions may display. Therefore, the problem is within the framework of tripartite cooperation by means of discussions, mutual concession and compromises to adopt realistic proposals, taking into account the real economic and social situation actually prevailing in the country, which are likely to be accepted by the relevant decision-making competent authority. Finally, the adoption of the proposals so made is due to the good will and fairness innate of the tripartite cooperation. That is why, normally, these proposals are accepted and ratified by the competent authorities. Despite this, the elaborated proposals by tripartite bodies are not legally binding.

Part I. The Institutions

Chapter 1. Introduction

54. The effective legal regulation of those institutions which administer the application of social security law was gradually introduced through the legislative reform of 1998–2003 and the subsequent numerous amendments to the SIC and the HIL. The administration it establishes is differentiated into two levels. On the one hand, the administration and its institutions are differentiated by subjects of insurance. As for this feature, they are divided into institutions for administering social insurance and institutions for administering health insurance. On the other hand, within the framework of these two major parts of social security, the administering institutions are differentiated by the type of insurance – State or private. The operative legislation provides for setting up nationwide systems for administering only the basic mandatory State social insurance and the mandatory health insurance. They are the only ones to have national public institutions. As for the administration of mandatory State social insurance, the institutions are the Ministry of Labour and Social Policy and the NII; and as for the mandatory health insurance, the institutions are the Ministry of Health Care and the NHIPCDO. They will be discussed later in those parts of the work which deal with mandatory State social insurance (*see infra*) and mandatory health insurance (*see infra* Part III, Chapter 1), respectively.

55. As for the administration of additional – mandatory and voluntary – social insurance, and additional voluntary health insurance, it is assigned to private shareholding commercial companies. It is administered by the bodies of these companies. They will be discussed in the part dealing with additional – mandatory and voluntary – social insurance (*see infra* Part VII, Chapters 4 and 5) and additional voluntary health insurance (*see infra* Part III, Chapter 3).

56. And yet, in view of the high social value of the interests fulfilled by these activities, the State does not leave them 'out of sight'. It exercises State supervision of their activities through its national specialized State body – the Financial Supervision Commission (FSC), which was set up under the FSC Law (promulgated in the OJ, No. 8 of 2003, amended). As for those commercial shareholding companies which carry out voluntary health insurance, the State supervision of their activities is exercised by the Ministry of Health Care. These matters will be discussed in the part dealing with additional social and health insurance (*see infra* Part III, Chapters 2 and 3).

57. Ministry of Labour and Social Policy. Its functions regarding State social insurance are determined in Article 32 of the SIC. They consist in 'developing, coordinating and conducting the State policy in the field of State social insurance'.

'State social insurance' is an important part of the social policy of the State. As its name shows, the Ministry of Labour and Social Policy is the specialized body of the government, as a supreme body of executive power, for the social policy of the State. The functions of the Ministry in the field of State social insurance comprise three main components:

(a) Developing the State policy on State social insurance. What this means is determining the basic directions of its development in short-term, middle-term and long-term aspects, as well as specifying the legal provisions regarding its implementation by way of working out bills and drafts of sublegal normative acts and the like.
(b) Coordinating the policy in the field of State social security with the other components of social policy: employment, working and living conditions, social assistance, healthcare, tax policy, and so on. A part of these policies fall within the sphere of activities of the Ministry of Labour and Social Policy (employment, working conditions, social assistance), while others are within the competence of other Ministries – those of healthcare and finance, and owing thereto, their coordination requires strict distribution, differentiation and combination.
(c) Conducting the policy in the field of State social insurance. What this means is implementing administrative, financial and other measures for the application of State social insurance. An important share of this part of the functions of the Ministry of Labour and Social Policy is formed by the measures regarding the application of operative insurance legislation as an important instrument in the social policy of the State.

Chapter 2. Public Institutions

§1. National Insurance Institute

58. The NII is a new governing body of social security. It was established under the Social Insurance Fund Law (promulgated in the OJ, No. 104 of 1995, repealed). After the adoption of the Code of Mandatory Social Insurance (promulgated in the OJ, No. 110 of 1999) and after changing its title to SIC (promulgated in the OJ, No. 67 of 2003), the regulation of the NII is contained in Articles 33–39 of the above Code. The term 'institute' has been used for denoting the body that realizes social security. This appellation has long-lasting traditions in Bulgarian social security legislation. Historically, the prototype of the NII according to the operative social security legislation is contained in the Social Security Institute Law of 1941 (promulgated in the OJ, No. 50 of 1941). This Law was effective until the end of 1948 when it was repealed by the Social Security Law (promulgated in the OJ, No. 11 of 1949, repealed). The Social Security Law of 1949 assigned the realization of social security to the Social Security State Institute (Articles 1–3 of the quoted Law). The Social Security Law was effective until 16 November 1951 and was repealed by the Labour Code of 9 November 1951.

Here 'Institute' means an institution – public law organization – which manages the property of the Social Insurance Fund and conducts the activity of social security realization. It fulfils its functions through the bodies that act on its behalf. The administration, which is being under consideration here, has two aspects: institutional and functional. The institutional aspect consists in the establishment of a special State body ('institution') for administering the fund through its bodies, sections and subdivisions in the form of the NII, while the functional one consists in the activity performed by this body for social security realization. Social security cannot be realized outside or without the bodies, sections and subdivisions of the NII. What this actually shows is that the question is about two aspects of the administration of social insurance, which constitute two sides of one and the same entity.

59. The NII is a complex organizational formation. The NII is a public institution (State body), a legal entity having its administration and central department in Sofia, and having its twenty-eight territorial divisions in the district towns of the country. The NII administers the State social security in the country. It has broad competence and numerous functions that are listed exhaustively in Article 33 of the SIC, for instance: implementation of the State social security budget; establishment and collection of the State social security receivables resulting from insurance expenses made incorrectly; exercise of State supervision over the observance of social security laws and organization of the activity of establishing administrative violations and sanctions; payment of all types of pensions, compensations and benefits from State social security under the Social Security Code and the Law on Workers' and Employees' Claims Guaranteed in the Event of Their Employer's Bankruptcy, maintenance of an electronic register of patients' cards and decisions on appeals against them, etc. In recent years, the functions of the NII have been extended by adding new functions, such as: issuance of a personal identification code and access to the electronic administrative services provided by the NII; keeping a register of persons that have transferred funds from the Bulgarian pension scheme to the pension scheme of the European Union, the European Central Bank and the European Investment Bank; maintenance of a register of insurers' data and documents; keeping a register of the recognized contributory length of service bought by way of payment made by the persons under Article 9a of the SIC; maintaining a register of the decisions of medical commissions at the territorial divisions of the NII in cases of orders being issued for granting disability pensions and additional sums for assistance by another person under Article 98, paragraph 4 of the SIC and the like. It includes bodies at the national level and territorial (local) bodies and subdivisions. It constitutes a system of mutually connected bodies forming an organizational set through which social security is administered. The following are the governing bodies at the national level:

(a) Manager.
(b) Deputy Manager.
(c) Supervisory Board.

60. The Manager is a single-member body (Article 34, item 2, Article 37 of the SIC). He/she is elected by the National Assembly for a term of four years, and he/she can be discharged earlier on the grounds specified in detail in the Laws: conviction for intended crime of general character if the sentence has come into force, entry into effect of an act ascertaining a conflict of interests under the Law on Establishing and Prevention of a Conflict of Interests, systematic failure to perform his/her duties, obstacles to his/her performing the functions for longer than six months (in case of general sickness, long absence and other similar) or if he/she files his/her resignation.

61. The functions of the Manager are specified in Article 37, paragraph 5 of the SIC. They can be divided into two groups:

(a) Functions regarding the organization and governance of the activities of the NII. The Manager administers the current activity of the NII, approves the obligatory instructions and the model documents for State public insurance, opens and closes territorial subdivisions, approves their structure, reschedules the payment of arrears in the amount of BGN 10,000 up to BGN 100,000 (USD 7,100 up to USD 71,000)[33] for a period of three years, approves the allotment of the capital investments for the management of the NII, performs the functions of a body of assignment of civil servants (public officers) as well as of employer to employees in employment legal relationships, and so on.
(b) Functions regarding the preparation of important acts and projects for decisions on the activity of State social insurance, which are introduced for being discussed by the Supervisory Board – decisions on approving the draft budget of

33. The exchange rate at 31 Oct. 2013, BGN 1= USD 0.71.

State social insurance, projects for normative acts, a project for the Rules on the organization and activity if the NII, projects for using the reserve of the State social insurance budget, and so on.

62. A Manager's Council is set up under the Manager. It consists of the Deputy Manager of the NII and the Heads of the functional departments – the main Directorates of the NII. This Council is not a managing body of the NII, but rather a subsidiary consultative body under the Manager of the NII – his/her 'Cabinet'. It assists the Manager in his performing his functions, by studying those questions which he/she is authorized to take decisions on or to prepare projects for (Article 38 of the SIC).

63. The Deputy Manager is also a single-member body and a governing official in the system of the institute. He/she is elected and discharged for the term and in the course stipulated for the election and discharge of the Manager. He/she renders assistance to the Manager in performing his/her functions and replaces him when the latter is absent. During that time, he/she also exercises the Manager's powers to their full extent. The Manager is not barred from assigning to the Deputy Manager a part of the powers connected with the organization and administration of the institute's activity. Although the Code does not make explicit provisions for it, this can be derived from the fact that the Deputy Manager is elected and discharged in the same way and on the same grounds as the Manager (Article 34, item 2 and Article 37, item 4 of the SIC).

64. The Supervisory Board is a collective body set up on the tripartite principle. It comprises one member of each of the trade unions and the employers' organizations recognized as representative under Articles 3, 34 and 35 of the LC and the same number of State representatives.

The representative trade union organizations are Confederation of Independent Trade Unions in Bulgaria (CITUB) and Confederation of Labour 'Podkrepa'(CL 'Podkrepa').

The employers' organizations that are recognized as representative ones are as follows: (1) The Bulgarian Chamber of Commerce and Industry; (2) The Bulgarian Economic Chamber; (3) The Confederation of Employers and Industrialists in Bulgaria; (4) The Association of Industrial Capital in Bulgaria; The Union for Private Economic Enterprise. Where the representative trade union and employers' organizations differ in number, on the grounds of an agreement between them, the quota of the smaller number organizations is increased so that it becomes equal to the quota of the larger-number organizations. If no agreement between them is reached, the Supervisory Board is composed of one representative of each of the representative trade union and employers' organizations.

In the current situation, where the number of the representative trade union organizations is two, and the number of the representative employers' organizations is five, such an agreement has been reached, and the number of representatives of the representative trade union organizations in the Supervisory Board is five, as is the number of the representatives of the representative employers' organizations. The representatives of the representative trade union organizations and employers' organizations are appointed by their national governing bodies in compliance with the articles of association of the respective organization. The number of the State's representatives is equal to the total number of representatives of the representative trade union organizations and the representative employers' organizations, which is actually ten. They are nominated by the Council of Ministers. Thus, the total number of the members of the Supervisory Board is twenty. This number is subject to being increased or decreased in the future depending on the number of the representative trade union organizations and employers' ones. The Supervisory Board elects among its members the President who organizes and presides at the meetings of the Supervisory Board.

65. The Law specifies the functions of the Supervisory Board (Article 36 of the SIC). They can be divided into two main groups – management and control.

The management functions of the Supervisory Board prevail over the control ones. This shows that the Supervisory Board is actually a body that solves important issues which are connected with the organization and activities of the institute. The following management functions of the Supervisory Board deserve being mentioned: it approves the basic directions in the activity of the NII, approves the projects for the annual budget of State social insurance and the report thereof, approves the projects for normative acts concerning State social insurance prior to their being introduced for adoption by the respective State bodies, adopts the Rules on the organization and activity of the NII and the Rules on the activity of the Supervisory Board, upon the request of debtors, in exceptional circumstances, it may reschedule the payment of arrears exceeding BGN 100,000 (USD 71,000) for a period of three years, takes decisions on striking off uncollectible arrears, takes decisions concerning the acquisition and disposition of the Institute's property, takes decisions on the use of the reserve funds of the State social insurance budget, and takes decisions regarding the acquisition of real estates on the part of the NII in return for liabilities to the State social insurance funds (Article 36, items 1–2, 4–10 of the SIC).

The control function of the Supervisory Board is only one. It is broadly formulated in Article 36, item 3 of the SIC: exercising control over the activity of the Institute, the Management Board, the Manager and the Deputy Manager. This laconic formulation assigns to the Supervisory Board the control over the entire activity of the Institute and its governing bodies, such as the Management Board, the Manager and the Deputy Manager of the Institute.

66. The operative activity of the institute concerning the social security realization is performed by its sections in the Central Department (departments, sections, offices and other similar) and those in its territorial subdivisions.

67. The Central Department has separate directorates, chief directorates, sections and offices. They are established, transformed and closed by resolution of the Supervisory Board of the Institute. Those sections in the Central Department of the Institute that exist now have been specified under Articles 2 and 7 of the Rules of the Institute.

68. The territorial subdivisions of the Institute are the Social Security Regional Departments. There are twenty-eight territorial subdivisions – Social Security Regional Departments in the country. They are seated in the district centres of the country (Article 2 of the Rules of the Institute). These bodies have territorial competence. It extends over the insured and insurers in the territory of the district centres, that is overinsured and insurers that are residents in or have their registered office in the territory of the municipality or the settlements within the region of the respective Social Security Regional Department. They are assigned the performance of the activity connected with social security realization.

The territorial subdivisions of the NII are headed by Directors being the second-degree appropriators of the Insurance Funds' budget and performing a number of functions relating to the social security realization. These subdivisions are established, transformed and closed by resolution of the Supervisory Board of the Institute (Article 33, paragraph 2 of the SIC). The Directors of the territorial subdivisions of the NII have been nominated on the grounds of a competitive examination.

Part II. Contribution and Financing

Chapter 1. Introduction

69. The social security system is a costly system requiring great financial resources. The way of raising them depends on the system adopted in the national legislation regarding the financing of social insurance. Three such systems are known in world practice: an expense-covering, a capital-covering and a State budget one.

70. During the socialist epoch of the country's development, for almost fifty years (1949–1996), the social insurance in Bulgaria was financed on the grounds of the State budget system. This system was introduced through the Social Insurance Law of 1949, affirmed through Article 203 of the 1951 LC, and through Article 170 of the 1951 LC in its wording of 1957, it continued being operative. This system consisted in collecting the insurance contributions from the insurers and the insured, and the infusion of the contributions into the State budget's receipts. The budget of the State social insurance is used to form part of the single budget of the State. The then-existing insurance funds that have been built for decades (since 1924), as well as the collected insurance contributions, were infused into the common receipts of the State budget, along with the receipts from taxes, while the real estates and other property owned by the Social Insurance Institute (administrative buildings, rest homes, hospitals and the like) became State-owned property. The insurance contributions were infused and assimilated into the common stock of receipts and revenues of the State budget, together with the taxes and deductions from the profit of State-owned enterprises, and turned into a part of the single stock of State-owned property. The insurance benefits (pensions, indemnities and social insurance aids) used to be paid from financial means of the budget which were individualized therein as a State social insurance budget. As a result of its being included in the single State budget, the State social insurance budget lost its 'individuality', as well as the one of its revenues and expenses, and this destroyed its financial and organizational independence. It was a part of and a manifestation of the more and more complete State totalitarianism which was established in the country at the end of the 1940s.

71. After the changes that took place in the country in late 1989, this system was assessed as inefficient by the Law on the Social Insurance Fund of December 1995 (repealed), which started the reform of social insurance, and was replaced by the expense-covering system of financing it. The latter was affirmed through the Code of Mandatory Social Insurance of December 1999 and the SIC of July 2003.

72. On the grounds of the expense-covering system, the financial means required for covering the social insurance expenses are raised mainly from the insurance contributions, and also from other receipts in the social insurance funds, including subsidies from the State budget. The receipts from insurance contributions made by the insured and the employers cover the expenses on the payment of insurance benefits (pensions, indemnities on temporary incapacity for work, etc.). The main part thereof is formed by the pension expenses. By 2021, they are 65% of the insurance revenues of the consolidated budget of State social insurance,[34] used for the payment of pensions. Thus, the receipts from those who work 'today' cover the expenses of those who worked 'yesterday'. And tomorrow, when those working 'today' stop working and become pensioners, they will receive pensions from the insurance contributions of those who will be working tomorrow, and so on. Thus, along with the rotation of generations, the 'change of generations' from employees into pensioners, financial means are also provided to the insurance funds, covering the expenses on social insurance. As Prof. Durand used to say, 'The efforts of the working adults are the ones which feed, clothe and heat the non-working elders.'[35]

---

34. Report of the Manager of the NII on the performance of the State social insurance budget for 2021, 11.
35. P. Durand, *La politique contemporaine de la sécurité sociale* 166 (Dalloz 1953).

Chapter 2. Insurance Funds

§1. Notion and Types

73. The financial means necessary for the realization of social insurance are distributed by insurance funds within the framework of the State public insurance budget. These funds are set apart and grouped by separate types of social risks depending on their type and closeness to each other. The financial means of the separate insurance funds are raised for and spent on the payment of the insurance indemnities upon the occurrence of the respective social risks, which the separate types of funds are designated for.

74. According to Article 18, paragraph 1 of the SIC, the financial means of the State public insurance budget have been separated and distributed among six independent types of insurance funds: (1) the fund of pensions related to labour activity; (2) the fund of pensions for people under Article 69 of the SIC. This Fund covers the military staff, the civil servants under the Law on the Ministry of the Interior, the Law on the Execution of Penalties and Detention, the Law on Special Means of Surveillance, the civil servants carrying out activities of safeguarding the judiciary under the Law on the Judiciary, and the civil servants of 'Fire Prevention and Population Protection' General Directorate; (3) the fund of pensions unrelated to labour activity; (4) industrial accident and occupational disease fund; (5) general sickness and maternity fund; (6) unemployment fund (UF).

§2. Revenues and Expenses of Insurance Funds

75. Each insurance fund has its specific sources from which its financial means are raised, as well as its specific purposes on which these financial means are spent. These specific sources are determined in accordance with the nature of social risks. And the specific purposes on which these financial means are spent are the insurance benefits paid upon the occurrence of the respective risks (pensions, pecuniary indemnities and aids), upon the occurrence of the respective occupational risks covered by the respective funds, and the financing of measures for their prevention (Articles 21–26'b' of the SIC).

76. The revenues to the Fund of pensions related to labour activity are raised from the insurance contributions of insurers, insured persons and self-insured ones, and the insurance contributions for insurance against disability, general sickness, old age and death, these contributions being remitted from the State budget for insuring civil servants, regular military staff (generals, officers and sergeants) under the Law on Defence and Armed Forces, as well as the insurance contributions for civil servants under the Law on the Ministry of the Interior and the Law on the Execution of Penalties, as well as amounts from the judiciary budget for insuring the judges, public prosecutors and investigating magistrates, the executive magistrates, the entry judges and the administrative assistant personnel of the judiciary, national budget transfers and health insurance contributions for pensioners, as well as ones from donations, testaments and other sources provided for in various laws.

77. The financial means of this fund are spent mainly on the payment of pensions for labour activity. These are the pensions for length of insurance and old age, for disability due to general sickness, for survivors' pensions, and the additional sums to the above-mentioned types of pensions – for updating, indexation and compensation of these pensions and the like.

78. The funds for insuring the persons under Article 69a (*see supra* paragraph 74) are provided from the insurance contributions paid for insuring these persons.

79. The revenues to the Fund of pensions unrelated to labour activity come from the national budget transfers, fees determined by the Council of Ministers, donations and testaments and the like.

80. The financial means of this fund are spent on the payment of pensions which are not related to labour activity. According to the operative pension legislation, such pensions are the following ones: pensions for military or civil disability, social pensions for old age and disability, personal pensions, additional sums to the pensions of war veterans, and so on.

81. The revenues to the Industrial Accident and Occupational Disease Fund are raised from the insurance contributions for these two insured social occupational risks, amounts from the State budget, amounts from the budget of the judiciary for insuring the judges, public prosecutors, investigating magistrates, the executive magistrates, the entry judges and the administrative assistant personnel of the judiciary, as well as revenues provided for in other laws, donations and testaments and the like.

82. The financial means of this fund are spent on the payment of pecuniary indemnities on temporary incapacity for work, pensions for disability caused by an industrial accident or occupational disease, the updating of these pensions and their indexation and compensation, measures for the prevention of industrial accidents and occupational diseases, improving the working conditions, financial aids for technical relief devices (prostheses, wheelchairs for the disabled and the like).

83. The revenues to the general sickness and maternity fund are raised from the insurance contributions, amounts from the State budget for insuring the civil servants and those equalled to them, for insuring the employees of the judiciary (judges, public prosecutors, investigating magistrates, etc.), other revenues for insuring these two general risks, donations and testaments and the like.

84. The financial means of this fund are spent on the payment of pecuniary indemnities and aids, as well as on their updating, indexation and compensation upon the occurrence of these two risks, the insurance benefits for these two general risks, the provision of technical relief devices (prostheses and the like) which are connected with the injury suffered from the general sickness, and so on.

85. The revenues to UF are raised from the insurance contributions, amounts allotted from the State budget specifically for indemnities on discharging regular military staff from military service, as well as from donations and testaments and the like.

86. The financial means of this fund are spent on the payment of indemnities on unemployment, and indemnities upon discharging generals, officers and sergeants from regular military service, and so on.

87. Since 1997 the revenues and expenses of these funds are determined in the annual budgets of State social insurance (Article 18, paragraph 2 of the SIC). They are approved for each calendar year and are effective from 1 January until 31 December of the year they refer to (*see supra* paragraph 42).

88. By virtue of the fund principle they are built upon, the financial means of each one of the six insurance funds are raised only from the sources and are spent only on the purposes provided for them in Articles 21–26'b' of the SIC. The law lays them down in detail. It is inadmissible for the means and revenues provided for a certain fund to be misused and directed to another fund, and the same applies to spending the financial means raised by a certain fund for purposes and insurance payments of another fund, where, for instance, the financial means of the second fund are insufficient. No managing body of the NII is entitled to do so, although these funds are under its 'general management' and supervision. This principle of lawfulness and purposefulness in raising and spending the financial means of the insurance funds expresses the legislator's concern for establishing a strict procedure for their management and supervision, and thus, to preserve them for their being used only in accordance with their designation, to protect the rights of the insured, and to create certainty about the enjoyment of these rights. This is also an expression of the NII insurance funds' autonomy and independence which were introduced following the model of the European legislations.

89. As it is evident from the preceding exposition (*see supra* paragraphs 75–88), the insurance contributions are supposed to be the main source of revenues for the largest part of the insurance funds, with the exception of the Fund of Pensions Unrelated to Labour Activity (*see supra* paragraphs 79–80). They are paid by the insurers, the insured persons and the self-insured ones, and are determined by the extent of the insured persons and the scope of social risks the persons are insured against. In this regard, a negative tendency has been observed over the last three or four years: a decrease in the revenues from insurance contributions as proceeds to the budget of the State social insurance. This requires that the State budget subsidies be augmented, so that the insurance benefits are paid out and, first and foremost, the pensions of the pensioners be regularly paid out each month. The actual revenues from insurance contributions in the budget of the State social insurance are not sufficient to cover the insurance payments. There are two reasons for it: the economic crisis which has brought about a considerable slump in the activity of the economic entities, and the unemployment growth, on the one hand, and, on the other hand, the difficulties in collecting the revenues from the insurance contributions due. Insurance contributions are collected by the National Revenue Agency and are forthwith credited to the account of the NII. At the end of October 2016, the accumulated liabilities of uncollected insurance contributions amounted to BGN 500 million (about USD 355 million). This sum is equal to the contributions of all the country's employees for pensions, indemnities for temporary incapacity for work and maternity and health for one month.[36] In 2018 and 2019, the portion of revenues from the collected insurance contributions was 52% and 47%, respectively, and the difference, which was covered by State budget subsidies for providing the insurance payments in 2020, was 52%, i.e., more than one-half of the budget of the State social insurance. This impairs the nature of the expense-covering system, which is based on the budget revenues of the insurance body – the NII. That puts the normal operation of the country's insurance system on a serious trial. Owing thereto, in order for a better idea of the financial position of State social insurance to be formed, it is also necessary to discuss the following: (1) The extent of the insured persons in State social security and the risks the persons are insured against; (2) The insurance contributions and their distribution between the insured and the insurers. This is what the exposition below will deal with (*see infra* Chapter 2 and Chapter 3).

36. M. Kostova & L. Kuyumdzhieva *Five Hundred Million Insurance Contributions Unpaid, Pressa Newspaper* (9 Oct. 2013).

Chapter 3. Extent of Insured Persons in State Social Insurance

90. Insured persons are the ones to which social insurance is applied. These might only be individuals who either exercise or are able to exercise labour activity, from which they receive labour remuneration for providing their own and their family members' maintenance. The absence of such incomes or the reduction thereof places the insured persons in a vulnerable financial position and a state of financial deficiency. It is overcome by the provision of an indemnity from the social insurance for the absent or reduced incomes. This is an expression of the application of social insurance to the insured.

91. In law, the extent of the persons insured in State social insurance is specified in detail through imperative legal norms. Social insurance is obligatory both for the persons it concerns and for the bodies of State social insurance, which are assigned the realization thereof. This shows that the legislator regards social insurance as being of public interest, spreads it over a large extent of people and attaches great importance to it. And the larger this extent is, the broader the personal field of application of State social insurance is and the more developed the insurance system is. This determines the practical significance of the extent of insured persons.

92. The extent of persons insured by mandatory insurance in State social insurance is large; however, it is not homogenous. The operative legislation does not provide for one and the same amount of insurance protection for the State social insurance as a whole. On the contrary, it establishes various 'internal' differentiated extents of insured persons with different amounts of insurance protection for each of these extents. Some of them are fully insured (*see infra* paragraph 94), while others are partially insured (*see infra* paragraphs 95–98). In each of these extents of persons, both the categories of insured individuals and the types of social risks which are applicable and relevant to the individual are specified, these being the risks the individuals are insured against.

93. The criterion on the grounds of which the differentiated determination of the various extents of insured persons was made is a reflex one; that is, it is a consequence of the difference in the legal nature of the primary legal relationships which precede the insurance ones: labour, business, civil, commercial and other relationships under which the labour activity is performed. In spite of their type differences, which determine their different legal nature, all these relationships are employment ones. This imparts elasticity to State social insurance and determines the differences in the amount and intensity of the insurance protection provided to the various groups of insured persons. These matters are regulated in Article 4 and 4a of the SIC. As far as this feature is concerned, the extent of persons insured with mandatory insurance in State social insurance is distributed among five groups:

(1) Insured against all social risks (Article 4, paragraph 1, items 1–4, 5, sentence 1, items 6–10 of the SIC).

(2) Insured against all insured social risks with the exception of the unemployment risk (Article 4, paragraph 1, item 1, sentences 1 and 2, item 5, sentence 2 of the SIC).
(3) Insured against old age, death, general sickness resulting in disability, industrial accident and occupational disease (Article 4, paragraph 2 of the SIC).
(4) Insured only against old age, death and general sickness resulting in disability (Article 4, paragraphs 3, 5 and 7 of the SIC).
(5) Insuring of seafarers (Article 4a of the SIC).

94. Persons insured against all social risks. The insurance protection for them is the broadest and the most complete one. Besides, the groups included in it are the most numerous ones. They have the same amount of insurance protection. What is common to all these insured is that all of them are persons exercising labour activity, holding an office in a constant and permanent way, getting regular labour remuneration or other payment for the work they do or the office they hold. The legal nature of the specific legal relationship on the grounds of which the insured persons do the assigned work or perform the duties of their office is different and, in view thereof, a distribution in several groups is made in Article 4, paragraph 1 of the SIC. These groups are as follows:

(1) *Employees working under employment relationships.* This is the most numerous part of the persons insured against all social risks. It comprises two main groups:
   (a) Employees working under an employment relationship, which is the only one for them, or under a main employment relationship in those cases where they also work under a second employment contract for additional labour (*see infra* item 'b'). These are persons employed for more than five working days or more than forty hours per calendar month. The nature of the work done and the way of payment are of no importance. Over the last three years, the scope of these persons has enlarged due to the addition of a new group of persons insured against all social risks – the postgraduate students in medicine and dentistry who receive remuneration under a training contract for acquiring specialization from the nomenclature of specializations as per Article 181, paragraph 1 of the Health Act.
   (b) The employees working under a second or an additional labour contract. A 'second' labour contract is present where an employee works in two places part-time, so that the total duration thereof exceeds eight hours a day. A 'second labour contract' is either a subsequent one or one of a shorter duration. And the 'additional labour contract' is the one either with the same employer (the so-called internal appointment – Article 110 of the LC) or with another employer (the so-called external appointment – Article 111 of the LC). As for the second employment contract and the additional labour contract, the employees are insured against all social risks.
   (c) According to Article 114a, paragraph 8 of the Labour Code, those workers who work under an employment contract of short-term seasonal work and are registered as farmers or tobacco producers are subject to mandatory

social security on the conditions and in accordance with the procedure laid down in the Social Security Code. In pursuance of this renvoi provision, these persons are insured according to Article 4, paragraph 10 of the Social Security Code against the social risks of disability resulting from general sickness, old age, industrial accident and occupational disease (*see infra* paragraph 124).

(2) *Civil servants*. These are civil servants under the Civil Servant Law, The Ministry of the Interior Law, the Defence and Armed Forces Law, as well as judiciary employees – judges, public prosecutors, investigating magistrates, executive magistrates, entry judges and administrative assistant personnel, members of the Supreme Judicial Council and inspectors of the Inspectorate at the Supreme Judicial Council.

(3) *Cooperative members*. Predominantly, these are members of cooperative societies, their subject of activities being 'production of goods for sale'– producers' cooperatives, producers' cooperatives of disabled persons, and so on. Their legal status is regulated under the Cooperatives Law.

(4) Persons working in commercial companies under management contracts or supervision ones. They perform management and supervision activity, which has the nature of labour activity. This group includes the contractors under management contracts, and contracts of supervision of commercial companies under the Commercial Law, regardless of the type of property these companies are established upon – private or public property.

(5) Persons carrying out labour activity and receiving labour remuneration from elective office without being in an employment relationship and without working under management contracts or contracts of supervision of commercial companies in carrying out this labour activity, as the persons specified in the above items '1' and '4' are. Such persons are municipal councillors, the Presidents of Municipal Councils who do not hold an elective office, and so on.

(6) The clergymen of Bulgarian Orthodox Church and other religions, registered under the Ecclesiastical Matters Law – Catholic, Muslim, and so on.

(7) Candidates for junior judges and junior prosecutors under the Judiciary Act.

95. Persons insured against all social risks with the exception of the unemployment risk. This category of insured persons includes the following two groups:

(1) Persons involved in the social benefits programmes for employment promotion. This legislative solution could be challenged as during that time the persons keep working under an employment relationship and, on general grounds, they should be entitled to all insurance rights, just like all other citizens working under an employment relationship of a full-time job for more than five working days, or forty hours per calendar month (*see supra* paragraph 94, item (1)).

(2) Cooperative members who work in cooperative societies without an employment relationships contract. These are cooperative members working under a freelance contract, the unemployment insurance being provided, in principle, for persons working under an employment relationship. As these persons have no such quality, they are not insured against unemployment.

96. Persons insured against disability caused by general sickness, old age and death (Article 4, paragraph 3 of the SIC). Here the particularity is that the insurance against the risk of general sickness is not a full one, and covers only one of the possible consequences thereof – disability – and does not cover the cases of temporary incapacity for work. The insurance against all these social risks concerns pension insurance, as the indemnities paid upon the occurrence thereof consist in granting the respective pensions (Articles 68, 80–83 of the SIC). The insured persons of this category are divided into four groups:

(1) Persons registered as exercising freelance practitioners' or craftsmen's activity. 'Freelance' professions are the ones regarding intellectual work of high professional level and creative nature. These are writers, painters, musicians, actors, lawyers, translators, and so on. They carry out their labour activity autonomously, beyond the strict regulations. And that is what their nature of 'freelance' professions is expressed in. While the 'craftsmen's activity' consists in the activity of exercising a craft. The 'craft' is a system of practical knowledge, habits, skills and dexterity. Such is the craft of the tailor, the shoemaker, the blacksmith, and so on. The persons exercising these activities as freelance practitioners or craftsmen have to be registered in accordance with the respective procedure and to obtain a permit for the exercise of the respective activities.
(2) Sole traders, owners or partners in commercial companies (unlimited partnerships, limited partnerships, etc.)
(3) Private farmers. These are landlords who own their private land, and cultivate it on their own, and deal with agriculture and livestock-breeding, and so on.
(4) Persons working without an employment relationship. What is typical of this category of persons is that they carry out labour activities without a labour relationship. This category comprises two relatively independent groups of insured persons:
    (a) Persons who do not work under an employment relationship and receive a monthly remuneration in the amount of one minimum monthly salary or exceeding one minimum monthly salary (for 2006 – BGN 160, which is about USD 114).
    (b) Persons who work without an employment relationship, but are insured for the respective calendar month on other grounds – as employees, and so on, regardless of the amount of the received labour remuneration.

97. There are two groups of persons who have the right, on their own initiative and at their own expense, to be insured against the risks of disability caused by general sickness, old age and death, the insurance contribution being assessed with respect to the amount of the self-insured persons' minimum insurance income laid down in the LSSSB, the said amount for 2016 being BGN 420 (about EUR 210) for an income of up to BGN 5,400 (Article 9, item 2, letter 'a' of the quoted Law):

(a) the husband (the wife) of an employee sent on a long-stay business trip to a diplomatic mission abroad – for the period of the employee's overseas mandate (Article 4, paragraph 7 of the SIC);

(b) the spouses of persons who are registered as exercising freelance activities' or craftsmen's activities as well as tobacco producers. The insurance contributions are assessed with respect to the amount of the minimum insurance income for self-insured persons laid down in the Law on the State Social Security Budget, the said amount for 2016 being BGN 300 (Article 4, paragraph 9 of the SIC).

98. Some of the partially insured persons (*see supra* paragraphs 95–97) are also entitled to voluntary insurance against other risks, apart from those against which they have mandatory insurance (Article 6, paragraphs 4–6 of the SIC). The insurance is made in the NII:

(a) The freelance practitioners, craftsmen, sole traders or partners in commercial companies, as well as the farmers-producers (*see supra* paragraph 95'1'–'2') are entitled to voluntary insurance against all other insured social risks with the exception of industrial accident, occupational disease and unemployment.
(b) The working pensioners who conduct activities under Article 4, paragraph 3 of the SIC are entitled to voluntary insurance against the risk of general sickness causing disability, as well as against old age and death (Article 4, paragraph 6 of the SIC).
(c) The persons sent to work abroad by a Bulgarian agent are entitled to insurance against general sickness causing disability, as well as against old age and death. They are insured in accordance with the State Social Insurance Budget Law on the grounds of the insurance income they have specified for the respective calendar year (Article 4, paragraph 5 of the SIC).

99. Seafarers. That is a new group of self-insured persons. It was introduced through the new Article 4'a' of the SIC in the course of amending the SIC in December 2009.

100. This is a radical innovation in Bulgarian social security legislation. As a rule, up to now, the self-insured persons used to be only self-employed ones, that is, persons who perform the so-called independent job and work in their own interest and at their own risk. On general grounds, seafarers are employees under an employment legal relationship; however, they make their mandatory insurance contributions entirely at their own expense, covering general sickness, maternity, disability due to general sickness, old age, death, industrial accident and occupational disease, upon the monthly insurance income they have chosen, which ranges between the minimum insurance income of BGN 460 up to BGN 5,500 and the maximum insurance income of BGN 7,500. In addition, on the grounds of their own choice and desire, the seafarers are entitled to insure themselves against unemployment upon the insurance income they have chosen as self-insured persons.

101. In spite of being employees, the seafarers have been 'converted' by the law into persons of mandatory self-insurance, while their employers are released from the obligation to pay insurance contributions for them. Their inclusion into the scope of persons of mandatory self-insurance places them into an unfavourable position in comparison with the other employees who are obligatorily insured by their employers, the latter taking up a significant portion of the insurance contributions paid for them. This puts seafarers into a disadvantaged position compared to all the other persons of mandatory insurance who work under an employment legal relationship and in whose insurance the employers necessarily have their share (*see infra* paragraphs 122, 123, 133). An expression of the inequitable treatment of these persons is their exclusion from the scope of persons insured against unemployment. Their disadvantaged position is also expressed in imposing upon them the obligation to pay on their own the entire insurance contributions, including those for the risks of industrial accident and occupational disease, which is unknown to any other insured persons who work under an employment legal relationship. Thus, the employers-shipowners turn out to be released from any obligations relating to the social security of these employees – all these obligations are imposed on the seafarers who are obligatorily self-insured. The new regulation raises the question of its constitutionality and, particularly, its consistency with the principle of equality of the citizens before the law under Article 6, paragraph 2 of the Constitution, as well as the question of its consistency with Article 52, paragraph 1 of the Constitution, which lays down the mandatory insurance against unemployment of those persons who have temporarily remained out of job. The new legislative solution is unfair and has been criticized in law literature and has been classified as a departure from the insurance protection of seafarers.[37]

102. As for the seafarers' insurance, there exists specific regulation and differentiation regarding the distribution of insurance contributions and the establishment of the amount thereof in the funds of the State social insurance. The amount of the insurance contributions due to the Pensions Funds varies depending on the date of birth of the insured persons: for those born prior to 1 January 1960, this amount is 17.8% and for those among them who work under the conditions of the 1st or the 2nd category of work it is 20.8%; for the persons born after 31 December 1959 the amount of the insurance contributions is 12%, and for those working under the conditions of the 1st or the 2nd category of work it is 15.8%. The insurance contributions due to the other funds are as follows: 3.5% for the 'General Sickness and Maternity' Fund, 1% for the 'Unemployment' Fund, and 0.4%–1.10%, depending on the specificity of the activity and working conditions in the separate branches of economy, for the 'Accident and Occupational Disease' Fund.

37. V. Mrachkov, *Social Security Law*, 129–131; Y. Genova, *Insured Persons in the State Social Security* 40–54 (Ciela Publishing House 2010).

Chapter 4. Insurance Contributions and Their Distribution

§1. Significance and Legal Infrastructure

103. Insurance contributions constitute the main revenues of the budget of the social insurance funds. Thus, out of the 2021 budget revenues amounting to BGN 15,566,455 (USD 9,259,684) in total, the insurance contributions are BGN 8,887,110 (USD 5,280,536). This also determines their great practical importance.

104. The legal infrastructure of insurance contributions into the State social insurance is regulated in law. The main part of the regulation is contained in Articles 6–7 of the SIC. As far as certain matters explicitly provided for in the SIC are concerned, this legal infrastructure is annually amended and specified in the laws on the annual budget of State social insurance per each calendar year. This creates stability of both the legal regulation of insurance contributions and the exercise of parliamentary supervision of the determination, collection and spending thereof, and that, in its turn, shows the importance the legislator attaches to their legal regime.

105. The determination of the insurance contributions into the SIC and the annual laws on the budget of the State social insurance comprises three main questions: (a) determining the monthly insurance contributions into the insurance funds; (b) the distribution of the insurance contributions among the legal subjects they are due by; (c) the distribution of the insurance contributions among the legal subjects they are payable by. These questions will be dealt with in the following exposition (*see infra* paragraphs 106–134).

§2. Determination and Distribution of Insurance Contributions

106. Here, determination of insurance contributions means the determination of their monthly amount. The latter is differentiated in accordance with the scope of the insured social risks against which the persons are insured. And this is reasonable and explicable: the more the social risks against which the persons are insured, the greater the expenses on insurance indemnities on their realization. And this requires greater revenues from insurance contributions for covering these expenses. This differentiation of the amount of insurance contributions follows the differentiation of the extent of the insured persons in accordance with the amount of insurance protection provided to them (*see supra* Chapter 2) and is set up according to this protection.

107. Amount of the insurance contributions of the persons insured against all insured social risks. This is the most numerous group of insured persons.

According to the operative insurance laws, the insured social risks under the mandatory State social insurance are eleven in number (Articles 1–2, 40–105 of the SIC). They are as follows:

(1) General sickness.

(2) Insured social risks equalled to general sickness:
 (a) Sanatorium and resort treatment.
 (b) Quarantine.
 (c) Removal from work.
 (d) Attending on a sick member of the family.
(3) Industrial accident.
(4) Occupational disease.
(5) Maternity: pregnancy, childbirth and raising a young child.
(6) Old age.
(7) Death.
(8) Unemployment.

108. On their part, the amounts of the insurance contributions of this group of broadest insurance protection are differentiated in accordance with an additional criterion: the working conditions the insured persons work under. The grounds for introducing this additional criterion for differentiation of insurance contributions are economically and socially justified. The grounds are – the more severe, harmful and dangerous the working conditions, the more common the cases of realization of a large part of the insured social risks, and, usually, the greater their seriousness, expressed in the consequences of injuring the health, capacity for work and life of the insured. For instance, such are the industrial accident risk, the occupational disease risk, and so on. And the greater the frequency and seriousness of the realization of the insured social risks, the greater the expenses on covering the insurance indemnities on them. And this, in its turn, requires higher amounts of insurance indemnities for meeting them.

109. According to the operative insurance laws, the working conditions the insured persons work under are divided into three categories depending on the nature of the work done, as well as on the severity and harmfulness of the working conditions. By delegation of Article 104, paragraph 1 of the SIC, the categorization of labour depending on the nature thereof and the working conditions is made by way of a regulation of the Council of Ministers (promulgated in the OJ, No. 123 of 1998, amended).

The first category includes nine types of work and activities whose working conditions are the most severe and harmful ones (underground work, working with radioactive substances, etc.). The second category includes forty-four types of work and activities of severe and harmful working conditions (work in open mines and quarries, work in foundries, etc.), and the third category includes all the rest. The idea of the Law is as follows: the higher the degree of particularities, heaviness and harmfulness of work (first and second category of work), the larger the amount of insurance contributions, because there is higher probability of injuring the life, health and capacity for work of the insured persons employed under those conditions.[38]

38. S. Malakova, *Mandatory Pension Insurance, in 2016 Social Security* 719–720 (Labour and Law Publishing House 2016).

110. The amount of the insurance contributions is differentiated for the various insurance funds within the NII (Article 6, paragraph 1 of the SIC). The said differentiation is grounded on the number and type of the insured social risks upon the realization of which insurance indemnities are paid from these funds, and on the number of persons insured against the respective risks. The greater the risks, the larger the amount of the insurance contributions and vice versa.

111. The amount of the insurance contributions is determined as a percentage of the insured persons' insurance income (Article 6, paragraph 1 of the SIC). This is the income derived from the labour activity of the insured individual. The income comprises any remuneration as well as any other income from labour activity upon which insurance contributions are due, including the allotted, yet unpaid gross-monthly labour remuneration (Article 6, paragraph 3 of the SIC). Therefore, the basis of the insurance income is formed by the remuneration for the work activity, regardless of the legal grounds on which it is carried out – labour, service, freelance or another one. The types of payment for work activity that the insurance income consists of are set out in the Ordinance on the Remuneration Elements and the Incomes upon Which Insurance Contributions Are Made, issued by the Council of Ministers at the proposal of the NII on the grounds of the legal delegation under Article 6, paragraph 13 of the SIC (promulgated in the OJ, No. 1 of 2007, amended).

112. The LSSSB specifies the total maximum and minimum monthly insurance income. The maximum monthly insurance income for 2021 was BGN 3,000 (about USD 1,781) (Article 8, paragraph 1, subparagraph 4 of the LSSSB). And the minimum amount of the monthly insurance income was BGN 650 (about USD 387). It is laid down in the LSSSB through the so-called minimum insurance thresholds. They were first introduced in 2003.

113. The minimum monthly social security income of farmers who cultivate their land themselves and practise agricultural activity, including stockbreeding, and tobacco producers is BGN 420 (about USD 250). These categories of persons who perform work on their own are explicitly included in the scope of persons insured under Article 4, paragraph 4 of the SIC. Their registration is made under Ordinance No. 3 dated 29 January 1999 of the Minister of Agriculture (promulgated in the OJ, No. 10 of 5 February 1999, amended and supplemented). It is under the same Ordinance that tobacco producers are registered as well (Article 19 of the said Ordinance).[39]

114. The amount of the insurance contributions for the 'Pensions' Fund is the highest one (Article 6, paragraph 1, subparagraphs 1–2 of the SIC). This is due to the fact that the grounds for the pensions paid from this Fund are different social risks insured against (old age, death), which, because of their nature, are widespread ones and cover all the insured persons under Article 4 and 4'a' of the SIC. And that requires a large stock of money for the payment thereof, this money being raised primarily from insurance contributions.

39 V Mrachkov, *Social Security Law* 128 (Sibi Publishing House 7th ed. 2019).

115. The amount of the insurance contributions for the 'Pensions' Fund is subject to further differentiation depending on the category of labour under the conditions of which the insured persons work (*see supra* paragraph 109) and the age at which they are 'found' by the entry into effect of the 1999 SIC.

116. For the persons working under the conditions of the 3rd category of labour, the said amount is 17.8% for those born prior to 1 January 1960. And for the persons working under the conditions of the first or second category of labour and those equalled thereto under Article 4, paragraph 1, subparagraph 4 of the SIC and for the investigators under the Judiciary Law the said amount is 20.8%.

For the persons born after 31 December 1959, that is, from 1 January 1960 onwards, this amount is 12.8%. And for the persons working under the conditions of the first or second category of labour and the insured persons under Article 4, paragraph 1, subparagraph 4 of the SIC and for the investigators under the Judiciary Law the said amount is 15.8%.

117. The participation of the State in the financing of the 'Pensions' Fund has necessitated a new distribution of the insured persons' insurance contributions. For the persons born prior to 1 January 1960, that is until 31 December 1959 inclusive, from 1 January 2011 these contributions are 7.9%, while for the self-insured persons these contributions are 17.8%, and for the insurer they are 9.9%, and where the person works under the conditions of the first or second category of labour they are 12.9%. For the persons born after 31 December 1959, that is from 1 January 1960 onwards, these contributions are as follows: 5.7% at the expense of the insured person, and if the latter is a self-insured one – 12.8%, and 7.1% at the expense of the insurer, and where the person works under the conditions of the first or second category of labour – 10.1%.

118. The total amount of the insurance contributions to the 'General Sickness and Maternity' Fund is specified in the SIC and amounts to 3.5% (Article 6, paragraph 1, subparagraph 3 of the SIC), and the contribution to the 'Unemployment' Fund amounts to 1% (Article 6, paragraph 1, subparagraph 4 of the SIC).

119. Unlike it, the insurance contributions' portion in 'Industrial Accident and Occupational Disease' Fund is a differentiated one and is added thereto. Its amount ranges from 0.4% to 1.1% and is determined each year by the State Social Insurance Budget Law – Supplement No. 2 to Article 11, paragraph 1, item 3 of this Law. For 2021 it specifies in detail the seventy-six branches of economic activity in national economy. This percentage is the highest (1.1% of the gross labour remuneration) for those working in branches of harmful and severe working conditions, such as extraction of ores and metals, transport, building industry and the like, and is the lowest (0.4% of the gross labour remuneration) in the branches of less severe working conditions, such as education, real estate transactions, insurance and the like.

120. Insurance contributions are due by the insurers, the insured, the State and the self-insured persons. However, each of these legal subjects owes insurance contributions of different amount.

121. Insurers are individuals or legal entities and subdivisions thereof which are economically and organizationally separate ones and employ persons under employment relationships on their own.

122. The insurers owe and pay insurance contributions for the persons they have employed under an employment relationship, as well as in the following two cases explicitly provided for in law:

(a) where the insurers are obliged in law to pay the full amount of insurance contributions for the insured persons against specific types of insured social risks. Such is the case provided for in Article 6, paragraph 6 of the SIC, by virtue of which the full amount of the insurance contributions for the insurance against industrial accident and occupational disease are 'at the expense of the insurers'. As it has already been pointed out, the amount of these contributions is specified in the State Social Insurance Budget Law for the respective year, and for 2021 it ranges from 0.4% to 1.1% for the various groups of economic activities (*see supra* paragraph 111);
(b) part of the insurance contributions for the other insured social risks is distributed among the insurers and the insured. In this respect, the insurance legislation has undergone an interesting development, which deserves being described in brief.

123. In the socialist epoch of development of Bulgarian society (1949–1989) and in the course of several years after the beginning of the democratic changes in the country (1990–1995), the insurance contributions were paid entirely by the employers. For the first time, since March 1996, the employees have been obliged to pay insurance contributions of minimum amounts – 2% of their gross labour remuneration. However, since that time this obligation kept increasing. Article 6, paragraph 3 of the SIC, adopted in December 1999, provided for gradual increase of the participation of the insured employees in the payment of insurance contributions and the decrease of the employers' insurance contributions. In 2000–2001 the ratio of the insurance contributions paid by the insurers to those paid by the insured employees was 80:20 ('80%' per the insurers and '20%' per the insured employees), in 2002–2004 the ratio was 75:25, and in 2005 it is 70:30. In the coming years this ratio will increase as follows: in 2006 – 65:35, in 2007 and the years following it, including 2021 – 60:40. By the way, the perspective in the development of the legislation in the forthcoming years is to have the insurers' participation in the insurance contributions decrease, and the insured persons' participation therein to increase, so that in the next years these two shares will be equal to each other.

124. The insurance contributions at the expense of the insurers are paid neither from their own financial means and may not be deducted from the remuneration of the insured nor may the insured persons' remuneration for work done be reduced in any way by the amount of the insurance contributions paid by the insurer for the insured person (Article 6, paragraph 12 of the SIC). At first sight, social security contributions resemble tax liabilities in their nature of public liabilities which the insured persons and the insurers must periodically pay to the State body – the National Social Security Institute – which administers the State social security on the grounds of Article 33 of the SIC (*see supra* paragraph 59). However, they are considerably different from tax liabilities and form a separate and independent type of public liabilities when considering their grounds, purpose, legal nature and legal regime. While tax liabilities are citizens' and legal entities' constitutional liabilities under Article 60, paragraph 1 of the Constitution and their payment is unrecoverable and gratuitous, and its purpose is to provide the State with funds for its maintenance and, specifically, for the maintenance of its bodies in the course of their performance of the State's socially significant activities and to ensure these activities[40], the social security contributions are made by natural persons (insured persons) and their insurers (natural persons and legal entities) solely for achieving a specific objective and for a specific purpose, namely, to provide the funds necessary for social security and to guarantee the exercise of the citizens' constitutional subjective right to social security under Article 51, paragraph 1 of the Constitution. On the other hand, it is from the social security contributions paid by the insured persons and their insurers that the insured persons receive social security benefits when certain prerequisites are present: in cases of short-term and long-term (pension) insurance, through which the insured persons provide their own subsistence in temporary or permanent incapacity for work. In this regard, social security contributions are recoverable public liabilities, which is one of their significant differences from tax liabilities which, in their legal nature, are 'irrecoverable' tax liabilities to the State. This is the dominant view in the legal doctrine that has also been supported by the unanimous and constant practice of the Constitutional Court for decades (D. No. 5 of 29 June 2000 on c.c. No. 4 of the year 2000; D. No. 8 of 4 July 2012 on c.c. No. 16 of the year 2011; D. No. 2 of 4 February 2014 on c.c. No. 3 of the year 2013, etc.). And, as for its legal effect, the non-compliance of legal provisions with decisions of the Constitutional Court is equivalent to non-compliance with the Constitution itself, with all the consequences arising from it for the social State governed by the rule of law as set out in indent 5 of the Preamble and Article 4, paragraph 1 of the Constitution; therefore, it forms grounds for declaring such a provision unconstitutional as per Article 149, paragraph 1, item 2 of the Constitution. In this regard, the categorical position taken by the Constitutional Court in its D. No. 14 of 21 December 2010 on c.c. No. 17 of the year 2010 is indicative. In the motives for the decision, it is stated that: 'Any action of the legislative body which is not compliant with a decision of the Constitutional Court or fails to give consideration to its legal consequences is a violation of the Fundamental Law itself, because it concerns the fundamental principles laid down in Art. 4,

40. A. Angelov, *Financial Law of the People's Republic of Bulgaria* 301–306 (Science and Art Publishing House 2nd ed. 1967); M. Kostov, *Tax Law and Civil Law*, *in* 49 *Yearbook of Sofia University – Faculty of Law* 155–276 (University Publishing House 1957); E. Eichenhofer, *Sozialrecht* 5–10 (C.F.Müller Verlag 10th ed. 2017); J.-J. Dupeyroux et al., *Droit de la sécurité sociale* 828–834 (Dalloz 14th ed. 2001).

para. 1 regarding the rule of law and the State governed in accordance with the Constitution and the laws of the country.' Anyone reading these lines will recognize the literal reproduction of Article 4, paragraph 1 of the Constitution. Actually, the decisions of the Constitutional Court form a constituent part of the supremacy of law as 'the most significant and authoritative achievement of the constitutional thought … The supremacy of law is the fundamental concept upon which the building of the political and legal system in our country is built and sustained' (D. No. 12 of 13 October 2016 on c.c. No. 132 of the year 2015).

125. The insured persons pay a part of the insurance contributions in the ratio specified above, the tendency thereof being to increase (*see supra* paragraph 117).

126. Apart from its participation in financing the 'Pensions' Fund (*see supra* paragraph 113), the State pays entirely the insurance contributions in the following two cases:

(a) It pays the entire insurance contribution of civil servants, including those of the civil servants of the Ministry of the Interior and the Ministry of Justice who are employed in the bodies dealing with the application of the Law on the Execution of Penalties (the Central Administration of the Ministry of Justice and in the administration of prisons and probation hostels), the regular military staff under the Law on Defence and Armed Forces (generals, admirals, officers and sergeants), as well as those of the judges, public prosecutors, investigating magistrates, executive magistrates, entry judges and the administrative assistant personnel of the judiciary. The insurance contributions of the civil servants and those equalled thereto are paid at the expense of the State budget, while the insurance contributions of the judges, public prosecutors, investigating magistrates and the other employees of the judiciary are paid from the judiciary budget, which also forms a separate part of the State budget (Article 6, paragraph 5 of the SIC).

(b) The State takes part in financing the State social insurance through the means it provides for the payment of all non-contributory pensions, such as the pensions for civil and military disability, special merits pensions and personal pensions. As far as these pensions are concerned, no insurance contributions are made for them and the State subsidies constitute the only financial source of the payment thereof. These pensions are granted from the State budget.

127. The insurance contributions of self-insured persons are entirely paid by them (Article 5, paragraph 2 and Article 6, paragraph 7 of the SIC). These are individuals who conduct activities as freelance practitioners, craftsmen, sole traders, partners and owners in commercial companies and other similar activities in agriculture, tobacco industry, building industry, and so on. They are not involved in any legal relationships with other persons they either depend on, or work under the supervision of, or receive instructions from in the course of exercising their labour activities. In the course of developing the private initiative and economic activity, for which the State creates and guarantees equal legal conditions for the legal entities (Article 19, paragraph 2 of the Constitution), the number of self-insured persons has considerably increased. In 2021 there were about 250,000 people.[41]

128. The self-insured persons pay insurance contributions in the amount specified in the State Social Insurance Budget Law for the respective calendar year (Article 6, paragraph 2, items 1 and 2 of the SIC). As for 2021, this is a fixed amount of BGN 650 (*see supra* paragraph 112).

129. Under the new legal regulation – according to Article 4'a' of the SIC – the category of seafarers is added to the scope of self-insured persons, who pay the entire insurance contributions on their own, although the seafarers work under an employment legal relationship (*see supra* paragraph 99).

130. The persons pay the due insurance contributions to the NII by monthly remittances to its account. The insurance contributions due by the insurers and the insured are paid together with the due labour remuneration for the preceding month not later than the tenth day of the subsequent month (Article 7, paragraphs 1 and 2 of the SIC). The insurance contributions due by the State for civil servants and other persons equalled thereto are also paid monthly. And the financial subsidies of the State for the payment of the non-contributory pensions are remitted to the NII at the beginning of the budget year. The insurance contributions of the self-insured persons are paid either personally by them or through the insurance cash desks[42] not later than the tenth day of the month they refer to (Article 7, paragraph 3 of the SIC).

131. One of the main problems of the legal regulation of insurance contributions is the regular collection thereof. Only if the insurance contributions are regularly collected and paid to the accounts of the NII does the NII dispose of them and is the NII capable of making the payments of the insurance indemnities. This problem becomes extremely topical and practically important in view of the financial embarrassment of the insurance system and the difficulties encountered in the collection of the insurance contributions.

132. The payment of the due insurance contributions is made by way of a writ of payment drawn by the insurers, remitting financial means from their accounts to the account of the respective insurance fund which the insurance contributions are

41. Statisticheski Spravochnik 2016, 41.
42. The insurance cash desks are bodies assisting in the implementation of State social insurance. Their legal status is regulated in Art. 8 of the SIC and the Ordinance of the Council of Ministers issued on the grounds thereof (promulgated in the OJ, No. 89 of 2001). They are set up by the self-insured persons and those legal entities which have up to ten employees. The insurance cash desks are registered with the respective territorial department of the NII and deal with the insurance of its members by collecting the insurance contributions due by them, remitting them to the respective accounts of the NII, paying the due money indemnities and benefits to the insured persons upon the occurrence of an insurance event, as well as executing and keeping the documents connected with the insurance of the members of the insurance cash desks.

designed for (*see infra* paragraph 133). In order for the regular payment of the insurance contributions to be made, the banks in which the financial means of the insurers are, undertake not to grant to the insurers amounts for the payment of labour remuneration if the insurers have not submitted a writ of payment for the remittance of the insurance contributions due by them to the accounts of the respective funds of the State social insurance. The idea is as follows: the insurers, in their quality of employers, should not be able to draw labour remuneration or other amounts prior to having paid the insurance contributions due by them to the NII.

133. Except for the insurance contributions for seafarers under Article 4'a' of the SIC, the insurance contributions to the 'Industrial Accident and Occupational Disease' Fund are paid entirely by the insurers (Article 6, paragraph 6 of the SIC). This legislative solution has its justification in the nature of these risks. These are occupational social risks faced by the employees who either work under the Labour Code or, although working under some other legal relationship (under a service one – as civil servants, or under an administrative one – as regular military persons, sergeants, officers of the Ministry of the Interior, and so on, or under a freelance one – under contracts of commercial companies' management and control), carry out labour activity or perform a public service of permanent employment and subordination to the respective manager. On the other hand, the industrial accident often – and the occupational disease always – occurs or is caused by the unfavourable conditions of labour and service. And the obligation to have them improved is imposed upon the employer, the respective public administration, and so on. Owing thereto, upon the occurrence of these risks, for covering the expenses resulting from their realization, it is natural for the resources of this Fund to be raised from the employer or from the appointment bodies, because they have the obligation to create such conditions for work and performance of the service as are necessary to eliminate or limit considerably the realization of these insured occupational risks.

134. One of the most important problems in the practice of applying the legal regulation of insurance contributions is their collectability. Only when the insurance contributions have been really paid does the NII dispose of them and can make the payment of the insurance benefits to the insured persons. Since 2004, the insurance contributions have been collected by the territorial directorates of the National Revenue Agency and are credited to the accounts of the NII's insurance funds within twenty-four hours. In recent years there still have been problems and difficulties in the collectability of insurance contributions. In 2019, 2020 and 2021, the amount of the collected insurance contributions reached 89%–92% of the insurance contributions payable by employers and insured persons. That is due both to the difficulties resulting from the economic crisis in the last two years and to the ongoing concealment – on the part of the insurers, commonly with the consent of the insured persons – of the actual insurance incomes. The efforts aimed at overcoming these difficulties continue in 2021 as well.

Chapter 5. Unemployment Fund

§1. Legal Infrastructure

135. UF has existed since 1989. Until the end of 2001, its legal framework was contained in Articles 6–15 of the Law on protection in unemployment and employment promotion. Since 1 January 2002 the legal infrastructure of UF has been transferred to Article 26‘a’–26‘b’ of the SIC, which is its proper systematic place.

136. The transfer of the legal infrastructure of UF to the SIC is not only a matter of logical arrangement of the legal infrastructure of social insurance. It is also connected with two other legal consequences of practical importance. They are as follows: (a) in this way UF became a part of the insurance funds of the State social insurance and was placed under the management of the NII; (b) the purpose of UF was limited. Until the end of 2001, that is until it was transferred to the NII system, UF used to have a double purpose: on the one hand, as an insurance fund against the unemployment risk, and on the other hand, as a source of financial means for financing the vocational training and retraining of the unemployed. The new legal infrastructure has limited its purpose only to the insurance one (*see supra* item ‘a’). This has consolidated the purpose of UF as being an insurance fund of the mandatory State social insurance.

§2. UF’s Revenues and Expenses

137. The sources of revenues to UF are explicitly regulated in Article 26‘a’ of the SIC. They are:

(a) *Insurance contributions*. Their monthly amount is specified in the annual State Social Insurance Budget Law for the respective year. As for 2005, this amount is laid down in Article 11, paragraph 1, item 4 of the State Social Insurance Budget Law for 2016 and is equal to 1% of the gross labour remuneration of the insured. According to Article 6, paragraph 3 of the SIC, the insurance contributions are distributed between the insurers and the insured in the ratio of 60:40. In this situation, the insurer pays insurance contributions in the amount of 0.60% of the gross labour remuneration of the insured, while the insured pay 0.40% of their gross labour remuneration.
(b) Amounts remitted to the State budget for the payment of indemnities under Article 233 of the Law on Defence and Armed Forces. These are indemnities amounting to the minimum monthly salary established in the country, which are paid to the wives of regular military staff persons, these wives having suspended their employment relationships in order to move to another place together with their husbands who have been officially moved to another place in order to hold a position there. This indemnity is paid for the period of time during which the wife has remained out of job in the new place; however, the indemnity may not be paid for more than twelve months, and the wife should

have registered herself in the job centre of the new place within one month following the arrival there. The indemnity is paid by the respective territorial department of the NII. These amounts, remitted to the NII by the State budget, are 'purposeful' ones as they are used only for the purpose specified in law – the payment of the indemnities under Article 233 of the Law on Defence and Armed Forces.

(c) Interest and dividends from financial means of the fund derived from depositing them in a bank, or investing them, and so on.
(d) Other sources provided for in separate laws.

138. The financial means of UF are spent on strictly defined purposes. They are specified in detail in Article 26'b' of the SIC. They are:

(a) Payment of unemployment benefits. The procedure for their payment is laid down in Article 54'a'–54'h' of the SIC and will be considered later (*see infra* Part VI, Chapter 3). This is the main expense of the fund.
(b) For the payment of indemnities under Article 233 of the Law on Defence and Armed Forces (*see supra* paragraph 94, item 2). They have limited application.
(c) For the payment of insurance contributions for mandatory health insurance of the unemployed. They will be dealt with later, within the framework of the presentation of mandatory health insurance (*see infra* Part III, Chapter 3).

Part III. Health Care

Chapter 1. Introduction

139. Medical care in the country has been free of charge since 1951. It includes all ambulatory, polyclinic and home medical examinations, manipulations, surgical operations and treatment including dentistry in medical establishments or at home, meals and medicines during any stay in hospitals and sanatoriums, prophylactic medical examinations, serums and vaccines (Article 2 of the Ukase on Nation-Wide Free Medical Care, promulgated in the OJ, No. 23 of 1951).[43] The only thing free medical care does not include is medicines for treatment at home (Article 4 of the quoted Ukase).

140. Taking into account the new situation established in the country after the changes at the end of 1989 and the transition to market economy, the new Constitution of 12 July 1991 introduced radical changes in this field. Article 52, paragraph 1 thereof stipulated – 'The citizens are entitled to both health insurance that guarantees them accessible medical care and free medical services under the terms and in the due course determined by the law.'

141. Since the Constitution took effect (13 July 1991), a painful transition has begun from the free medical care that had existed for decades and had created traditions and customs, to the health insurance system. This transition has been seriously hampered and delayed because of the severe shortage of financial means for subsidies for public health. There has been a serious crisis in the health services for the population and a deterioration of the quality thereof. These features of public healthcare have not yet been overcome.

142. In the course of this transition, several amendments were made to the Public Health Law of 1973: in 1993, 1994, 1995 and 1997. It was not until the amendments to the Public Health Law at the beginning of 1997 (OJ, No. 12 of 1997) that free medical care was definitively abandoned and health legislation started being brought into conformity with the quoted Article 52, paragraph 1 of the Constitution.

43. The Ukase (Decree) on Nation-wide Free Medical Care was repealed by the Public Health Law of 1973 (OJ, No. 88 of 1973). However, this Law affirmed the free medical care. This situation actually continued until the end of 1997.

In the month of December 1997, the Minister of Public Health issued Regulation No. 22 on the terms and course in which medical care at the patient's choosing is paid for (OJ, No. 122 of 1997).

143. It does not mean that free medical care is totally and absolutely abolished, it only means that, after the HIL took effect, free medical care is no longer the basic form of provision of medical care for the citizens. Pursuant to Article 52, paragraph 1 of the Constitution, 'free use of medical services' for citizens is admissible on general grounds and is applied 'under the terms and in accordance with the procedure set out in law' as a form of the exercise of the citizens' fundamental right to health. Such is the Health Law of 2004 (promulgated in the OJ, No. 70 of 10 August 2004, amended), effective since 1 January 2005. Article 82 of the said Law provides for 'free medical services' in certain cases which are explicitly specified, such as the following: provision of urgent medical care, psychiatric care for inpatients, supply of blood and blood products, transplantation of organs, tissues and cells, medical care in case of pregnancy, childbirth and maternity, and so on. However, free medical care is not a form of health insurance and, because of that, it is not dealt with in this exposition and is only mentioned for the sake of completeness.

144. The changes to the Public Health Law in 1990–1998 ensued from the changing social conditions in the country and the provision of Article 52, paragraph 1 of the Constitution. However, these changes were accompanied by the adoption of other important laws in the field of healthcare. The following ones of them deserve being mentioned.

145. In November 1997 the government introduced the Bill of the HIL into Parliament and after long discussions the Law was adopted on 4 June 1998 (promulgated in the OJ, No. 70 of 1998). It established the general legal framework implementing citizens' rights to health insurance under Article 52, paragraph 1 of the Constitution. The Law has become fully operative in practice from 1 July 1999 (§2 and §3 of the quoted Law). Because of that the following exposition of health insurance as a branch of social insurance is based on the effective insurance law.

146. The HIL introduces two basic forms of implementing health insurance in the country: mandatory and voluntary health insurance. They will be considered in succession (*see infra* Chapters 1–6).

147. Certain matters of healthcare are regulated in a number of other laws. Here are the most important of them:

(a) The Law on Professional Organizations of Physicians and Dentists (promulgated in the OJ, No. 83 of 1998, amended). This Law has provided for the establishment of professional organizations of physicians and dentists – the Union of Bulgarian Physicians and the Union of Bulgarian Dentists, respectively, this restoring the traditions of their professional organizations dating back to the beginning of the twentieth century (years 1903 and 1905). Their legal status has been regulated, as well as their participation in the implementation of healthcare and the health policy of the State (Articles 5–43). The membership in these organizations is obligatory for those physicians and dentists who exercise the profession of a physician or dentist (Articles 3 and 4 of the quoted Law). Later on, these organizations were involved in the implementation of mandatory health insurance (*see infra* Chapter 2).

(b) The Law on the Professional Organization of Nurses, Midwives and Associated Medical Specialists (promulgated in the OJ, No. 46 of 2005). This Law regulated the structure, organization, management and activity of this professional organization of medical specialists, the conditions under which they conduct their activity, the Bulgarian Association of Health Care Professionals they have established (Articles 1 and 2 of the quoted Law) and its participation in the implementation of healthcare and the healthcare policy of the State, and in health insurance, in particular. The membership in this association is voluntary for the nurses, midwives and associated medical specialists (medical and roentgen laboratory assistants, rehabilitation therapists, physician's assistants, orthopaedic technicians and masseurs).

(c) The Law on Drugs and Pharmacies in Human Medicine (promulgated in the OJ, No. 36 of 1995, amended). This Law regulates the conditions and procedure for the permission and supervision of the manufacture, application, clinical studies, import, export, wholesale trade and retail trade in drugs for human medicine in the country, including the procedure for opening new pharmacies in the country, which is permitted only to pharmacists holding the Master's Degree, thus ensuring the high quality of the offered drugs and their efficient and safe use in the best interests of the health of citizens (Articles 1–142 of the quoted Law).

(d) The Law on Medical Treatment Institutions (promulgated in the OJ, No. 62 of 1999, amended). It regulates the structure and activity of medical treatment institutions for outpatients (dispensaries, individual and group practices, medical and dental centres), for inpatients and their types (hospitals for active treatment, post-treatment, continuous treatment, rehabilitation, general and specialized hospitals), the territorial distribution thereof in accordance with the population of the country, the procedure for their establishment, organization and closure, their management, and so on (Articles 8–81 of the quoted Law).

(e) And last but not least among the laws of this group is the Health Law adopted in 2004 (promulgated in the OJ, No. 70 of 2004). The numerous amendments that were made to the 1973 Public Health Law in the period after 1989 (*see supra* paragraph 144) have contributed to resolving some urgent specific matters in the reorganization of healthcare legislation; however, they have not contributed to a radical legislative change of its philosophy. And the latter has been created for and under social conditions grounded on the right to free healthcare (*see supra* paragraphs 139 and 142). The 1991 Constitution placed healthcare on the grounds of health insurance. The Public Health Law of 1973 did not correspond to these new conditions and social needs. This necessitated the adoption of an entirely new Health Law. This new general Law, which is an organizational one in its nature, regulates the legal grounds of healthcare in the country. It provides the legal infrastructure of basic matters, such as the establishment of a national healthcare system, basic healthcare activities (provision of healthy living environment, influence upon health risk factors, control over infectious diseases, protection against the effect of ionizing radiation, etc.), medical services, mental health of the nation, unconventional methods of favourable influence upon the individual's health, medical education, and so on (Articles 1–236 of the quoted Law).

148. The laws mentioned above create the required legal and medical (public and private) infrastructure for the implementation of the health policy of the State, which is directed to the exercise of the citizens' right to health. Health insurance has its important place in this infrastructure and is a matter of special interest in this exposition.

Chapter 2. Mandatory Health Insurance

149. The mandatory health insurance is regulated under Articles 4–80 of the HIL. It is the basic type of health insurance. Its nature is determined by the wide extent of insured persons, the scope of medical care and the importance of its financial and organizational structure and management. This is confirmed by its detailed legal infrastructure.

150. This health insurance is mandatory because it directly ensues from the law: it applies regardless of whether the persons it covers wish it or not. No contractual, administrative or other act of will is necessary in order for these persons to become insured.

§1. Personal Field of Application of Mandatory Health Insurance

151. The extent of insured persons is extremely wide (Article 33 of the HIL). It comprises four large categories of persons: (1) all Bulgarian citizens who are not citizens of another State as well; (2) Bulgarian citizens who are also citizens of another State permanently residing in the territory of the Republic of Bulgaria; (3) foreign citizens and apatrides who are permanent residents in Bulgaria; (4) persons who have been granted either the status of refugees or the right to asylum.[44]

§2. Rights of Insured Persons

152. Insured persons have rights established by the Law (Article 35 of the quoted Law). These rights can be divided into two groups.

The first of them consists of the insurance rights of the insured persons. These are the following rights: (a) to receive medical care in the extent stipulated under the law, the NFC's and the contracts between the Regional Health Insurance Pay Cash Desk Offices (RHIPCDO) and the providers of medical care (*see infra*); (b) to choose one provider of primary medical care among the providers that the RHIPCDO has made a contract with; (c) to have their costs for medical care abroad recovered in case of obtaining advance permission thereof from the NHIPCDO; (d) to receive information from the regional pay offices concerning the contracts concluded between the RHIPCDO and the providers of medical care.

The second group comprises the 'administrative rights' of the insured persons. These rights are as follows: (a) to participate through their representatives in the management of the NHIPCDO; (b) to file complaints to the Director of the NHIPCDO through the Director of the respective RHIPCDO, these complaints concerning violations of the law and contracts.

44. As to the legal status of the refugees, *see infra*, Part IX, S. 2.

§3. Obligations of Insured Persons

153. Insured persons have three basic obligations:

(1) According to Article 37 of the HIL, the insured persons pay a fee in the amount of BGN 2.90 (about USD 1.72) for each visit to the doctor or the dentist. Those persons who have exercised their right to pension for contributory length of service and old age pay BGN 1 (about USD 0.70) for such a visit. The insured persons pay BGN 5.80 for each day of hospital treatment, yet not for more than ten days per year. The amount of these payments is determined by the Council of Ministers (Decree of the Council of Ministers 193/year 2012, OJ, No. 68/year 2012; Ordinance No. 8 of 3 November 2016, promulgated in the OJ, No. 92–93 of the year 2016). These fees are not payable by persons suffering from certain diseases specified in a list maintained by the NHIPCDO, juveniles and minors (persons younger than 18), the unemployed, military persons during their regular military service, the poor who receive aid under the Social Assistance Law, and so on.
(2) To make insurance contributions within seven days of their becoming due (*see* below).
(3) To notify the RHIPCDO of any change in the circumstances of their health insurance.

§4. Content of Health Insurance

154. Health insurance consists of different types of benefits that the insured persons are provided with in order to establish, protect, restore and improve their health status. What is common for all these benefits is that they relate to the health of the insured persons. They are enumerated in Article 45 of the quoted Law and include the following:

(a) Medical and dental activities for prevention of diseases.
(b) Medical and dental activities for early diagnosing of diseases.
(c) Medical care in diagnosing and treating inpatients' and outpatients' diseases.
(d) Medical rehabilitation.
(e) Urgent medical care.
(f) Medical care in the cases of pregnancy, childbirth and raising children.
(g) Abortions for medical reasons and in the case of pregnancy resulting from a rape.
(h) Dental medical care.
(i) Medical care where treatment is conducted at home.
(j) Medicines and consumables for treatment at home.
(k) Prescribing the granting of medical products and dietary foods for special medical purposes.
(l) Examination by a medical expert in case of temporary incapacity for work.
(m) Transport services for medical reasons.

155. The provision of different types of medical care is specified in the NFC and in the contracts between the RHIPCDO and the providers of medical care. Health insurance medical care has to be in compliance with the rules on good medical practice. These rules are adopted by the professional organizations of the physicians, dentists and the NHIPCDO, and they are approved by the Minister of Health Care. These rules comprise requirements for timeliness, accessibility and quality of medical care.

Chapter 3. National Health Insurance Pay Cash Desk Office

§1. Administrative Organization

156. The NHIPCDO is the body that implements the mandatory health insurance. This Office is the insurance body in the system of health insurance. The NHIPCDO is an administrative body, and it may not be the owner of medical establishments, consulting rooms, laboratories, pharmacies and the like. Neither may it conduct voluntary health insurance (*see* Chapter 6 *infra*). This Office is set up under Article 6 of the quoted Law and it is a legal entity. The NHIPCDO comprises a Central Administration and twenty-eight RHIPCDO situated in the regional towns of the country.

157. The amendments to the HIL made in December 2010 (promulgated in the OJ, No. 98 of 14 December 2010) introduced important changes into the governing bodies of the NHIPCDO. These changes have simplified its governance and have made the latter somewhat symmetrical to the governance of the NII, while preserving its specificity of a health insurance body. The governing bodies are: (1) Supervisory Board; (2) The Manager (*see infra* paragraphs 158–165).

158. Supervisory Board (Article 6, paragraph 3, subparagraph 1; Articles 13–19'a' of the HIL). It has a quadrilateral composition and consists of nine members, distributed as follows: one representative of the representative patients' organizations for patients' rights, two representatives of the representative trade union organizations, two representatives of the representative employers' organizations and four representatives of the State, one of them being the Director of the National Revenue Agency.

159. The representative of the representative patients' organizations is elected by those patients' organizations which the Minister of Health Care has recognized as representative non-profit-making legal entities – under the Law on Non-Profit Making Legal Entities – carrying out activities for the public good under the said Law, in accordance with the procedure and criteria set by the Minister for a term of three years. The representatives of the representative trade union and employers' organizations are designated by their national governing bodies.[45] The stronger representation of the representative employers' organizations under Article 35 of the LC (each of them has two representatives, while each representative trade union organization has one representative) in the Supervisory Board of the NHIPCDO is due to the fact that the lawmaker has taken into account the considerable participation of the employers in the health insurance contributions (*see infra* paragraph 174). The participation of the State in the Supervisory Board has also been greatly strengthened. The representatives of the State are five: four members and the President. They are nominated by the Council of Ministers. Thus, in crucial votes, the representatives of the State have majority in the decision-making process.

45. As for the representative trade union and employers' organizations, *see* V. Mrachkov, *Labour Law*, 749–760, 766–772.

160. The President and the members of the Supervisory Board are elected for a term of five years.

161. The Supervisory Board has important governance functions: it takes part in drawing up and adopting the NFCs for medical and dental activities, approves the Bill on the budget of the NHIPCDO prior to its introduction before the Council of Ministers, approves the annual financial statement of the NHIPCDO, and so on.

162. The new regulation concerning the Supervisory Board and its functions shows a clear tendency to the State's greater participation in the governance of the NHIPCDO. The representatives of the professional organizations of physicians and dentists, who used to form part of the governing bodies of the NHIPCDO prior to the changes of December 2009, are no longer included in the composition of the Supervisory Board. The designation of the patients' organizations as representative ones is granted by the Minister of Health Care.

163. The Manager of the NHIPCDO. He/she is elected by the National Assembly for a term of five years. This election by the Parliament – which is introduced for the first time – results in a rise in his/her official status and makes him/her equal to the Manager of the NII.

164. As a single-person body, the Manager of the NHIPCDO is vested with important functions. He/she organizes and manages the activity of the NHIPCDO, he/she concludes, changes and terminates the employment contracts of the Directors of the RHIPCDO, makes the project for the annual budget of the NHIPCDO, makes the report on the execution thereof, performs the employer's functions in relation to the employees of the Central Administration of the NHIPCDO, acts as a first-degree appropriator of the budget of the NHIPCDO, and so on.

165. The Directors of the RHIPCDOs represent the NHIPCDO at the territorial level; they organize and manage the activity of the RHIPCDOs, conclude, change and terminate the employment contracts of the employees in the respective Offices, and so on. They are second-degree appropriators of the budget of the RHIPCDOs.

§2. Financial Structure

166. The NHIPCDO keeps its autonomous budget separate from the State budget. It is a financial plan for raising and spending the finance of the mandatory health insurance.

The annual budget of the NHIPCDO is approved by the National Assembly by way of a Law. The Bill is introduced by the Council of Ministers along with the Bill of the State Budget and the one of the Social Insurance Fund. The first Law on the Budget of the NHIPCDO was adopted for 2000 because 1 January 2000 was the commencement date for the performance of the contracts between the RHIPCDOs and the providers of medical care.

167. The revenues for the budget of the NHIPCDOs are raised from insurance contributions (*see infra*), interest and incomes from managing the Office's property, fines and penalty interest, fees, donations, wills, and so on. According to the Law on the 2021 Budget of the NHIPCDO, their total amount is BGN 5,446,919.3 thousand (USD 3,238,731 thousand), which is about BGN 1,091,608 million (USD 649,980 million) more compared to the 2020 budget, in spite of the crisis that the country continues being under.

168. The finances of the NHIPCDOs are spent on payment for the medical care the insured persons have been provided with in accordance with the NFC (*see infra*), financing the health insurance administrative activities, acquisition of movables and immovables, fees for the collection of health insurance contributions by the NII, and so on. The total increase in the revenues of the 2021 budget of the NHIPCDO (*see supra* paragraph 167) compared to 2020 is a humble one and is highly insufficient for the needs of health insurance. And yet, in view of the said increase and a better internal distribution of the budget funds, a considerable increase (of about BGN 350 million) (USD 201 million) of the expenditure on hospital treatment has been provided for. This amount will be used for increasing the spending on intensive treatment, urology, neonatology, radiotherapy and haematological diseases.

169. The NHIPCDO is obliged to form a reserve. It is raised from – 10% of the collected insurance contributions into the Office and from other revenues as well. The financial means of the reserve cover expenses in the cases of considerable diversions from the uniform spending of financial means, or territorial imbalance in the consumption and payment of medical aid. The pecuniary amounts provided for in the annual Law on the Budget of the NHIPCDO are used solely and exclusively for the implementation of the citizens' constitutional right to health, part of it being the constitutional right to health insurance under Article 52, paragraph 1 of the Constitution. These pecuniary amounts have a strictly defined purpose. It is inadmissible for these amounts or any part thereof to be transferred and made available to State bodies for other purposes, including constitutional ones, e.g., for use by healthcare authorities of the executive power and the like. This issue became extremely topical in 2011–2012 when the 41st National Assembly – the first legislature in which the political party CEDB had parliamentary majority – decided, on the grounds of Article 1, paragraph 2, line 5 of the Law on the 2011 budget of the NHIPCDO, to provide the Ministry of Health with BGN 100 million (about USD 54,484,861) from the budget of the NHIPCDO for the payment of medical activities, medicines, products and articles provided by the said Ministry, through monthly transfers (§ 5, paragraph 2 of the quoted Law). This provision was challenged by a group of deputies – from the opposition, as usual – as unconstitutional as per Article 149, paragraph 1, item 2 of the Constitution. Through its Decision No. 8 of 4 July 2012, the Constitutional Court declared it unconstitutional because it contravenes the principle of the rule of law (*see also* D. No. 17 of 6 November 1997 on c.c. No. 10 of the year 1997; D. No. 13 of 15 December 2012 on c.c. No. 12 of the year 2012, etc.).

170. Those financial means which are temporarily spare, as well as those of the reserve of the NHIPCDO can be deposited in bank accounts or State securities. The banks which have the right to operate with the financial means of the NHIPCDO are determined jointly by the Bulgarian National Bank and the Ministry of Finance. It is among the banks thus determined that the Supervisory Board of the NHIPCDO chooses the banks to which the right of operating with the financial means of the NHIPCDO is assigned.

Chapter 4. Health Insurance Contributions

171. Health insurance contributions for mandatory health insurance are the main revenues for the NHIPCDO. According to Article 1, paragraph 1 of the Law on the Budget of the NHIPCDO for 2021, out of all the revenues amounting to BGN 5,105,493 thousand (which is about USD 3,325,415 thousand) are revenues from insurance contributions. This determines their practical importance.

172. According to Article 29, paragraph 3 of the HIL, the amount of health insurance contributions for mandatory health insurance is determined annually under the Law on the Budget of the NHIPCDO. The Bill of this Law is introduced in the Council of Ministers by the Supervisory Board of the NHIPCDO through the Minister of Health Care, and the Council of Ministers introduces it in the National Assembly within the terms provided for submitting the Bill of the State Budget (three months prior to the end of the calendar year, that is prior to 1 October of the current year). For the purpose of establishing consistency and coordination in the budget legislation of the country, this Bill is discussed in the National Assembly along with the Bills of the State Budget and the State social insurance budget. According to Article 2 of the Law on the Budget of the NHIPCDO for 2021, the amount of health insurance contributions is 8%.

173. As for those persons who receive incomes from employment relationships, civil services relationships or other relationships connected with exercising labour activity, which are grounded on special laws (cooperative members, persons working under contracts of management or supervision of commercial companies, etc.), the amount of health insurance contributions is calculated on the grounds of the insurance income upon which the insurance contributions for mandatory State insurance are paid, this income being determined in compliance with Article 6 of the SIC (*see supra* paragraph 117). As for the self-insured, these contributions are determined on the grounds of the insurance income they have stated within the limits of the minimum and maximum insurance income, provided for in the State Social Insurance Budget Law for the respective calendar year. According to Article 8 of the State Social Insurance Budget Law for 2021, the minimum insurance income for the self-insured was BGN 650, and the maximum one was BGN 3,000 (*see supra* Chapter 3, §2).

174. The health insurance contributions for those persons who work under employment or self-employment relationships, or under relationships which have occurred on grounds provided for in special laws (*see supra* paragraph 157), the health insurance contributions are remitted either by the employer or by the institution in which these people work and the insured person in the ratio specified in Article 40, paragraph 1 of the HIL. In 2017 this ratio is 60:40, the 60% being paid by the employer or the institution, and the 40% being paid by the insured person. By the way, the ratio and rhythm assumed for this change are aimed at achieving in the future an equal participation in the payment of health insurance contributions on the part of the insurer and on the part of the insured, which also applies to the insurance contributions in State social insurance (*see supra* Chapter 3, paragraph 2).

The health insurance contributions of the self-insured are remitted by them in person and are wholly at the expense thereof.

175. Health insurance contributions are paid monthly. They are paid to the respective territorial department of the National Revenue Agency, and afterwards they are remitted to the account of the NHIPCDO not later than the tenth day of the month they refer to.

176. The great and difficult economic, social and legal problem existing with regard to health insurance contributions is the amount thereof. The rising cost of medical aid due to the introduction of new and modern methods of examination and treatment brings about an increase of the expenses on paying for it. Each year this causes serious financial problems in the NHIPCDO and strain in its budget. In recent years, this problem has been in the centre of parliamentary discussions in the course of preparing the budget laws of the NHIPCDO.

Chapter 5. Contracts for Provision of Medical Care

§1. Introduction

177. One of the most important novelties introduced by the Social Security Law is the principle of contracts in providing medical care. This is a negation of the free medical care introduced in 1951, which used to be wholly financed by the State budget. The said principle is one of the mainstays (fundaments) that health insurance is based on. The contract is a mechanism of market economy and introducing it in health insurance means bringing health insurance in line with the requirements of market economy. On the other hand, the introduction of health insurance imparts social character to market economy.

178. The principle of contracts is used in the provision of medical care. This principle finds its expression in two main types of contracts: (1) NFC; (2) contract between the NHIPCDO and the RHIPCDO and the providers of medical care. These will be considered in brief.

§2. National Frame Contracts

179. In December 2009, the amendments to the HIL (promulgated in the OJ, No. 101 of 18 December 2009) introduced substantial changes into the legal regulation of the NFC, which took effect on the day of their promulgation in the OJ. These are changes in several important directions.

180. First of all, there was abandoned the conclusion of a unitary general NFC between the NHIPCDO and the professional organizations of physicians and dentists, which was provided for in the 1998 HIL (Article 35 of the HIL, 1998 version) and used to cover both medical and dental activities. The conclusion of a unitary NFC used to create major difficulties in achieving common consent between the representatives of the professional organizations of physicians and dentists, on the one hand, as well as between them and the NHIPCDO, on the other hand. Because of these difficulties, over the last three years (2007, 2008 and 2009) no consent has been reached and no NFCs have been signed, and the 2006 NFC was applied instead. The new regulation 'divided' the conclusion of the unitary general NFC into two NFCs: one for medical activities, which is concluded between the NHIPCDO and the Union of Bulgarian Physicians, and another one for dental activities, which is concluded between the NHIPCDO and the Union of Bulgarian Dentists (Article 53, paragraph 1 of the HIL, 2009 version). This legislative solution was welcomed with relief and was adopted by the representatives of the two professional organizations.

181. The NFCs are concluded for a term of three years (Article 53, paragraph 2 of the HIL) and not for one year as the previous regulation provided for. If changes have occurred, each year the parties sign an agreement, updating it for the respective calendar year.

182. There are both general and specific matters for the contracting parties to discuss when concluding each of the two separate NFCs. The NFC for medical activities is drawn up in the course of negotiations involving ten representatives of the NHIPCDO and ten representatives of the Union of Bulgarian Physicians, while the negotiations for the NFC for dental activities involve seven representatives of the NHIPCDO and seven representatives of the Union of Bulgarian Dentists. The NHIPCDO is represented by members of the Supervisory Board and the Manager of the NHIPCDO, while the two professional organizations are represented by members of their national governing bodies.

183. The negotiations for the conclusion of the NFCs are conducted during the period laid down in law, starting at the time of bringing in the Bill on the NHIPCDO budget for the next calendar year (usually, November–December of the current year) and continuing during the time of discussing the Bill, until it is finally adopted and promulgated in the OJ. This parallel discussion of the Bills allows for mutual provision of information among the representatives of the parliamentary bodies and those of the professional organizations and the NHIPCDO, and the synchronization (the consideration in view of time) thereof, as well as the alignment in view of their content.

184. The NFCs are adopted by a majority of seven representatives of the NHIPCDO and seven representatives of the professional organizations of the physicians and dentists.

185. The NFCs are concluded in writing. This is the '*ad solemnitatem*' form of their validity.

186. The NFCs are signed by the Minister of Health Care and are promulgated by him/her in the OJ. The NFCs for medical services and for dental services for 2016 are also published in OJ, No. 2 of 8 January 2016.

187. The NFCs regulate the basic issues of health insurance implementation. They establish the due course and terms for determining the providers of medical care, types of medical care – its provision and payment, the accessibility and quality, the list of medicines payable by the NHIPCDO, the control over the performance of the contract, sanctions in the case of non-performance, and so on.

188. In March and December 2015, some amendments and supplements were made to the procedure for concluding and changing the NFCs on medical and dental activities (promulgated in the OJ, Nos 48 and 98 of 2015):

a) The national frame contracts on medical and/or dental activities are concluded not later than the last day of February and take effect on the first of April of the respective calendar year. They must comply with the budget of the NHIPCDO for the calendar year they take effect in and apply to (Article 53, paragraph 6 of the HIL);

b) In those cases where the legislation has undergone changes which require that changes in the national frame contracts are made as well, the changes required are introduced through a decision of the Supervisory Board of the NHIPCDO at the proposal of the Director of the NHIPCDO. This quick and simple way of introducing changes is conditioned by the obligatory nature of the legislative changes concerning the national frame contracts and the need for timely application of these changes through the national frame contracts (Article 53, paragraph 9 of the HIL);

c) The Minister of Health Care coordinates the decision of the NHIPCDO under Article 53, paragraph 9 of the HIL within seven days following its submission by the Director of the NHIPCDO and promulgates it in the Official Journal (Article 53, paragraph 11 of the HIL).

189. The NFCs may not lay down requirements regarding – the minimum number of persons with health insurance registered by the providers of primary medical care for outpatients, conditions interfering with the insured person's free choice of the provider of medical care, conduct of highly specialized medical activities apart from those specified in law and provided from the budget of the NHIPCDO, additional requirements regarding pharmacies, wholesale traders and drug manufacturers apart from those specified in the Law on Drugs and Pharmacies in Human Medicine, maximum number of conducted activities, and limitations in the amount of the activities distributed among medical treatment institutions.

190. The new regulation has given greater clarity to the legal nature of the NFCs. This matter was not explicitly regulated by the previous legal framework and used to create difficulties and disputes. The changes in the HIL of December 2009 – Article 4'a' of the HIL – explicitly specify the NFC as 'a normative administrative act which is operative on the territory of the whole country for a certain period of time and is binding on the NHIPCDO, the RHIPCDOs, the providers of medical care, the insured persons and the insurers'.[46]

191. The NFCs are sublegal normative acts which concern the application of the HIL. This nature of theirs is clearly expressed in Article 53, paragraph 1 of the HIL, according to which they are adopted 'for the performance of the activities provided for in this Law', that is in the HIL. These activities form the subject matter of regulation of the said Contracts. What is special about this sublegal normative act is its negotiated origin, as it constitutes an agreement between the NHIPCDO and the professional organizations of physicians and dentists, respectively. That does not change its normative nature. The latter is determined by its content, effect and purpose imparted to it by the law, and not by the subjects that conclude it.

46. V. Mrachkov, *Social Security Law,* 470–474; K. Sredkova, *Social Security Law, supra*, 90–99.

192. The changes in the regulation of the NFCs have evoked reassurance. In conformity with this regulation – and following long-continued and heated discussions – the NFCs for the last four years (2013–2016) are regularly signed and are operative during the calendar year they concern.

§3. Contracts Between the NHIPCDO, RHIPCDOs and the Providers of Medical Care

193. The contracts between the NHIPCDO, the RHIPCDOs and the providers of medical care are regulated in Articles 58–62 of the HIL. Their main purpose is to ensure the provision of medical care for the insured persons. And that is what determines their great importance.

194. The following are the providers of medical care: medical establishments, physicians, dentists and other specialists in medicine who have the right to practise medicine as physician's assistants, midwives, nurses, dental technicians and the like who give medical treatment to outpatients.

195. The contracts between NHIPCDO and the providers of medical care are concluded by the Manager of the NHIPCDO, while the contracts between the RHIPCDOs and the providers of medical care are concluded by the Director of the respective RHIPCDO. These contracts specify the conditions of the NFCs. The content of these contracts may not be less favourable than the content of the NFC. These contracts are made for the period of time the NFCs are effective and they are in force until either the NFCs are changed or new NFCs are adopted. The contract with the providers of medical care is changed or a new one is concluded in those cases where the effective NFCs are changed or new NFCs are adopted.

196. The RHIPCDOs may also conclude contracts with physicians and dentists working in hospitals for providing medical care for outpatients in the case of shortage of physicians of the same speciality, who treat outpatients in the territory of the RHIPCDOs, if that does not disturb the activity of the hospital.

197. The NHIPCDO and the RHIPCDOs are obliged to inform the providers of medical care about any changes ensuing either from decisions of their managing bodies or from changes in the NFC, as well as to give the necessary instructions in relation to these changes. These obligations of the NHIPCDO and the RHIPCDOs are regulated in the NFCs and in the contracts between the RHIPCDOs and the providers of medical care.

Chapter 6. Control and Disputes in Mandatory Health Insurance

§1. Control in Mandatory Health Insurance

198. Constant control is exercised over the provision of mandatory health insurance. It is designed to guarantee the provision of mandatory health insurance of the scope and content established by the HIL and the contracts concluded for the implementation thereof (*see* Chapter 4 *supra*).

199. There are three types of control over the provision of mandatory health insurance, these types depending on the bodies exercising the control and the issues it subtends: (a) administrative; (b) financial; (c) medical.

200. The overall administrative control (inner office control) over the mandatory health insurance is exercised by the Manager of the NHIPCDO. The Directors of the RHIPCDOs exercise control over the offices of the Central Administration and the territorial departments of the NHIPCDO. This control extends over the current operational activity of the offices in connection with mandatory health insurance.

201. The financial control over mandatory health insurance is exercised by the Chamber of Accounts, the Supervisory Board and the financial inspectors specially charged therewith.

202. The Chamber of Accounts controls the budget of the NHIPCDO. This is control over the raising and spending of the financial means of the annual budget of the NHIPCDO, these financial means being public ones. The control is exercised in the due course provided for under the Chamber of Accounts Law.

203. The Supervisory Board exercises control over the activity of the NHIPCDO, the Manager of the NHIPCDO and the Directors of the RHIPCDOs. This control extends over the disposition of and spending of the financial means of the NHIPCDO and the RHIPCDOs and it is exercised by the said bodies and officials.

204. The financial inspectors, being specialized financial bodies, exercise direct control over the finances of the RHIPCDOs. Their control activity comprises checks on the revenues into the NHIPCDO, the accounting documents of the providers of medical care, payments made and their compliance with the law as well as checks relating to complaints of insured persons and employers in the realization of mandatory health insurance, and so on.

205. Medical control is exercised by two types of specialized medical control bodies: (a) the Minister of Health Care; (b) physicians-controllers of the NHIPCDO and the RHIPCDOs.

206. It is through the Specialized Medical Supervision Directorate of the Ministry of Health Care that the Minister of Health Care exercises control over the quality of the conducted health activities and services, and over the access to medical care in mandatory health insurance. In performing its control functions, the Directorate examines the observance of medical standards and rules regarding good medical practice in the contracts signed between the RHIPCDOs and the providers of medical care. The Directorate also examines the access of the insured to high-quality medical and dental care for outpatients and inpatients. The Directorate draws up a report to the Minister of Health Care on the overall state of health insurance, and so on. The controllers of the Directorate are entitled to check the contracts between the RHIPCDOs and the providers of medical care, to make *in-situ* checks in the NHIPCDO and the RHIPCDOs, and so on.

207. Medical control is exercised by physicians-controllers of the RHIPCDOs. The medical care provided within the frames of health insurance is the subject of their control. This control extends over the rules on good medical practice, the type and scope of the medical care rendered, the type and quantities of prescribed medicines, the correlation between the medical care provided and the sums paid for it and other similar.

Medical control is exercised either accidentally – by way of checks in connection with complaints, or in cases of excessive expenses on medical care or routinely – over the activity of the providers of medical care of the separate RHIPCDOs.

208. When the physician-controller, who exercises control, establishes a violation, he draws a statement of facts, which specifies the respective violation. One copy of this statement of facts is given to the person under check, a second one is sent to the respective RHIPCDO and a third one to the regional college of the professional organization of physicians and dentists.

§2. Disputes in Mandatory Health Insurance

209. The person under examination is entitled to file a written objection against the statement of facts, which specifies the respective violation act, within three days of its being signed (Article 74, paragraph 4 of the HIL). In these cases the physician-controller sends the records including the statement of facts, the objection against it and the other related materials to the administrative penalty body, that is, to the Director of the RHIPCDO who rules upon it. If the latter finds that the objections are well founded, he/she terminates the procedure (Article 54 of the Law on Administrative Violations and Sanctions); otherwise, he/she issues a penalty decree for imposing an administrative sanction in the form of a fine on the person under examination (Article 105'h' of the HIL).

210. The performance of the contracts between the NHIPCDO, the RHIPCDOs and the providers of medical care might give rise and does give rise to disputes between the parties. These are contractual-civil law disputes arising out of the contracts under Articles 58–62 of the HIL. They are dealt with in accordance with the standard procedure of sentencing claim proceedings under Articles 103 et seq. of the Civil Procedure Code.

Chapter 7. Contemporary State of Additional Voluntary Health Insurance

211. The 1998 HIL, which introduced the new legal regulation of health insurance in performance of Article 52, paragraph 1 of the Constitution, has laid down two forms of its implementation: basic obligatory and additional voluntary health insurance (*see supra* paragraph 146). In the subsequent years – 2002, 2005, 2007, etc. – the regulation of voluntary health insurance was amended and expanded considerably. The health insurance companies started being created and began functioning. In 2012 their number reached nineteen, as was the number of the health insurance funds they managed. On the whole, in the period 1998–2012, the voluntary health insurance established itself as a form supplementing the obligatory health insurance.[47]

212. However, along with it, after the 2003 amendments to the HIL, the additional voluntary health insurance started departing – discreetly at the beginning and more tangibly later on – from the social security model and drew closer to insurance. This tendency in the development of legal regulation was expressed in the renvoi to insurance law in case of unsettled matters (the insurance contract (Articles 380–418 of the Commercial Law, 1996 version), and to the Insurance Code (IC) after 2005), the transfer of the State financial supervision on voluntary health insurance – exercised under the FSC Law – from the FSC Deputy Chairperson in charge of social security supervision to the FSC Deputy Chairperson in charge of insurance supervision, etc.

213. This tendency has found its most vivid manifestation in the radical change made to the HIL in August 2012 (promulgated in the OJ, No. 60 of 7 August 2012). Taking effect on the date of its promulgation in the Official Journal – 7 August 2012 – this change has almost totally repealed the detailed social security law regulation of voluntary health insurance, which has been gradually built up in the preceding years. The regulation of Chapter III of the HIL, which preserved its ambitious title – 'Voluntary Health Insurance' – was reduced to four legal regulations only (Articles 81, 82, 83 and 85) out of all the forty Articles that used to exist until that time. This has abruptly impoverished the social security regulation of the Law and has changed its legal countenance: the changes of August 2012 have turned it from a sectoral social security regulation into an insurance regulation of a special part of the personal insurance.

214. A summarized expression of this profound change which transformed the previous social security law regulation into an insurance law regulation is Article 82, paragraph 1 of the HIL, according to which: 'Voluntary health insurance is performed on the grounds of a medical insurance contract within the meaning of Article 222a of the Insurance Code.' The fact that the said legal regulation is contained in a social security Law, namely in the HIL, does not change its insurance law nature.

47. V. Mrachkov, *Social Security Law* 444 (Sibi Publishing House 7th ed. 2019).

Leaving alone the juridical imperfection of the normative wording of this provision, it lays down a normative oxymoron, i.e., an internally discrepant regulation made up of heterogeneous, contradictory and juridically inconsistent legal solutions, which cannot be combined into a unified regulation because of their significant differences. Social security may not be expressed by way of insurance legal mechanisms, such as the medical insurance contract. Leaving alone the logical mutual exclusion of the terms 'insurance' and 'social security', the medical insurance contract under Article 222a of the IC – instead of providing social security in accordance with the rules of additional voluntary health insurance – lays down the insurer's obligation to provide indemnity for damages resulting from the occurrence of an accident or a disease risk (general sickness, occupational disease and industrial accident) through ensuring certain health services and goods provided by the insurer to the insured person in return for the insurance premium paid by or in favour of the latter. This contract may also cover the financial provision of health services and goods connected with the prophylaxis of the insured person, including special attendance and palliative care. It may as well set forth the maximum amount of the insurer's liability in the form of an insured value or an amount and scope of health services, the term of which is stipulated in the contract. It may also lay down the insurer's obligation to reimburse the expenses incurred by the insured person or to provide the latter with goods and services through contractors with whom the insurer has made a contract. The medical insurance contract may be concluded for an indefinite period of time (as a contract of unlimited duration). In the latter case, the insurance premium stipulated in the insurance contract may not be augmented by the insurer along with the advancement of the insured person's age or the impairment of his/her health. The contract under Article 222a of the IC may stipulate the indemnity for damages caused by loss of income resulting from an accident (an industrial or a household one, etc.) or a disease.

215. Those health insurance companies and health insurance funds established under the legal regulation of voluntary health insurance prior to 7 August 2012 which perform only health insurance activities are subject to closure. They have no part to play in the new insurance model; however, they can be relicensed by the FSC within a year if they file the documents required for it.

216. The new regulation provides that the currently existing insurance companies may as well perform activities under Article 222a of the IC. As these companies are financially stronger and have gained large experience in the insurance activity after Article 222a of the IC (7 August 2012) took effect, they are making their way in medical insurance and competing the health insurance funds and companies, making it difficult for them to perform their activities, and will inevitably take them over. Actually, that is the ultimate goal of the legislative reform of August 2012.

217. In this difficult situation, the existing insurance companies and funds are not enthusiastic about taking the opportunity – provided by the new legal regulation – to be relicensed by the FSC within a year, i.e., until 7 August 2013 (*see supra* paragraph 215) in order to perform insurance activity. That is what the data show.

Twelve out of all the nineteen existing health insurance companies have filed their documents; however, until 15 October 2013, none of them has received a reply from the FSC.[48] The practical result of this liquidation reform is the abolishment of voluntary health insurance in its social meaning, and its complete commercialization by way of replacing it with the medical insurance contract.

218. The change made in August 2012 is positively perceived neither by those legal entities which have performed voluntary health insurance until now nor by the persons having additional voluntary health insurance, and is regarded as unsuccessful. The change in the legal nature of additional voluntary health insurance means destruction of the additional voluntary health insurance and its social nature in the interests of the big insurance companies. Actually, this change replaces voluntary health insurance with a special personal medical insurance for health within the limited framework set out in Supplement No. 1A, section II, items 1 and 2 of the IC. It is taken out of the social security law and is transferred to the subject matter of insurance law regulation. And, owing thereto, it does not form part of the subject matter of social security law regulation any more.

48. S. Terziyska *No Health Fund Has Been Relicensed*, 24 Hours Newspaper, 15 Oct. 2013.

Part IV. Family Allowances

Chapter 1. Introduction

219. In recent years, the legal framework concerning the insurance benefits for children has undergone considerable changes. Under the 2002 Law on Family Allowances for Children (promulgated in the OJ, No. 32 of 2002, amended), they changed from insurance indemnities, as they used to be for decades – since 1949[49] – into family allowances for children.

220. The new legal framework necessitated a change in the management of children's allowances. They were taken out from the social insurance of the system of the NII, where they used to be until that time, and were integrated into the matters administered by the Agency of Social Assistance of the Ministry of Labour and Social Policy.

221. According to the new legal provisions, the family allowances for children are financed by the State budget (Article 5 of the quoted Law). They are specified annually in the Law on the Budget of the Agency of Social Assistance, along with the Law on the State Budget of the Republic of Bulgaria. The budget of the Agency of Social Assistance forms part of the budget of the Ministry of Labour and Social Policy.

222. According to Article 2 of the quoted Law, the following are the family allowances for children:

(1) A lump sum benefit for pregnancy.
(2) A lump sum benefit for childbirth.
(3) Monthly children's allowances until the child graduates from Secondary School, but not after he/she becomes 20 years old.
(4) Monthly allowances for raising a child until he/she attains the age of one year.
(5) Amounts allotted to schoolchildren.

223. Depending on the grounds on which they are payable, the family allowances for children under Article 2 of the quoted Law form three groups:

49. V. Mrachkov, *Social Security Law – Bulgaria, International Encyclopaedia of Laws* 67–72 (1999).

(1) A lump sum benefit for pregnancy (Article 2, items 1 and 2 of the quoted Law).
(2) Periodical monthly allowances for children until the child attains a certain age (Article 2, items 3 and 4 of the quoted Law).
(3) Amounts allotted to schoolchildren (Article 2, item 5 of the quoted Law).

This is the sequence in which they will be considered below (*see infra* Chapters 2, 3 and 4).

224. The new legal framework of social benefits for children cannot be evaluated unambiguously. In certain aspects, it introduces more favourable social solutions (*see infra* paragraph 225). However, it also lays down some restrictions on using the monthly children's allowances (*see infra* paragraph 226). This legal infrastructure adopts another conception of granting the children's allowances, this conception having certain negative aspects, which will be pointed out in the course of consideration.

225. The more favourable social solutions in the new legal infrastructure refer to the lump sum benefits for pregnancy, the monthly allowances for raising a child until he/she attains the age of one year, the established final age of 20 for granting monthly allowances for children, while under the preceding legislation this age was 18, and so on.

226. The most considerable change which was introduced through the quoted Law consists in making the monthly allowances for raising children dependent on the monthly income of the child's family. While the repealed legal framework used to provide that monthly allowances were payable for each child until he/she attains a certain age (16 years of age, and 18 for schoolchildren and students) regardless of the monthly income of the family, the new legal framework provides that these allowances are payable only for children whose families have a certain lower average monthly income per member of the family for the preceding six months. The amount of this income is specified annually in the State Budget Law (SBL; Article 4 of the quoted Law). This new solution introduces a restriction in the right to family allowances for children. This is a consequence of the change in the legal nature of these allowances: instead of being insurance indemnities due because of the decreased income of the family resulting from the newly born children, as the monthly children's allowances until 1 April 2003 used to be, the new legal framework turns them into a form of social support. And, as far as its purpose and legal nature are concerned, social support is granted to low-income families, who are financially embarrassed and need social support. And lastly, the limit above which the family allowances for children are not paid is too low, and thousands of families living in financial embarrassment are deprived of this right. Besides, this does not comply with the traditional nature and purpose of monthly allowances for children as being insurance benefits which express the participation of the State and society in raising the children, which is not only a personal problem of the parents, but also a problem of society as a whole.

Chapter 2. Lump Sum Benefits for Pregnancy and Childbirth

227. The benefits under this chapter (*see infra* §§1–2) are lump sum ones. They are paid only once to the pregnant woman and the mother if the legal prerequisites provided for them are present.

§1. Lump Sum Benefit for Pregnancy

228. The lump sum benefit for pregnancy was introduced through an amendment to the Family Allowances Law which was made in June 2004 (promulgated in the OJ, No. 69 of 2004). It has been effective since 1 July 2004. The legal framework of this benefit is contained in Article 2, item 1 and Article 5'a' of the quoted Law.

229. Pregnant women have the right to the lump sum benefit in 2021 if the following prerequisites are present:

(1) To be Bulgarian citizens.
(2) To be permanently residing in the country.
(3) To have a monthly income per family member not exceeding BGN 510 (about USD 303).

230. Pursuant to Article 63 of the Law on State Budget of the Republic of Bulgaria for the year 2021, the amount of monthly child care allowances for children raised until completion of their secondary education, yet not over 20 years of age (Article 7 of the Law on Child Care Allowances), depends on the number of children (*see infra* paragraph 236) as follows: 1) one child – BGN 40 (about USD 24); 2) two children – BGN 90 (about USD 54); 3) three children – BGN 135 (about USD 81); 4) four children – BGN 145 (about USD 86), the child care allowance for each subsequent child growing by BGN 20.

231. If the pregnant woman is insured against all social risks with the exception of industrial accident, occupational disease and unemployment, or against all social risks with the exception of unemployment only, but does not receive insurance indemnity for pregnancy and childbirth because of not having the insurance length of service required under Article 48'a' of the SIC (*see supra* paragraph 229), the lump sum benefit is paid to her in proportion to the number of the calendar days from the beginning of the pregnancy and maternity leave until the acquisition of the insurance length of service required under Article 48'a' of the SIC, however, for no longer than forty-five calendar days.

§2. Lump Sum Benefit for Childbirth

232. The right to a lump sum benefit for childbirth is regulated in Article 2, item 2 and Article 6 of the quoted Law. This right existed under the repealed legislation as well.

233. The right to a lump sum benefit for childbirth arises in the presence of the following prerequisites:

(1) The family in which the child is born should be a family of Bulgarian citizens. If one of the parents is not a Bulgarian citizen, it is necessary that he/she live in Bulgaria and the child be a Bulgarian citizen.
(2) The child should be raised in Bulgaria.

234. A pregnant woman – foreign citizen, and the families of foreign citizens are entitled to this benefit if they permanently reside in Bulgaria, raise their children in Bulgaria, and the granting of such a benefit is provided for in an international treaty, Bulgaria being a party thereto.

235. The right to this benefit arises on the birth of a viable child according to the medical statements thereof. This benefit is designed for supporting the child's parents in meeting the initial expenditures on the child.

236. The amount of the benefit is specified depending on the consecutive number of the children born alive from the mother: for the first child – BGN 250 (about USD 143), for the second – BGN 600 (about USD 345), for the third – BGN 300 (about USD 172), for the fourth and each consecutive child – BGN 200 (about USD 115) (Article 60, paragraph 7 of the 2021 SBL). When twins are born, the benefit is BGN 1,200 (about USD 689) per each child (Article 60, paragraph 9 of the 2021 SBL).

The benefit is in the form of a lump sum, and it is payable once for each child born alive.

Chapter 3. Monthly Children's Allowances

237. The allowances considered in this chapter (*see infra* §§1–3) are periodical ones. They are paid if the prerequisites provided for them in law are present.

§1. Monthly Children's Allowances until the Child Graduates from Secondary School

238. The right to these allowances is regulated in Article 2, item 3 and Article 7 of the quoted Law.

239. The right to these allowances arises in the presence of the following prerequisites:

(1) The child has not been placed in a specialized institution for children in order to be raised at the expense of the State.
(2) The child attends school regularly – either primary school (first through eighth class) or secondary school (ninth through twelfth class), unless that is impossible because of the state of his/her health.
(3) The child is below the age of 20. This solution is more favourable than the one provided for in the preceding legislation, according to which the maximum age monthly children's allowances could be received until was the attainment of 16 years of age, and for schoolchildren and students, this age was 18.
(4) The child is permanently residing in Bulgaria.
(5) The child's family has a monthly income per family member not exceeding BGN 400 (about USD 230) (*see supra* paragraph 229).

240. The amount of this allowance is annually specified in the SBL for the respective year. For 2021 this monthly allowance was BGN 37 (about USD 21) for a family with one child, BGN 87 for a family with two children, BGN 130 for a family with three children, BGN 140 for a family with four children and BGN 20 for each subsequent child (Article 60, paragraph 7 of the 2021 SBL).

241. As for children with permanent impairments established by the competent health bodies, in the presence of the conditions specified above (*see supra* paragraph 222), this allowance is paid in its double amount, that is it amounts to BGN 100 (about USD 57) per month regardless of the income per family member.

§2. Monthly Allowance for Raising a Child until He/She Attains the Age of 1 Year

242. This allowance has first been regulated in Article 2, paragraph 3, item 1 and Article 8 of the quoted Law.

243. The right to this allowance arises in the presence of the following prerequisites:

(1) The mother (the adoptive mother) is neither insured nor she receives indemnity under the SIC for pregnancy, childbirth or raising a young child.
(2) The child has not been placed in a specialized institution for children in order to be raised at the expense of the State.
(3) The child is residing in Bulgaria.
(4) The child's family has a monthly income per family member not exceeding the one specified in the SBL for the respective calendar year. For 2021 this income was BGN 400 (about USD 230) (*see supra* paragraph 229).

244. Under the conditions laid down in the quoted Law (*see supra* paragraph 243) the adoptive father in a single-parent family is also entitled to this allowance.

245. The amount of the monthly allowance for raising a child until he/she attains the age of 1 year is BGN 100 (about USD 71).

§3. Procedure for Determining the Monthly Children's Allowances

246. The family allowances for raising a child (*see supra* §§1–2) are granted, upon the request of the persons concerned, by the Social Support Directorate of the municipal administration through an ordinance of the Director of the Directorate, if the prerequisites provided for in law are present.

247. The refusal of the Director of the Social Support Directorate to grant the requested allowance has to be motivated. This refusal is communicated in writing to the person who has filed the request, within a term of seven days following the day of filing the request.

248. The Ordinance for granting the monthly allowance for children (as for its amount, terms of payment and the like) as well as the refusal of granting the allowance are appealed against, under the Administrative Procedure Code (APC), to the mayor of the municipality, while the decisions of the latter are appealed against to the respective district court. The mayor's decision may also be appealed against to the Supreme Administrative Court.

Chapter 4. Lump Sum Benefits for Schoolchildren

249. This benefit is regulated in Article 2, item 5 and Article 10'a' of the quoted Law. It was introduced for the first time through the amendments to this Law which were made in June 2004 and have been effective since 1 January 2005.

250. This benefit is a lump sum one; that is, it is paid only once. The prerequisites in the presence of which the right to this benefit arises are as follows:

(1) the child is registered in the first class of a State or municipal school;
(2) the child has enrolled in and attends school;
(3) the child's family has a monthly income per family member not exceeding the one specified in the SBL for the respective calendar year. For 2021 this income was BGN 400 (about USD 230) (section 12, paragraph 1 of the Interim and Concluding Provisions of the SBL for 2017; *see supra* paragraph 229).

251. In principle, the benefit is pecuniary. Its amount is specified annually by the Council of Ministers under the proposal of the Minister of Labour and Social Policy. However, this benefit may also be granted in kind, in the discretion of the Social Support Directorate and with the assistance of the board of trustees of the school. As for the school year 2016/2017, the amount of this benefit is BGN 200 (about USD 115). It is specified in Decree No. 58 of the Council of Ministers dated 20 July 2016 (promulgated in the OJ, No. 56 of 2016). This benefit is granted for a specific purpose – for covering the schoolchild's needs during the school year – clothes, shoes and the like. If the child does not enrol in school, the benefit is reimbursed by the parents it has been paid to.

Part V. Incapacity to Work

252. Incapacity for work is an important part of Bulgarian security law. Its importance is determined by the large number of social insured risks causing the incapacity, the high frequency of their occurrence, the wide extent of insured persons as well as by the benefits the insured are granted when those risks occur. The latter are regulated in the SIC, effective since 1 January 2000.

253. General social risks are those arising in the development and existence that are common for and inherent to the biological nature of man and are caused by the objective social conditions man is placed to live in. They are called general because they are common to all people regardless of the work they do and the conditions thereof. Such risks causing temporary incapacity for work are the following: general sickness, the cases equalled to it and maternity. Of course, for some of these risks (e.g., general sickness), the working and living conditions and the nature of work affect the provoking, course, development and recovery of the insured sick person's capacity for work. However, in the end, the decisive factors are still those originating in the biological nature of man, his/her individual physiological and anatomical structure and functioning, his/her immune sufficiency and resistance, the objective social conditions he/she lives in and not the ones originating in his/her occupation or the professional work he/she does under the employment relationship.

Chapter 1. General Sickness

254. The legal provisions relating to general sickness are contained in Articles 1, 11, 21–22, 25–26, 40–42, 71–77 of the SIC and others.

255. General sickness consists in the impairment of the structural and functional characteristics of the human body due to its insufficient adaptability to the changeable conditions of external and internal environment of man. It occurs regardless of the working environment and the specific effect thereof, and it is due to the said external and internal factors in the development of the human body and insufficient adaptability to the external and internal environment conditions.

256. As an insured social risk, general sickness is not an impairment of the structural and functional characteristics of the human body. It is only the impairment that has led to a certain high degree of incapacity upon the occurrence of the risk. This makes general sickness a legal fact relevant to social security law.

257. Incapacity, as a constituent element of the insured social risk of general sickness, is marked here only for the sake of completeness of the exposition. However, incapacity is not a unique feature of general sickness only – it is also a general unfavourable consequence of the occurrence of a number of other social risks: industrial accident, occupational disease, maternity, and so on. Because of that, incapacity for work will be considered later (*see infra*).

258. The slump in the standard of living of a large part of the population in the period of severe economic and social crisis that the country is undergoing, and the deterioration of working conditions, decrease the 'resistance' and 'immune' power, in the broad sense of the word, of Bulgarian citizens against general sickness, and so the number of people suffering from general sickness gets larger, people get ill more often and for a longer time.[50] As a whole this results in increasing the number of cases in which the social risk of general sickness occurs.

259. The extent of persons insured against the risk of general sickness is large. It comprises two main categories of persons:

(a) Persons of mandatory insurance against all social risks under Article 4, paragraph 1 and Article 4a of the SIC: employees under employment relationships, civil servants under service relationships, regular military staff, officers and sergeants in the Ministry of the Interior, employees under the Law on the Execution of Penalties, judges, public prosecutors, investigating magistrates and other employees in the judiciary, cooperative members, contractors under management and supervision contracts with commercial companies, seafarers.
(b) Persons of mandatory insurance only against the risks of old age, death and general sickness causing disability. These are the persons specified in detail in

50. Statisticheski spravochnik 2021, 22–23.

Article 4, paragraph 3 of the SIC: freelance practitioners, craftsmen, sole traders, owners or partners in commercial companies, and the like.

260. General sickness has important social security legal consequences. They are manifested in several directions:

(a) The general sickness is the reason for the state of incapacity. General sickness is such a deteriorated health state of the insured person in which he/she cannot and should not (because of danger of further deterioration of his/her health) continue working. The judgment about that is made in the due course by the competent medical expertise bodies.
(b) If the incapacity for work is a temporary one, the insured is allowed a sick leave for as long as the temporary incapacity for work subsists. This leave is allowed regardless of whether it is due at all or not and, should it be due, regardless of the amount of temporary incapacity indemnity (Articles 40–42 of the SIC). When a temporary incapacity leave is allowed, this means that the insured person is absent from work for valid reasons, because of his/her state of temporary incapacity for work.
(c) During the temporary incapacity for work, the insured gets no earnings as he/she does not work. Insurance benefits (indemnities, aids, etc.) replace the missing earnings. These insurance benefits are paid to the insured from the insurance body in performing its duties under the insurance relationship. Pursuant to the law the risk of unintentional failure to work is transferred to the insurance body.
(d) During that time, the insured is entitled to medical care for his/her treatment, recovery of his/her capacity for work and his/her convalescence (*see infra*).

261. The legal consequences of the occurrence of the general sickness risk causing temporary incapacity for work are as follows:

(a) Suspending (stopping) the fulfilment of the employment relationship or the fulfilment of the other relationship that working activity is performed under, this activity being the one for which insurance is made. This means suspending the consideration of the working force (under the employment relationship) or suspending the performance of other labour activity, respectively. This suspension is temporary and it lasts as long as the temporary incapacity for work subsists.
(b) Transferring to the insurance body the risk of failure to provide working force, this failure being due to objective impossibility, or transferring the risk of innocent non-performance on the part of the employer.
(c) An obligation of the insurance body arises by virtue of the risk transferred to it, this being the risk of failure to provide working force due to objective innocent impossibility. This is the obligation of paying certain insurance benefits (indemnities, etc.) in lieu of the missing earnings to the temporarily incapacitated person (*see infra*).

262. Where the general sickness causes permanent incapacity for work (disability), the legal consequences thereof are:

(a) The employment relationship with the insured employee is suspended (Article 325, paragraph 1, item 9 of the LC) or the insured person is reassigned to another suitable job (Articles 314–321 of the LC).
(b) Where, without having worked under an employment relationship, or under another relationship where working activity is performed, the insured person who performs freelance practice, or the like, has become permanently incapacitated because of general sickness, the said person suspends the respective activity in accordance with the degree of loss of his/her capacity for work.

Chapter 2. Social Risks Equalled to General Sickness

263. Bulgarian security law provides for a number of insured social risks equalled to general sickness and this is one of its particularities. In this way it extends the scope of insurance protection.

264. The legal provisions concerning insured social risks equalled to general sickness are contained in Articles 43–45 of the SIC.

265. The risks equalled to general sickness are insured social risks and they possess the features thereof. What is specific to these risks is that the insured person actually has the capacity for work, he/she is capable of work, but he/she is 'prevented' from work.

266. This 'prevention from work' means that the law has given superior legal protection to other rights and interests of the insured person. It does not mean that there are any obstacles to the insured person to work that he/she cannot overcome. What it means is that favourable legal opportunities have been given to the insured, releasing him/ her from the obligation to work, so that other rights and interests of his/her can be protected. This finds its expression in the stronger legal protection of other basic personal rights of the insured and in giving preference and priority thereto over his/ her obligation to work. It is because of this priority that the law 'releases from work' the insured person 'as though' he/she is not capable of work as it would have been in the case of his/her real incapacity for work. This is a 'favourable prevention' of the persons from work, this prevention being provided by the insurance protection they are entitled to.

267. The insured social risks equalled to general sickness can be divided into two groups depending on the sphere to which the interests belong, these interests being the ones for whose protection the insurance is provided:

(a) Equalled risks where the object of insurance protection is the personal health state of the insured.
(b) Equalled risks where the object of insurance protection is the urgent care for the insured person's relatives.

§1. Risks Connected with the Personal Health State of the Insured Person

268. Sanatorium and resort treatment (Article 44 of the SIC). This treatment is carried out in special medical establishments – sanatoriums, where natural medicinal factors, such as climate, mineral waters, atmospheric pressure and others are used along with drug treatment, sports, and so on. Patients suffering from tuberculosis, nervous and mental diseases undergo such treatment. The sanatorium and resort treatment is the continuation of their treatment in clinics and polyclinics or at home. The state of the insured persons during their sanatorium and resort treatment is a continuation of their state of being ill (in the broad sense of this term) and a continuation of their state of temporary incapacity for work. The person is regarded as being incapable of work for that period of time and, if not being sent to sanatorium and resort treatment, he/she is entitled to a sick leave. Yet, the sanatorium and resort treatment has its specificity that makes it a separate social risk, distinct from general sickness. This treatment is specific and the law fixes its duration of the state of temporary incapacity for work – this duration is equal to the length of the person's stay at the sanatorium or the rest home, where the stay is usually twenty days, including three calendar days for travelling.

269. Quarantine (Article 43, item 1 of the SIC). Quarantine is an isolation, seclusion, separation of the ill and suspected ill with contagious diseases by keeping them at home so that the contagious disease cannot spread. The insured persons are quarantined for the time they are contagious disease carriers or for the maximum incubation term, this being the period within which the respective contagious disease develops although it does not show. The duration of quarantine is determined by the attending physician in compliance with modern epidemiological achievements relating to the respective disease. The 'prevention' from work of the insured person is evidently a consequence of the home isolation imposed on him/ her by the attending physician.

270. Removal from work by the order of health bodies (Article 43, item 2 of the SIC). By virtue of Article 19, paragraph 1, item 5 of the Health Law (promulgated in the OJ, No. 70 of 2004), effective since 1 January 2005, the State sanitation control bodies remove from work persons suffering from contagious diseases, carriers of contagious diseases and carriers of parasites that are dangerous to other people's health. Persons who have been in contact with those suffering from contagious diseases are put in quarantine or under medical observation. The removal from work by the order of health bodies, being a compulsory administrative measure, is studied by labour law.[51]

271. The removal from work has its specific importance as an insured social risk. The specificity consists in the fact that the presence of this risk results in the person's prevention from work. A compulsory administrative measure is carried out, this measure actually being an 'order' that the person should not perform his/her work because he/she is a carrier of contagious disease or parasites that are a source of disease to other insured persons. That is why this prevention from work is imposed on him/her. The insured person is prevented from work for the time he/she is removed from work and this insured social risk is present for him/her for this period of time.

51. V. Mrachkov, *Labour Law* 305–309 (Sibi Publishing House 10th ed. 2018).

§2. Risks Connected with Urgent Healthcare for Insured Person's Relatives

272. Nursing or urgent attendance on a sick member of the family (Article 45, paragraph 1, item 1 and paragraphs 3–4 of the SIC). There are two hypotheses.

273. The first hypothesis is nursing a sick member of the family. The essence of this hypothesis is that the person is prevented from working in order to take care of the sick member of the family at hospital or at home. For the purposes of Article 45, paragraph 1, item 1 and paragraphs 3–4 of the SIC 'members of the family' are the spouse, lineal descendants within the second-degree of the insured or the spouse thereof, adoptive parents, children (including recognized, adoptive and step ones, the grandchildren where they either have no parents or the parents are prevented from looking after them, brothers and sisters if they live in the insured person's household and are his/her dependants). In these cases, the health bodies allow the insured person a leave, the duration thereof being dependent on the capacity of the sick person who needs care and nursing: for nursing a sick member of the family older than 18 – up to ten calendar days within one calendar year per each insured person.

274. The second hypothesis is urgent attendance on a sick member of the family (Article 45, paragraph 1, item 1 of the SIC) and it also includes two separate cases.

The first one is the attendance on a sick member of the family for going to a medical establishment situated in another town in order that the sick member of the family be examined or treated there.

The second one is the attendance on a sick member of the family for his/her medical examination or treatment abroad. In both cases the attendance has to be urgent; that is, it should be necessitated by the care for the sick person or for the person who needs examination or treatment. The attending physician makes the judgment about both this need and the duration of the attendance. The prevention of the insured person from work is expressed in this necessity of attending on a family member who is either ill or in need of medical examination or treatment. This is the essence of the insured social risk. The duration of the attendance is determined by the attending physician depending on the distance between the place of residence and the medical establishment where the examination will be carried out (either in Bulgaria or abroad), the time necessary for the examination or the patient's placement for being treated at the respective medical establishment, the time for going to and coming back from the medical establishment, and so on.

275. Attendance on a child aged below 18. It also comprises two hypotheses (Article 45, paragraph 1, items 2 and 3 of the SIC).

276. The first one is – attending on and due accompanying of a child aged below 18 for a medical examination or treatment in Bulgaria or abroad. 'A child' means both an own and an adoptive child. The only particularity is that a child aged below 18 is concerned. As for the other elements of this hypothesis, they tally with the requirements under Article 45, paragraph 1, item 1 of the SIC, and owing thereto, we are making a renvoi to the preceding exposition (*see supra* paragraphs 272–274).

277. The second hypothesis is – attending on a child aged below 18 who is ill with a contagious disease and is quarantined.

278. Attendance on a young child aged below 7. Here again two cases are comprised as follows:

(a) The first one concerns the attendance on a child aged below 3, who has been placed in a hospital together with the insured member of the family under Article 45, paragraph 4 of the SIC. Usually it is the mother of the child. As for the other requirements regarding 'attendance on a child' by a member of the family, they were considered above, and owing thereto, we are making a renvoi to the preceding exposition (*see supra* paragraph 274).
(b) The second case concerns the attendance on a child who is not ill but has been returned from a children's establishment because of quarantine. Here 'a children's establishment' denotes a nursery (for children aged below 3) and a kindergarten (for children aged 3 to 7). The announcement of the quarantine in the children's establishment is a medical question, which is solved by the healthcare bodies when a contagious disease has appeared.

279. What is important in the last two groups of cases (*see supra* paragraphs 277 and 278) is that the respective insured member of the family has to take over the care of raising the child, and this prevents him/her from work. And that is what the essence of the insured social risk consists in for him/her. This circumstance, as well as the attending on and accompanying of a sick member of the family under Article 45, paragraph 1, item 1 of the SIC (*see supra* paragraph 274), is determined by the attending physician, who issues a patient's card to the insured member of the family, and on the grounds thereof the respective insurance indemnities are paid (*see infra*).

280. The insured social risks that 'prevent insured persons' from work are equalled to the general sickness risk with respect to the bodies and the due course for establishing the occurrence of the risk (by way of a patient's card), their duration, prerequisites and amount of indemnities (*see infra*). This is also the sense of the renvoi that is made in Articles 43–45 of the SIC to Articles 40–42 of the SIC. These risks create only 'temporary prevention' from work. Moreover, they have short duration, which is different depending on the nature of the risk. Sometimes this duration is also specified in calendar days.

Chapter 3. Maternity

281. Maternity risk has 'double value' as an object of security legal protection: the pregnant woman with the foetus in her womb and the mother of the newly born child. Each of them has its unique value of human life and health. This value gets 'twice' greater during pregnancy because then the two values form an inseparable biological, legal, social and emotional unity.

282. Maternity as an insured social risk has undergone dynamic and progressive development for the last fifty years. Its very start was the protection of 'pregnancy and birth' risk by way of the legal regulations contained in the Labour Code of 1951, providing for thirty days' leave before and sixty days' leave after childbirth (Articles 156–157 of the LC of 1951, version 1951). These provisions have several further amendments. The main landmarks in this development are 1957, 1968, 1973 and 1986 when the Labour Code (Articles 163–165), which is operative now, was adopted, as a result of which its large-scale development of today was achieved, this development far exceeding the unpretentious start in 1951 (*see infra*).

283. Extent of insured persons. Because of the nature of maternity risk and the biological nature of maternity and birth, it is women only that are insured against this risk. According to Article 48'a' of the SIC, which has been effective since 1 July 2004, these are the following women in particular: (a) insured with mandatory insurance against all social risks; (b) insured against all social risks with the exception of industrial accident, occupational disease and unemployment; (c) insured against all insured social risks with the exception of unemployment.

284. The supplements to the SIC of December 2009 (promulgated in the OJ, No. 103 of 2009) have strengthened the insurance protection of maternity risk. That is expressed in extending the said protection even to the women in an advanced stage of in vitro treatment given through the assisted reproduction method. This stage of treatment covers the period of follicular reproduction until the human embryo is transferred into its natural biological environment the female womb (§1, item 13 of the Supplementary Provisions of the LC and Article 48, paragraph 1 of the SIC). Thus, the insurance protection of maternity was 'carried forward' in time, prior to the insured woman's being biologically pregnant. The insured women who are at this stage of treatment enjoy insurance protection of the same content as the one enjoyed by the biologically pregnant women. In this way, the length of insurance protection of maternity as an insured social risk has been extended.

285. Maternity risk has its own dynamic and uneven internal development. It has had different stages. Each of them is characterized by different intensity of insurance protection, and so its development 'in stages' has been formed. The separate stages in the development of maternity risk have their specific 'risk charge' and content. This specific risk charge has the respective intensity of insurance protection. The relation is, so to say, 'directly proportional' – the greater the risk charge of the insured woman during the maternity period, the greater the 'legal intensity' and insurance protection provided by the operative law. This relation contains certain symmetry in one more aspect – the insurance protection provided for the separate stages in the dynamic development of the maternity risk has its beginning, ascent, apogee and abatement.

Thus, the following four stages can be outlined in the development of maternity risk in view of its insurance protection.

286. Advanced stage of in vitro treatment. That is a 'pre-pregnancy' stage. Its presence is a medical question and is determined by physicians of the medical establishment in which the treatment takes place. In view of the insurance protection, this is a stage of short duration: from the follicular puncture until the transfer of the embryo into its natural biological environment – the mother's womb. On the grounds of scientific medical studies, this period is fixed at twenty calendar days.

287. Pregnancy. It begins at conception and lasts until the forty-fifth day prior to the day specified for the childbirth (the term). This is the initial development of pregnancy which takes about seven and a half months. In this stage, the insurance protection of maternity is expressed under 'general sickness' under the operative law. Thus, operative law 'fits' this first stage of the development of maternity risk (the first seven and a half months of the pregnancy) into the general sickness risk. Thus, regardless of the pregnant woman's right to pecuniary indemnity for pregnancy and childbirth, the pregnant woman is allowed a leave, and she is entitled to pecuniary indemnity at the amounts provided for temporary incapacity for work in case of pathological pregnancy and in case the health bodies find it necessary for the correct development of pregnancy.

288. Where the work performed by the employee at an advanced stage of in vitro treatment or by the pregnant employee is unsuitable for her state and may have an unfavourable effect upon the development of her pregnancy and health, under the instructions of the health bodies, the employer implements the necessary measures for the temporary adaptation of her working place and/or her working time in order for the safety and health of the pregnant employee to be ensured. And if this turns out to be impracticable or unjustified, under the instructions of the health bodies, the employer reassigns her to another job which is suitable for her state (Article 309 of the LC and Article 48 of the SIC).

289. The close of pregnancy, childbirth and a certain time thereafter. This is the next stage in the development of the maternity risk. The close of pregnancy normally begins on the forty-fifth day prior to the specified term and continues for a certain period of time after the childbirth. This stage marks the apogee in the development of maternity insurance protection. In other words, it marks the stage of the greatest and most intensive insurance protection, because during this period of time, the employee receives 90% of her average monthly labour remuneration (Article 49 of the SIC – *see infra* Chapter 4, §5).

290. This leave has the duration of 410 calendar days per child, regardless of the consecutive number of the child. Out of them, forty-five calendar days are taken prior to the childbirth term determined by the healthcare bodies. Where, due to an inexact estimation of the healthcare bodies, the childbirth takes place prior to the expiry of forty-five days following the beginning of the leave, the remainder to the 410 days is taken after the childbirth. And if the childbirth takes place later than the estimated term, the mother is entitled to the remaining part of the pregnancy leave (Article 163, paragraphs 1 and 2 of the LC and Article 53 of the SIC).

291. The next stage in the development of maternity risk covers the period of time after the maternity and childbirth leave has elapsed until the child becomes 2 years old – for the first, second and third child, or six months old – for the fourth and each consecutive child (Article 164 of the LC). This leave is provided for the upbringing of the little child. Its intensity of insurance protection is lower compared to the one of the preceding stage because during that time the insured mother receives BGN 340 (about USD 241) per month (Article 53 of the SIC).

292. The last stage in the development of maternity risk includes the period of time when the child is 2–8 years of age (Article 167'a' of the LC). This leave was introduced through the amendments to the Labour Code of June 2004 (promulgated in the OJ, No. 52 of 2004) and has been applied since 1 August 2004. The said leave is granted to both parents (adoptive parents) working under an employment relationship. Each one of them has the right to take six months of it. According to the latest amendments to Article 167a, paragraph 1 of the Labour Code (promulgated in the OJ, No. 7 of 2012), each parent (adoptive parent) may use up to five months of the leave of the other parent (adoptive parent) if the latter has given his/her consent thereto. A parent who takes care of the child on his/her own (where he/she is not married to the other parent, or does not have a common household with him/her, or the parents are divorced and the parental rights have been assigned to one of them, or the other parent is deprived of parental rights or has died) is entitled to a leave of twelve months. It has the lowest degree of insurance protection: this time is regarded as length of service for the mother only (*see infra*).

293. The last two stages in the development of maternity insurance are possible but not obligatory: they occur if the mother wishes to have these leaves. This is her subjective right. If she wishes to have this leave then the insurer-employer or the assignor of the work cannot refuse it. And it is a matter of her independent judgment if she takes it or not. This demonstrates the dynamic development of this risk, its possibilities and the lack of obligatory nature.

294. Maternity risk is established comparatively quickly and easily and it has certain particularities in view of the stage of its development. In order to establish the pre-pregnancy stage and the first stage of pregnancy – the one starting from the beginning and lasting until the forty fifth day before the term, the risk is established by way of a patient's card issued by the gynaecologist of the gynaecological ward of the polyclinic or the hospital where the woman at an advanced stage of in vitro treatment or the pregnant woman has been registered. The same is valid in the case of pathological pregnancy and where it may be necessary to ensure the normal development of pregnancy. Pregnancy leave and childbirth leave are allowed by the gynaecologist, by his/her assistant, by the midwife or by way of a patient's card. As far as leave for nursing a child aged two to eight is concerned, it should be requested by the parents by way of a written request addressed to the employer or the assignor of work and the latter is obliged to allow it under Articles 164 and 167a of the LC. Establishment and certification of maternity risk occurrence and the stages in the development thereof is easy because of the nature of the risk and the obviousness it has as a biological and physiological state of the mother and the child she has born.

295. The occurrence of maternity risk leads to both actual temporary incapacity for work and a state in which the mother is capable of work but, because of the supreme interest to which the law gives preference and the greater legal protection, she is temporarily entitled not to perform her obligations under her employment relationship. This puts her in the state of being 'prevented from work' in the sense that has already been discussed (*see supra*).

296. The first hypothesis – the actual incapacity for work refers to cases of pathological development of pregnancy, cases where it is necessary to ensure conditions for the normal development of pregnancy and, primarily – the cases of pregnancy leave and childbirth leave under Article 163 of the LC.

297. The second hypothesis – 'prevention from work' and cases equalled to temporary incapacity, refers to maternity risk where the mother, in spite of her being capable of work, is exempt from the obligation to work because she takes care of the upbringing of the child and thus she is provided leave for the upbringing of the child under Articles 164 and 167a of the LC. This is confirmed by the opportunity given by law concerning this leave. If the mother agrees so, this leave can be used by the child's father or by a child's grandparent (Article 164, paragraph 3 of the LC). Obviously, this would not be possible or admissible if the mother is actually incapable of work during that time because the actual incapacity for work is always a personal and non-transferable state and attribute of the insured person. It is, incidentally, the social considerations connected with the child's upbringing that form the foundation of these legislative decisions and not the real incapacity of the mother for work. Actually, scientific studies show that the real incapacity for work of the woman after childbirth and the need of her physiological recovery takes about forty-two days after the childbirth, provided that it had been a normal one, except for cases where the capacity for work has not been restored within that time because of particularities connected with childbirth. If such is the case, at the discretion of the health bodies this leave is extended for as long as the mother's capacity for work is missing. This 'medical attitude' has been adopted by the law under Article 163, paragraph 4 of the LC, according to which:

> When the child is still-born, dies or is freed for adoption or for full State maintenance, the mother is entitled to a paid leave until the forty-second day after the birth. If the mother's capacity for work has not been recovered until the forty-second day after the birth, this leave is extended at the discretion of the health bodies until her capacity for work is recovered.
>
> However, from the forty-second day after the childbirth until the end of the pregnancy and childbirth leave under Article 163, paragraph 1 of the LC, this

state of the mother is personal and it is not transferable to other persons under Article 164, paragraph 3 of the LC, except for the cases under Article 167 of the LC. This shows that the leave under Article 164, paragraph 1 of the LC even after the forty-second day is connected primarily with the mother's indispensable functions of upbringing the child (breast-feeding and other forms of feeding, emotional upbringing and the like) and it is not connected only with the child's upbringing and development as is the case with leaves under Articles 164 and 165 of the LC.

298. Since 2014, the insurance protection of maternity in the cases of adoption of a young child aged between 2 and 5 has been extended. The extension of the said protection was introduced through Article 164a of the LC (promulgated in the OJ, No. 104 of 2013). The objective of the new legal regulation is to make the protection of the insured female employees who adopt young children aged between 2 and 5 the same as the protection enjoyed by natural (biological) mothers and by adoptive mothers who adopt young children either immediately after they are born or before they attain the age of 2. What is common to these cases is that women – natural mothers and adoptive ones – provide care for raising a young child. The care of adoptive mothers who adopt children aged between 2 and 5 are of the same nature, and, apart from the mother's care that is inherently needed at this early age, these adoptive mothers must also provide specific care for introducing the child into the family environment that is new to him/her, and integrating the child as a new member of the family community. This new resolution of Bulgarian social security legislation deserves full support.

The essence of the insurance protection under Article 164a of the LC is that the said right is granted to the employee-adoptive mother of a young child aged between 2 and 5 under the conditions of full adoption. This is the adoption conducted by the court in which the family ties of the child and his/her biological parents are discontinued, and the child's adoptive parents become his/her parents by virtue of law; the child's family name and his/her father's name are changed, and the legal relationships arising between the child and the adoptive parents are the same as those between a child and his/her biological parents, including those regarding succession. The main content of the insurance protection of an adoptive mother is expressed in the fact that she is entitled to a leave of 365 calendar days starting from the surrender of the child for being adopted; however, this leave cannot be used after the child attains 5 years of age. The length of this leave is the same as the one for raising a child under one year of age, which is granted under Article 163, paragraphs 1 and 6 of the LC to natural mothers and adoptive mothers who adopt young children immediately after they are born.

Provided that the adoptive mother has given her consent thereto, the leave under Article 164a of the LC can also be used by the adoptive father; however, this is possible only after the expiry of six months following the child's surrender for adoption, and on condition that the person providing care for the child over this six months' period was the adoptive mother (Article 164a, paragraph 2 of the LC), and the child has not attained 5 years of age. The right under Article 164a of the LC can also be enjoyed by a male employee who adopts a child aged between 2 and 5. During the time the insured person-adoptive parent uses the leave under Article 164a of the LC, he/she receives compensation under Article 53a of the SIC on condition that he/she has twelve months' insurance length of service as regards the maternity risk. The amount of this compensation is equal to 90% of his/her average daily gross labour remuneration for the period of twenty-four calendar months preceding the month of the child's adoption. The said compensation is not paid in the event of death of the adopted child, or termination of adoption, or when the adopted child attends a children's establishment, including a nursery or an educational institution (Article 53a of the SIC).

299. The social security consequences of the occurrence of the maternity risk are the following three:

(1) If the insured woman at an advanced stage of in vitro treatment and the pregnant woman are employees under an employment relationship who perform work which is unsuitable for their health and pregnancy, the employer is obliged to implement the measures under Article 309 of the LC (*see supra* paragraph 288).
(2) The insured in vitro and pregnant woman and the insured mother are in a state of temporary incapacity for work. Depending on the stages the development of maternity risk goes through, the woman/mother is either in a state in which she 'cannot work' – in the case of pregnancy and childbirth leave under Article 163 of the LC, including the cases in which leave is granted for pathological pregnancy or for ensuring the normal development of pregnancy (*see supra*) (Article 158, paragraph 1 of the LC of 1951), or she is in a state in which she is 'prevented from work' – in the case of a child's upbringing leave under Articles 164 and 165 of the LC (Article 158, paragraph 1 of the LC of 1951).
(3) For the time the maternity risk is being realized, the insured mother receives indemnities and aid under short-term social insurance, which will be considered later (*see infra*).

Part VI. Industrial Accidents and Occupational Diseases

300. Occupational risks are those connected with the work performed and the conditions (most often the harmful, severe and dangerous ones) under which the work is performed. There exists a functional relationship between the work performed and the danger the insured risk involves. Such risks are industrial accidents and occupational diseases. Occupational risks are characterized by increased special insurance protection for the employees.

Chapter 1. Industrial Accident

301. Industrial accident is the basic and most frequently occurring insured social occupational risk. Its legal framework has its decades-long traditions and experience in Bulgarian security law. It is the 1918 Law on Sickness and Accident Insurance that has first regulated industrial accident as an insured social risk, and since that time it has constantly been a subject of legislative provisions.

302. The severe economic conditions that the country continues to be under have their unfavourable effect upon the improvement of the working conditions in the enterprises, and the number and seriousness of industrial accidents show a constant tendency. According to the data of the General Inspectorate of Labour for 2012, the number of registered industrial accidents was 3,027, and 82 out of them were lethal ones.[52] The largest number of industrial accidents has been registered in the branches of building industry, coal and peat extraction, and manufacture of machinery, equipment and domestic appliances.

303. The legal provisions of the operative social security law concerning industrial accidents recognize them as being insured social risks (Articles 1–4, 55–67, 78–79 of the SIC, Article 200 of the LC) and under the Ordinance on Establishing, Examining, Registering and Reporting Industrial Accidents (promulgated in the OJ, No. 6 of 2000).

304. The legal infrastructure of industrial accident was regulated in the SIC of December 1999. Thus, the juridical rank of its legal infrastructure was augmented, and the fragmentation of its framework of sublegal normative acts existing for over fifty years was overcome. The new legal framework also contains important changes and improvements in substance, which will be considered in the following exposition.

305. Industrial accident is legally defined under Article 55 of the SIC. It reads as follows: 'Industrial accident is any sudden impairment that has occurred during and in connection with or on the occasion of the work done as well as in the course of any work performed in the interests of the enterprise where the said work has caused incapacity for work or death.'

---

52. *Report of the General Inspectorate of Labour for 2020*, Labour and Law Journal, 2021, No. 3, Supplement, 28–37. 'As a result of the improvement of working conditions, in the recent years a tendency towards a decrease of industrial accidents has been observed: in 2001 their number was 5941, in 2002 – 5212, in 2009 – 4311, in 2012 – 3027' (the quoted Report); in 2020 – 2946 (Report *of the General Inspectorate of Labour for 2020*, Labour and Law Journal, 2020, No. 6, Supplement, 46–47).

§1. INDUSTRIAL ACCIDENT: SUDDEN IMPAIRMENT

306. The constitutive legal features of industrial accident are derived from its legal definition (*see supra* paragraph 305). They are as follows:

(a) Presence of a sudden impairment of health. It consists in breaking the continuity and disturbing the functions of tissues and organs of the human body under the influence of chemical, thermal (fire, solar irradiation, etc.) and electric agents (causes), Roentgen radiation, radium emanation, and so on. This sudden impairment is not limited to mechanical traumas only. Psychic traumas are also possible caused by the effect upon the nervous system (fear, fright, stress and the like). Sudden impairment is an external and direct effect upon the human organism which destroys the continuity or the normal functioning of the organs of the human body (decision 1107 dated 19 October 1971 on case 905/1971 – Civil Chamber, 3rd Division).
(b) The traumatic impairment should have occurred in connection with the performance of work or service under the employment or service relationship, or in the course of the insured person's performing other work or activity assigned within the framework of the legal relationship under which he/she is insured. This 'work' is both generally and explicitly specified in Article 55, paragraph 1 of the SIC – 'during and in connection with or on the occasion of the performed work'. There is no causality between the impairment and the work performed; that is, it is not the performed work that directly causes the sudden impairment. The connection between the work performed and the impairment is rather specific and of a different nature. It is a connection with the circumstances and situation in which the work or service is performed under the employment or service relationship. This makes the said connection not a causal, but rather a functional one.[53] Establishing this general connection with the work and service performed, Article 55, paragraph 1 of the SIC takes one more step to extending it by way of including therein any impairment which has occurred 'in the course of any work performed in the interests of the enterprise … '. This might also be work or service beyond the employment or service obligations of the insured person under the respective legal relationship, and it might also be work that has not at all been assigned to him/her; however, he/she has performed it on his/her own initiative. This is a new point in the functional relationship between the impairment and the work or service performed. As for the insured person, it does not matter for him/her whether this work has been assigned to him/her or he/she has taken it up on his/her own. What matters here is that the work is in the interests of the enterprise, and he/she has undergone a sudden impairment of health in performing it. The 'interests of the enterprise' may have its expression in various forms: saving or protecting the property of the enterprise in general, furnishing the enterprise with techniques, furniture and the like. By the way, the idea of the law directs us to a broader interpretation of the interests of the enterprise, considering the specific situation in each separate case. The court

53. V. Mrachkov, K. Sredkova & A. Vassilev, *Komentar na Kodeksa na Trouda* [*Commentary on the Labour Code*] 666–684, at 667–684 (Sofia: Sibi Publishing House 13th ed. 2021).

practice also directs us to this interpretation. *See* Decision No. 674/year 1999 of the 3rd Civil Department of the Supreme Court of Cassation. No innocent conduct of the injured insured person is required for the presence of an industrial accident. Industrial accident is an impairment of the insured person's health, which has occurred suddenly, against the wish of the insured person, even where he/she has shown negligence (or carelessness, or lack of knowledge or experience, or presumption and the like). Industrial accident is not present only where the impairment of health has been caused deliberately by the injured person (Article 55, paragraph 3 of the SIC). In the latter case no suddenness of the impairment is present, either. This impairment also contravenes the general principle of *Volenti non fit injuria*.

(c) Industrial accident is also characterized by its specific result. This result is incapacity for work (either temporary or permanent) or death of the injured, this being equivalent to total and permanent incapacity for work 'forever'. A constituent element of industrial accident is, however, necessary to be present – the occurrence of a severe harmful effect of a specifically high degree, not any sudden impairment – but such a sudden impairment that has affected (injured) the capacity for work of the person resulting in his/her incapacity for work or his/her death. If the impairment is a slight one and has not caused such a result, there is no industrial accident in the sense we are considering, that is the industrial accident as a social risk.

(d) Causality between the sudden impairment and the incapacity for work (either temporary or permanent) or death. Here we are facing actual causality – the incapacity for work or death has been caused by the traumatic impairment and are the consequences thereof.

§2. Accidents Equalled to the Industrial Ones

307. Accidents equalled to the industrial ones are those which do not have some of the constituent elements that industrial accidents have according to the regulation thereof contained in Article 55, paragraph 1 of the SIC (*see supra*). Most often, the missing elements are 'person insured against industrial accidents' or 'functional connection' between the impairment and the work assigned. However, the impairment (most often a traumatic one) of the injured person is present in all those cases.

308. This equalization is made for the purpose of giving these traumatic impairments the character of industrial accidents so that the injured persons be entitled to the favourable grants provided under Article 55 of the SIC for the cases of actual industrial accidents.

The equalization is carried out through legal fictions of presence of industrial accidents in certain cases provided for in law. These cases are specified in detail in Article 55, paragraph 2 of the SIC.

309. The three cases of equalled industrial accidents under Article 55, paragraph 3 of the SIC are as follows:

(a) The insured person's going from his/her place of residence to work and coming back from work. What matters here is that the place of residence should be a permanent one; that is, the insured person should be living there for the time of performing his/her employment duties. This may be a housing accommodation, a villa, a hotel, or the home of the person's friends or relatives in the cases of a business trip to another town, and so on.
(b) The insured person's going from his/her place of work to the place he/she has his/her meals, and coming back. This might be the canteen, or the home of the insured person, or his/her parents' home, and so on. It is required that the person go to this place during the working day. This makes one think that the lunch is envisaged here. However, it is not only the lunch, if the insured person performs shift work, and so on.
(c) The insured person's going from his/her place of work to the place of receiving his/her remuneration from the employer and coming back. Often the insured person receives his/her labour remuneration in a place which is different and distant from the place in which he/she performs his/her duties. The 'remuneration' comprises both the basic and the additional labour remuneration, various types of indemnities and other compensation payments – daily allowances and travelling allowances for business trips, and other similar payments.

310. The extent of persons insured against industrial accident is conditioned by the nature of the risk. Two different categories of persons are included here:

(a) Persons insured against all social risks, including the industrial accident risk. These are the persons specified in detail in Article 4, paragraph 1 of the SIC: employees working under employment relationships, civil servants, judges, public prosecutors and investigating magistrates, cooperative members, and so on (*see supra* paragraph 305).
(b) Employees employed for no more than five working days (forty hours) within the calendar month, regardless of the amount of their labour remuneration (Article 4, paragraph 2 of the SIC). They might be employed either by one or more employers.

311. The following persons do not belong to the extent of those insured against industrial accident: freelance practitioners, sole traders, persons working under a freelance contract at their own risk and responsibility (Article 4, paragraph 3 of the SIC). This ensues from the essence of industrial accident, which is historically connected with the work permanently performed by employees for the employer and in his/her interests, under an employment contract. And as far as the persons under Article 4, paragraph 3 of the SIC are concerned, no such legal situation is present.

312. Industrial accident is established in accordance with a particular procedure, which is different from the one laid down for establishing the other insured social risks. The 'establishment of an industrial accident' includes the establishment of the fact of the accident and the impairment as well as the legal qualification of the impairment as an industrial accident.

313. While the inclusion of the element symmetrical to impairment in the other social risks – sickness, pregnancy and the like, is made by medical bodies (the physician, the Medical Consultation Commission, etc.), in the cases of an industrial accident it is preceded by the actions of other persons and bodies. This also concerns the establishment of the accident as a fact. As for the establishment of the harmful effect – the incapacity for work or death caused by the accident – it is carried out in the way applicable to the general sickness risk – by the bodies of the Medical Expert Commission on employment matters, and by the healthcare bodies. However, once the accident has been established as a fact, there follows one more specific point of establishing the industrial accident – the legal qualification thereof as being an industrial one. All this makes it clear that the legal proceeding for establishing an industrial accident is a specific and complex one.

314. The procedure according to which this legal proceeding is conducted is regulated in Articles 57–60 of the SIC and the Ordinance of the Council of Ministers on establishing, examining, registering and reporting industrial accidents, which was issued on the grounds of Article 57, paragraph 3 of the SIC. This legal framework outlines two different proceedings which are conducted one after another: administrative and court proceedings.

315. As for the time it is conducted, the administrative proceeding is the first one. It is called 'administrative' because it is conducted with the participation of administrative bodies (the Labour Inspection and other official persons) and is governed by the administrative procedure. This proceeding is aimed at establishing the fact of industrial accident and the circumstances under which it has occurred. This proceeding is conducted in two stages: the establishment stage and the evaluation one.

316. The establishment stage is started at the time the industrial accident is declared before the territorial body of the NII, within which the insurer of the injured insured person has been registered. The industrial accident is declared by the insurer within a three days' term following the occurrence of the accident. If the insurer fails to do so, the industrial accident may be declared by the injured person or his/her heirs within a six months' term following the occurrence of the accident. These terms are instructive ones. They are aimed at having the accident declared as soon as possible in order for the proceeding of its establishment to commence. And the sooner it is declared, the more precise and complete the establishment of the circumstances of occurrence will be.

317. The declaration of the accident means the stating of the fact of its occurrence before the territorial body of the NII. It is the establishment of the circumstances regarding the occurrence of the industrial accident that commences after it. This part of the administrative proceeding is performed jointly by representatives of the territorial body of the NII, the Labour Inspection (the regional or the central one) and the working conditions committees of the enterprise in which the industrial accident has occurred, these committees being set up under Articles 27–28 of the Law on Healthy and Safe Working Conditions. The proceeding is conducted either in the presence of the injured person, or – if he/she cannot attend the proceeding – in the presence of his/her relatives and the representatives of the trade union committee of the enterprise. The idea is to have an objective and complete investigation carried out.

318. The establishment of the circumstances under which the industrial accident has occurred is obligatory in the cases of severe industrial accidents. Such are: lethal industrial accidents, those which have caused the injury of more than three employees, as well as those which are reasonably expected to cause the disability of the injured person or persons. This establishment is carried out in accordance with the procedure described above. It is necessary that an inspection of the place of the accident be made, and that the injured person and witnesses of the event be heard out, and the respective measures be made, photos be taken, and so on, all these truthfully reflecting the set of facts relating to the occurrence of the accident.

319. A record is drawn up of the actions taken in the course of the administrative proceeding, this record presenting the fact of the accident and describing the circumstances under which it has taken place. As for the established facts and circumstances stated in the record (*see infra* paragraph 321), great importance is given to the explicit description of the health impairment the accident consists in: breaking an arm, a leg, a pelvis, a thigh bone, or a traumatic shock and the like (D. No. 248-07-III C.D., D. No. 54-11-IV C.D., D. No. 123-12-III C.D., D. No. 218-21-III C.D., etc.). The description contains information about the specific industrial accident and the severity thereof. This is an official document which establishes the circumstances described in it, and the findings contained in it are presumed truthful unless they are disproved (Article 58, paragraph 6 of the SIC in connection with Article 179 of the Civil Procedure Code). Copies of the record are sent to the territorial body of the NII, the insurer, the injured person and his/her heirs.

320. A dossier is drawn up for each accident, this dossier containing all documents and data regarding the accident and the injured person. This dossier is kept in the territorial department of the NII

321. The evaluation proceeding consists in defining the legal qualification of the accident as an industrial one (Article 60 of the SIC). This proceeding is conducted by an administrative body – an official of the territorial department of the NII designated by the Head thereof. This official examines the dossier and, on the grounds of the documents contained therein and the legal framework of the industrial accident, he/she issues an order either recognizing the accident as an industrial one in the sense pursuant to Article 55, paragraphs 1 and 2 of the SIC, or not. The act – the order – he/she has issued is an authoritative act, an individual administrative act in the sense pursuant to Article 21 of the APC. It is handed down to the insurance body and the injured person or his/her heirs within a term of seven days following its issuance. Only an impairment which has been established and qualified as an industrial accident in accordance with the administrative procedure laid down in Article 60 of the SIC forms grounds for the occurrence of the social security law consequences provided for in the SIC (payment of insurance benefits to the insured person – *see infra* paragraph 324) or the employer's incurrence of his property liability for the damages suffered by the injured employee as a result of an industrial accident under Articles 200–202 of the LC (*see infra* paragraphs 352–362). This exclusiveness of the body which is competent to recognize the accident as an industrial one, and the procedure it follows for it are due to the specificity of the industrial accident and the insurance consequences it gives rise to (*see infra* paragraph 324). The steady practice of the SCC is to that effect (D. No. 1130-03-III C.D., D. No. 119-10-II C.D., D. No. 31-11-IV C.D., 169-12-IV C.D., 184-21-IV C.D., etc.), too.

322. The administrative proceeding ends with the exercise of the right to appeal against the order, under Article 60, paragraph 4 of the SIC, to the Head of the territorial department of the NII on the part of the insurer and the insured person or his/her heirs (Article 60, paragraph 4 in connection with Article 117, paragraph 1 of the SIC). This stage is facultative, and not mandatory, because it is also possible that the order is not appealed against under the administrative procedure. In this case, the proceeding ends with issuing and handing down the official's order under Article 60, paragraph 1 of the SIC to the insurance body and the insured person or his/her heirs (*see supra* paragraph 317).

323. The court proceeding is facultative. It is instituted where and if the order under Article 60, paragraph 1 of the SIC issued by the Head of the territorial department of the NII is appealed against. The right to appeal is assigned to the persons concerned. And these are: the insurer and the insured person and his/her heirs. Within a term of fourteen days, the statement of appeal is filed with the district court in the venue of which the accident has occurred. The court considers the statement of appeal in accordance with the procedure set forth in Articles 145–184 of the APC. The decisions of this court are subject to cassation appeal to the Supreme Administrative Court (argument under the APC and Article 5). Thus, judicial supervision of the act recognizing the accident as an industrial one is exercised. This is a court proceeding under administrative jurisdiction, and not under civil jurisdiction, because the subject matter of the proceeding is the lawfulness of an individual administrative act regarding the recognition or non-recognition of the accident as an industrial one (Decision No. 657/year 1999 of the 3rd Civil Department of the Supreme Court of Cassation).

324. The occurrence and the recognition of an industrial accident give rise to important insurance rights of the insured. These rights are as follows:

(a) The right to indemnity for temporary incapacity for work, sanatorium and resort treatment, urgent medical examination and/or treatment (Article 11, paragraph 1, item 1'a', Articles 40–42 of the SIC).
(b) The right to pecuniary indemnity in the cases of reassignment of a person with temporary incapacity for work to another suitable job (Article 11, paragraph 1, item 1'b', Article 47 of the SIC).
(c) The right to pension for disability caused by an industrial accident (Article 11, paragraph 1, item 4'b', Article 12, paragraph 1, item 3, Articles 71–73, Articles 78–79 of the SIC).

(d) The right to pecuniary aid for prophylaxis and rehabilitation, as well as for relief devices connected with the injury (Article 11, paragraph 1, items 2'b' and 2'c', Article 12, paragraph 1, items 2 and 4 of the SIC).
(e) In the case of death of the insured person – the right to pecuniary aid for the surviving spouse, the children and parents (Article 11, paragraph 2 and Article 12, paragraph 2 of the SIC).

These rights will be considered later (*see infra* Chapter 4 and §2).

Chapter 2. Occupational Disease

325. Occupational disease is the next insured social risk. Its significance is determined by the increasing number of occupational diseases resulting from the impairment of working environment. In 2020 the number of newly registered occupational diseases was 850 and as at 31 December 2020 the total number thereof amounted to about 27,940.[54]

326. The legal provisions on occupational diseases as an insured social risk in internal law are contained in Articles 56, 59, 61–67, 78–79 of the SIC, in the Occupation Diseases List adopted under the Decision of the Council of Ministers No. 175 of 16 July 2008 (promulgated in the OJ, No. 65 of 2008) and in the Regulation on Notification, Registration and Reports on Occupational Diseases issued by the Minister of Health Care (promulgated in the OJ, No. 65 of 22 July 2008), and so on. The legal provisions on occupational diseases have been created on the occasion of provisions on other matters, and they have mostly been created 'past' the legal provisions on industrial accidents. This puts the occupational diseases 'in the background' of industrial accidents.

327. The legal provisions on occupational diseases are in parallel with the legal provisions on industrial accidents. The two risks – occupational disease and industrial accident – are treated equally by social security law insofar as the insurance consequences for the insured persons are concerned (*see* Article 40, paragraph 2, Articles 41–42, 47, 64–67, 78–79 of the SIC, etc.).

328. Similarly to Article 55, paragraph 1 of the SIC, which concerns industrial accidents, Article 56, paragraph 1 of the SIC gives a legal definition of 'occupational disease'. According to it:

> 'Occupational' is a disease which has occurred exclusively or primarily under the effect of harmful factors of the working environment or the working process upon the organism.

329. Proceeding from this legal definition, two basic legal features of occupational disease can be pointed out:

(a) First of all, occupational disease is a type of disease. As such, it has all the characteristic features a disease has. Just like any disease, it is an impairment of the structural and functional characteristics of human organism and reflects its pathological (abnormal) state.

54. *Report on the Activities of the General Inspectorate of Labour for the Year 2020*, Labour and Law Journal, 2021, No. 3, Supplement, 46–47.

(b) Occupational disease has its aetiology (origin). This feature is ranked first in this part of the legal definition under Article 56, paragraph 1 of the SIC which provides that occupational disease is 'a disease which has occurred exclusively or primarily under the effect of harmful factors of the working environment or the working process upon the organism'.

330. According to law, these factors are twofold:

(1) The first type of factors are those of the working environment. These are the external conditions under which the work is performed: concentration of harmful substances in the air, temperature, movement and humidity of the air, lighting, noise and the like.
(2) The second type of factors are those of the working process. They are connected with the essence of the performed work. Examples thereof are: work on a computer and constant staring at the display, and the impact of the radiation from it, optic intensive work (with a microscope, a telescope, a camera and the like), work with isotopic and ionizing radiation, with pneumatic machinery causing strong vibrations of human body, and so on.

331. The novelties in the legal framework of occupational disease as an insured social risk continue further, in the procedure for the recognition of occupational diseases.

Depending on the procedure for their recognition as occupational diseases, under the insurance legislation which took effect on 1 January 2000 through the coming into force of the SIC, they are divided into two categories.

332. According to Article 56, paragraph 1 of the SIC, the first category comprises the diseases included in the Occupation Diseases List adopted under the Decision of the Council of Ministers No. 175 of 16 July 2008 (promulgated in the OJ, No. 65 of 22 July 2008).

The 2008 List sharply increases the number of occupational diseases from 30 – under the repealed Table of Occupational Diseases of 1958 – to 126. This shows, on the one hand, the increased number of occupational harmful factors under modern technical conditions of manufacture, and, on the other hand, the striving of the State for more comprehensive insurance protection of the insured against the occupational disease risk. This line deserves being fully supported.

333. Depending on their closeness by medical symptoms and the occupational harmful factors which cause them, the occupational diseases of the 2008 List are distributed into five main groups: (1) Diseases resulting from chemical factors – lead, mercury, manganese, and so on, and their compounds; (2) Diseases resulting from noise; (3) Diseases resulting from biological factors; (4) Diseases resulting from biomechanical factors; (5) Diseases resulting from other factors, materials and products.

334. The List comprises the following:

(a) The medical appellation, under which the disease has been discovered, described and known in medical science and treatment practice: tenosynovitis, coordination, dyskinesia, neurosis, and so on.
(b) Harmful factors of the working environment. Depending on their nature and source, they are divided into two groups: harmful factors of the surrounding working environment and harmful factors of the working process and the work performed:
   - Harmful factors of the surrounding working environment. Such are the external conditions in which work is done: concentration of harmful substances in the air, temperature and speed of air draft, humidity of the air, lighting, noise and its levels and the like.
   - Harmful factors of the working process and the work performed. Such are: work on a computer and constant staring at the screen and the impact of the screen radiation, work requiring eye strain (work on a microscope, a telescope, a camera and the like), work with isotopes and ionizing radiation, pneumatic machines causing strong vibrations of the human body, etc.
   - These factors unfavourably affect the human body and bring about pathogenic changes therein. That is what Article 56, paragraph 1 of the SIC envisages when considering 'the impact of harmful factors of the working environment and the working process'. The occupational diseases are a result of the said impact.
(c) The typical and most important occupational harmful factors causing the respective disease are listed. The new legal framework does not list the occupations or types of work in the performance or exercise of which the occupational disease occurs, but rather points out, in a general and flexible way, that these are all types of activities in which the occupational factors causing the disease are present. For instance, as far as the tenosynovitis is concerned, this is the heavy and systematic overstrain or pressure on the respective muscles and tendons, for radiation sickness – work connected with ionizing radiation, for vibration disease – work with pneumatic and other machinery and equipment causing local and general vibrations, and so on. The objective is to cover the widest scope of occupational activities causing the respective disease.

335. There should be causality between these occupational harmful factors and the disease specified in the list. This means that the occupational disease should have occurred as a result of the action of the said factors. This causality is envisaged under Article 56, paragraph 1 of the SIC which provides that the disease should have occurred 'exclusively or primarily under the effect of harmful factors of the working environment or the working process upon the organism', or that it should have been 'mainly and directly caused by the usual labour activity of the insured person' (Article 56, paragraph 2 of the SIC).

336. The effect of the occupational harmful factors 'upon the organism', which results in an occupational disease, should be long-term and permanent and not a momentary and single one. This implies a long-lasting contact between the insured employee and the working environment, in order for the occupational disease to occur. This feature of the harmful effect is determined by the nature of the occupational disease. It constitutes a profound and permanent impairment of the structural and functional characteristics of the human organism resulting from the long-term and permanent effect of the occupational harmful factor causing the disease.

337. The legal significance of the List under Article 56, paragraph 1 of the SIC is that the diseases specified therein are recognized as occupational ones on the grounds of their being included in the List. The causality regarding the respective disease should be established in each separate case – the disease should have occurred 'exclusively or primarily under the effect of harmful factors' of the specific working environment or the specific working process upon the organism of the injured insured person.

338. The occurrence of an occupational disease of this category might bring about temporary incapacity for work, permanent incapacity for work or death. Each of these three unfavourable outcomes of the realization of the risk under Article 56, paragraph 1 of the SIC results in the payment of the respective insurance benefits (*see infra* Chapter 4, §2).

339. Apart from the diseases specified in the List, other diseases may be recognized as occupational as well. According to Article 56, paragraph 2 of the SIC:

> a disease which is not included in the Occupational Diseases List under Article 56, paragraph 2 of the SIC may also be recognized as an occupational one if it is established that the disease has been mainly and directly caused by the usual labour activity of the insured person and has resulted in permanent incapacity for work or death of the insured person.

This is the second category of occupational diseases. It exists along with the first one and complements it. What is specific to this category of occupational diseases is the procedure for establishing the occupational nature thereof (*see infra* paragraph 340). This is the new, fair and modern solution, which deserves being fully supported. It has turned the operative national insurance system of Bulgaria from 'a List system' into a mixed system. It already accepts both the system of the Occupational Diseases List and the system of legal definition, on the grounds of which other diseases that are not included in the List may also be recognized as occupational ones if it is established that they have been caused by the harmful effect of the working conditions or the nature of the work performed by the insured person.

340. However, as for the recognition as 'occupational' of those diseases which are not included in the List, two important circumstances are worth being pointed out.

The first one of them concerns the recognition procedure. As for these diseases, in each specific case, it should be established that the disease 'has been mainly and directly caused by the usual labour activity of the insured person' (Article 56, paragraph 2 of the SIC). This wording contains several basic points.

First, there should be established causality between the disease and the usual labour activity of the insured person. The 'cause' is the usual labour activity, while the consequence (the result) thereof is the disease. As a cause, 'the usual labour activity' is the performance of the labour function which the person carries out on the grounds of the legal relationship that his/her insurance is based on. The said function should contain the harmful factors.

Establishing the causality means establishing that the disease has been caused mainly and mostly by the said labour activity. And the disease being 'directly' caused by the usual labour activity means it is being caused by the respective labour activity itself, without the interference of any intermediate factors.

This causality should be established in observance of the special proceeding provided for it in Articles 61–63 of the SIC (*see infra* paragraph 341).

The second point concerns the insurance consequences of these diseases. This way of establishing and recognizing may be used only for those diseases which have brought about permanent incapacity for work (disability) or death, and not for the ones which have brought about temporary incapacity for work. This is an improper solution in the law and a mistake therein. This mistake makes Article 56, paragraph 2 of the SIC obviously inconsistent with Article 40, paragraph 2 and Article 41, paragraph 1 of the SIC, the latter regulating the right and amount of the indemnity for temporary incapacity for work resulting from occupational disease. Article 24, paragraph 1 of the SIC also proceeds from the idea of indemnities being paid for temporary incapacity for work resulting from an occupational disease. This means that in a number of cases, the Commonwealth of Independent States (CIS) proceeds from the concept of payment of indemnities for temporary incapacity for work caused by an occupational disease. Owing thereto, this part of the provision of Article 56, paragraph 2 of the SIC should be subject to correctional construction, and it has to be assumed that, on general grounds, the insurance against occupational disease under the conditions of Article 56, paragraph 2 of the SIC also includes an indemnity for temporary incapacity for work caused by the said disease.

341. The establishment proceeding of any occupational disease (belonging to the first or second category) includes its notification, the execution of the documents thereof, and the confirmation or denial of its being recognized as an occupation one, as well as the appeal against the said confirmation or denial (Articles 61–63 of the SIC).

342. 'The notification' consists in the immediate communication, on the part of the practising physicians and dentists of the respective territorial department of the NII, of each separate case of suspicion for an occupational disease. The 'respective' territorial department of the NII is the one by the place in which the practising physicians and dentists exercise their profession. The obligation of notification is assigned to the practising physicians and dentists because, in the course of practising their profession, they are the first ones to receive the information of it in their everyday practice. The fulfilment of this obligation sets the beginning of the proceeding for establishing the presence of an occupational disease.

343. On the grounds of the notification under Article 61 of the SIC, the territorial department of the NII carries out an enquiry on its own. The enquiry is carried out by a commission headed by a representative of the territorial department of the NII, this commission also including a specialist in labour medicine, a representative of the insurer and a representative of the working conditions committee at the employer-insurer that the insured person is employed by. This commission studies the factors of the working environment and the working process, as well as other data required for confirming or denying the presence of an occupational disease of the insured person. The results of the enquiry are entered in a record drawn up by the commission, and this record is submitted to the Territorial Medical Expert Commission (TMEC).

344. The TMECs, which either confirm or deny the presence of occupational diseases, are set up by the Minister of Health Care. In these cases, their composition includes specialists in occupational diseases and work hygiene, and where the commission renders a decision on occupational diseases resulting from ionizing radiation, it also includes a specialist in radiobiology or radiation technology. These requirements are aimed at assigning the confirmation or denial of the presence of an occupational disease to medical expert bodies of professional competence.

The TMEC carries out a study and a clinical examination of the patient, examines the medical information and documentation – both the available and the additionally collected one – and renders its decision on the grounds thereof, either accepting or denying the occupational nature of the disease, doing so by way of its expert decision. The latter is communicated to the territorial department of the NII, the insurer and the insured person.

345. The decision of the TMEC may be appealed against to the National Medical Expert Commission (NMEC) by the territorial department of the NII, the insurer and the insured person within a term of fourteen days following the day of its being received by the territorial department of the NII, the insurer and the insured person. The NMEC renders its decision on the appeal on the grounds of a clinical examination of the insured person and the available documents. The NMEC may confirm the decision of the TMEC, or overrule it, or refer it back for having the person being examined anew, with instructions regarding the correction of the mistakes, or may overrule it and take a decision of its own on the merits.

346. The expert decisions of the NMEC may be appealed against, in accordance with the procedure set forth in the APC, to the Sofia City Administrative Court. The decisions of the latter are subject to cassation appeal to the Supreme Administrative Court. In this way, judicial supervision is exercised of the lawfulness of a specific individual administrative act, as the decision of the NMEC is, regarding the occupational nature of the disease under Article 56 of the SIC.

347. Occupational disease may only be established by the bodies and through the procedure shown above (*see supra* paragraphs 337–346). It may not be established by other bodies or through another procedure, including by the court through claim proceedings, questioning of witnesses, assessment experts and the like. This exclusiveness of the bodies and the procedure for establishing the occupational disease, which is also specific to the establishment of an industrial accident (*see supra* paragraph 321), is conditioned by the presence of a number of medical issues that the occupational disease poses, the clarification and resolution thereof requiring specialized medical knowledge and experience. The practice of the SCC is to that effect (D. No. 468-08-IV C.D., D. No. 207-10-III C.D., D. No. 298-21-III C.D., etc.), too.

348. The extent of the persons insured against the risk of occupational disease is the same as the one of those insured against industrial accident (Article 4, paragraphs 1 and 2 of the SIC). The reason for it is the common nature of industrial accident and occupational disease as occupational insured social risks. Owing thereto, we are making a renvoi to the above exposition on this matter (*see supra*).

349. The realization of an occupational disease as an insured social risk results in a temporary or permanent incapacity for work or death.

The establishment of temporary or permanent incapacity caused by an occupational disease is carried out in the general due course, valid for the other social risks – general sickness, accident, and so on, and will be considered later (*see infra* Chapter 3, §2).

350. Insurance rights. The realization of the risk of an occupational disease gives rise to insurance rights of the insured persons, these rights being the same as those on realization of the risk of industrial accident (*see infra* Chapter 4, §2).

351. In case of occurrence of an industrial accident (*see supra* paragraphs 301–324) or an occupational disease (*see supra* paragraphs 325–350) affecting an insured person, pursuant to Article 59 of the SIC, the respective territorial division of the NII is obliged to open, maintain and keep a record containing:

(a) a declaration of the industrial accident or a notification of the occupational disease;
(b) a protocol of investigation into the industrial accident in the event that such an investigation has been undertaken, or a protocol of examination of the specific occupational disease;
(c) an order regarding the admission or non-admission (recognition or non-recognition) of the accident as an industrial one, or an expert decision regarding the affirmation or the refusal (rejection) to regard the disease as an occupation one, and a registration card of the occupational disease;
(d) a copy of the primary sick-leave certificates related to the industrial accident or the occupational disease;
(e) other documents connected with the specific industrial accident or occupational disease.

The collected documents contained in the industrial accident record give clarity and orderliness as regards the occurrence of the respective social risk and its course and insurance consequences. In the event of litigation, these documents can be used as official written documents and written evidence before the court. It is at any time that both the injured insured person and the insurer have the right to get acquainted with the content of the record.

Chapter 3. Employer's Property Liability

352. A special employer's property liability in the case of death of an employee or damages to his/her health was established by Article 200 of the Labour Code. Until entry into force of this Code as of 1 January 1987, the responsibility of the employer in such a case was regulated by the general rules of common civil liability for unlawful inflicted damage as a consequence of the infringement of the common rule *neminem laedere* (do not damage another) according to Article 45 of the Law on Contracts and Obligations. Since then, Article 200 of the Labour Code has introduced important peculiarities which have created a new form of the employer's civil liability for damages caused to an employee. This responsibility consists in the obligation of the employer to indemnify the employee or his/her heirs by means of a lump sum the amount of which represents the difference between the damage caused – material (patrimonial) and moral.[55]

353. Material (patrimonial) damage includes not only actual losses (*damnum emergens*) but also missed opportunities (*lucrum cessans*) and compensations and/or pensions paid by social insurance funds:

(a) The actual losses incurred comprise those damages suffered by the injured person which concern: medicines, prostheses, rich diet food, sick-attendant, transportation charges and other expenses relating to the treatment. They are reimbursed to the injured person, including where he/she has reached the retirement age, until the end of his/her life (D. No. 109-1865-IV C.D., D. No. 74-99-III C.D., D. No. 1625-99-III C.D., D. No. 724-05-III C.D., D. No. 985-05-III C.D., D. No. 268-19-IV C.D., D. No. 48-19-III C.D., etc.).
(b) The missed opportunities are expressed in the lower remuneration and income the injured employee has while being in a state of temporary incapacity for work and will have in future because of the said incapacity. To some extent, though not completely, the missed opportunities are indemnified by social insurance. The indemnity for missed opportunities is aimed at covering the difference between the income that the injured person used to have prior to the industrial accident or the occupational disease, and the indemnities from the social insurance funds.

354. Moral damages. They are expressed in the injured person's pains, sufferings and mental discomfort. And in case the industrial accident or the occupational disease causes the injured person's death, these damages are expressed in the pain and sorrow felt by his/her relatives (spouse, children, parents) for his/her decease. These damages are not at all indemnified by social insurance. The law assigns to the employer – within the framework of the employer's insurance against civil liability – the whole indemnification for the moral damages suffered by the injured person. According to Article 52 of the Law on Obligations and Contracts, the

---

55. For more details on the employer's property liability under Art. 200 of the LC *see* V. Mrachkov, *Employer's Property Liability* 63–271 (Sibi Publishing House 2013).

amount of these damages is determined by the court in equity (D. No. 899-99-III C.D., D. No. 1854-2000-III C.D., D. No. 156-01-III C.D., D. No. 1180-02-III C.D., D. No. 292-03-III C.D., D. No. 181-04-III C.D., D. No. 786-05-III C.D., D. No. 248-07-III C.D., D. No. 749-08-II C.D., D. No. 95-14-III C.D., D. No. 161-14-III C.D., D. No. 62-15-IV C.D., D. No. 180-15-III C.D., D. No. 54-19-III C.D., D. No. 178-20-III C.D., D. No. 35-20-IV C.D., etc.).

355. The following prerequisites for the responsibility can be deduced from the law:

(1) The occurrence of an industrial accident or occupational disease of the employee as defined by law (Articles 55 and 56 of the SIC – *see supra* §§1 and 2). It does not matter whether or not the employer is at fault as regards the occurrence of an industrial accident or occupational disease. It is sufficient that the event has occurred. In this sense, the envisaged liability is objective and differs from the civil responsibility under Article 45 of the Law on Obligations and Contracts, which always requires the element of guilt bringing about the damage. The basic idea of this prerequisite and the property liability of the employer as a whole is that the industrial accident or occupational disease is a result of the employer's failure to secure normal hygienic and safe working conditions. The employer has this obligation by virtue of the law. The law not only lays down the accomplishment of hygienic and safe working conditions by the employer but also imposes on him the risk of failing to secure safe and healthy working conditions. That is why the law in Article 200, paragraph 1 of the Labour Code expressly provides that liability arises irrespective of fault on the part of the employer himself, somebody on his/her managerial staff or any other person in his/her employ as regards the occurrence of an industrial accident or occupational disease. The employer is also liable for an industrial accident due to an Act of God (force majeure), or occurring as a result of accomplishing or in connection with a task entrusted to the employee, or in connection with any job completed in the interest of the enterprise, even without an order to that effect by the employer. The employer is also liable if an industrial accident has occurred during a rest period spent in the enterprise (Article 200, paragraph 2 of the Labour Code). The only case in which the employer does not bear responsibility for damages caused to an employee during his/her work is when the employee causes the damage to himself with premeditation (Article 201, paragraph 1 of the Labour Code). But in such circumstances, there is no industrial accident in the legal sense of this term (Article 55, paragraph 3 of the SIC – *see supra* §§1–2). In the last case, the burden of proof (*onus probandi*) rests upon the employer. Also, the responsibility of the employer may be diminished if the employee by his/her serious misconduct has contributed to the industrial accident taking place (Article 201, paragraph 2 of the Labour Code).

(2) The industrial accident or occupational disease must provoke a temporary incapacity for work, disability or death of an employee. These are the legally recognized types of damages or injuries sustained by the employee. Only these

three forms are relevant to any employer's responsibility arising. They are established by the competent medical bodies in the manner prescribed by the law.[56]

356. According to Article 200, paragraph 4 of the LC, the amount of damage determined under Article 200, paragraph 3 of the LC is reduced by those amounts which the injured employee has received under obligatory insurance contracts concluded by the employer for the employees performing work that poses a danger to their life and health (Article 52 of the Law on Healthy and Safe Working Conditions). These contracts take into account the activity performed by the enterprise and the country's average rate of industrial accidents' frequency and severity, this rate being determined annually by the Minister of Labour and Social Policy. For example, according to Ordinance No. RD-01-865 of 30 October 2012 (promulgated in the OJ, No. 92 of 23 November 2012), the industrial traumatism rate in the economic activity of 'Extraction of Metal Ores' is 10.65, in the economic activity of 'Building Services and Landscaping' it was 0.84, and the country's average rate for 2013 was 0.75. The contract of employees' insurance is concluded in accordance with Articles 230–243 of the IC.[57]

357. The employees insured under Article 52 of the Law on Healthy and Safe Working Conditions are named in a written contract with the insurer following consultations with the Labour Medicine Office and the working conditions committees (groups), in compliance with the risk assessment (Articles 1, 2, 4 of the quoted Ordinance). Special attention should be given to several specific points:

(a) 'Insurance is at the employer's account'. This means that all the expenses on obligatory insurance and, primarily, those on the insurance premium as being the insurance price due to the insurer are paid out fully and solely by the employer, without any participation of the insured employee in whose favour and interest the insurance contract is concluded. As a 'pecuniary instalment', this premium is the aggregate of all the financial resources which the employer allots from his patrimony and pays to the insurer.
(b) This insurance covers the following insurance consequences of the industrial accident risk: the insured person's death resulting from the industrial accident, his/her permanently reduced capacity for work and his/her temporary incapacity for work.
(c) The insured value under the industrial accident insurance is determined on the basis of the monthly gross salary of the employees as at the time the insurance is taken out.
(d) The obligatory insurance is taken out by way of conclusion of an insurance contract under Articles 230–243 of the IC between the employer and the insurer for each calendar year. The duration of the contract may not be longer than twelve months or shorter than one month (Article 16, paragraph 2 of the quoted Ordinance).

56. V. Mrachkov et al., *Komentar na Kodeksa na Trouda*, 668–689.
57. P. Goleva, *Insurance and Reinsurance Law* 453–460 (Sibi Publishing House 2000).

(e) The insurance amount which is due upon the occurrence of an event insured against (occurrence of an industrial accident) is fixed in the insurance contract. It may not be smaller than the sevenfold amount of the annual gross salary of the respective employee (Article 8 of the quoted Ordinance).

358. Against the background of the preceding exposition (*see supra* Article 350b), the legislative solution contained in Article 200, paragraph 4 of the IC is logical and fair: the amounts received by the injured employee for an industrial accident under the insurance contract to which he/she is a beneficiary (third-person beneficiary) and to whom pecuniary amounts are paid as insurance indemnity from the accumulated instalments of insurance premiums the employer has paid in his/her interest. The amounts received by the insured person injured in an industrial accident have the same subject matter, legal grounds and purpose as those of the indemnity due by the employer under Article 200, paragraph 3 of the IC, namely: the fullest possible indemnification for the damages caused by the industrial accident, as is the aim and purpose of the indemnity under Article 200, paragraph 3 of the IC. Owing thereto, it is right – as Article 200, paragraph 4 of the 2005 IC provides – to offset the received amounts against the indemnity due by the employer, because the payment of the indemnity due has already been made, so it should be offset, or, as Article 200, paragraph 4 of the 2005 IC provides, 'the indemnity due under Article 3 is reduced' in order to prevent a twofold payment on the same grounds and twofold indemnification for the same damage. Court practice, including the practice of the Supreme Court and the Supreme Court of Cassation, has followed this solution (Decree of the Plenum of the Supreme Court (DPSC) No. 4 of 1961 and DPSC No. 4 of 1975, which the Resolution No. 2 of the Plenum of the Supreme Court (PSC) of 11 July 1995 lays down as obligatory for the employer's property liability under Articles 200 et seq. of the IC) even long before it was legislatively fixed (in 2005).[58] Its explicit legislative fixation deserves approval not only because it affirms and consolidates this practice but also because it eliminates any doubts and hesitations when determining the indemnity due by the employer within his property liability under Article 200 of the IC[59] and the insurance premium as per which the insurer's payment is made.

359. The above exposition on the offset of the received insurance amount against the indemnity under Article 200, paragraph 4 of the IC (*see supra* paragraphs 356–358) does not concern the insurance amount received under a personal insurance for accidents, as the grounds for paying the latter is a personal contract concluded by the insured employee and the insurer (DPSC No. 4 of 1961).

360. The employer's liability under Article 200 of the IC poses specific questions concerning the cases where the industrial accident or the occupational disease

58. The texts of these interpretative acts of the Supreme Court are quoted as per the Collection of Decrees and Interpretative Resolutions, *Civil Trials (1953–2011)*, Vol. I, 79–80, 85–97, 113–120 (Pleneia Publishing House 2011).
59. A. Vassilev & E. Mingov, *In: Komentar na Kodeksa na Trouda,* 692–695.

has caused the injured person's death. There are two questions: (1) the circle of relatives of the deceased employee; (2) the inflicted damages for the recovery of which the employer is answerable.

361. The law does not fix the circle of relatives in these cases. According to Article 52 of the Law on Obligations and Contracts, the court determines it by equity. Pursuant to item 2 of Decree No. 2 of the PSC dated 30 November 1984, these are only the closest relatives of the deceased employee and comprise: the children of the deceased person, his/her parents and the surviving spouse. The other relatives, e.g., the grandmother and grandfather, the grandchildren, brothers and sisters of the deceased are excluded.[60]

362. The damages suffered by the said relatives of the deceased person (*see supra* paragraph 361) are property and non-property ones. Property damages consist of the lost maintenance and material support which the surviving relatives used to receive from the deceased person. And the non-property damages consist of the pain, sorrow and suffering from the death of their deceased relative – a child, a parent, a surviving spouse. Each case has its specific circumstances, which determine the amount of the damages awarded: the age of the children (the younger they are and, therefore, the longer the years lying ahead for their raising, upkeep, healthcare, education and the like, the higher the amount of the maintenance awarded), the length of the matrimonial life with the surviving spouse, emotional attachment between the spouses, etc. The court determines the pecuniary amount of these damages by equity (Article 52 of the Law on Obligations and Contracts).

60. The legal doctrine criticizes this stringent and restrictive identification of the circle of relatives of the deceased person and pleads for its expansion in order for it to cover the grandmother and grandfather, the grandchildren, brothers and sisters, as according to Bulgarian family traditions they still keep the patrimonial and emotional closeness and attachment to each other (V. Tadjer, *Right to Indemnity for Non-Property Damages*, 2 *Pravna Misal* [*Legal Thought*] *Journal* 86–91 (1986)); S. Tassev, *Tortious Liability* 153–159 (Ciela Publishing House, 2010); V. Mrachkov, *Employer's Property Liability* 171–174 (Sibi Publishing House, 2013).

Chapter 4. Temporary Incapacity for Work

§1. The Notion of Temporary Incapacity for Work

363. Depending on the duration of incapacity for work and the presence or absence of prospects of its recovery, incapacity for work is of two types: temporary and permanent.

364. Incapacity for work and its two types – temporary and permanent are not legally defined. However, the operative legislation contains instructions concerning both general features of incapacity for work and specific features of temporary and permanent incapacity for work. Here we are interested in temporary incapacity for work. Permanent incapacity for work will be analysed later when pensions are concerned, as it constitutes the grounds of pension benefits (*see infra*).

365. Temporary incapacity for work is characterized by several main features. They concern the state of the insured person. These features are as follows: (a) an alteration of the health state and the general physiological state of the person; (b) impossibility for the person to perform his/her work; (c) the impossibility of performing the work is for a definite time, this time being of short duration and there should be a prospect of recovering the capacity for work; (d) temporary incapacity for work may be – (i) total temporary incapacity for work; (ii) reduced temporary incapacity for work, that is partial temporary incapacity for work; (e) as for its content, temporary incapacity for work may be actual or equalled; (f) temporary incapacity for work is a consequence of strictly specified reasons. These features will be briefly analysed below.

366. Altered health state and general physiological state. The altered health state is actually a diversion from the normal health state and an impairment of the physical or mental health of the insured person (e.g., general sickness or occupational disease). The altered general physiological state is expressed in a diversion from the usual state of the person (e.g., pregnancy of a woman).

367. Temporary incapacity for work is the state of impossibility of the insured person to perform his/her labour activity, this being the activity he/she receives his/her earnings from and makes his/her livelihood. This means: diversion from the usual good health state of the insured person and deterioration of his/her health state to such a degree that makes the person incapable of work. Therefore, this is not any indisposition or any physical, physiological, mental or emotional state of the insured person, but only such indisposition or discomfort that results in his/her incapability, due to contraindications or danger of unfavourable complications, of performing the specific work that the insurance is connected with.

368. The temporary incapacity for work continues for a definite period of time, which is short as a rule. Recovery of the person's capacity for work is expected. The incapacity subsists until the insured person recovers his/her capacity for work or until his/her temporary incapacity for work turns into permanent incapacity for work (disability) or until he/she is employed in work appropriate to his/her available capacity for work or until he/she dies.

The time this temporary incapacity for work subsists is either definable or definite. It is definable on the grounds of the incapacity because in certain cases it is well known how long the temporary incapacity for work will last. In general, the duration of this period depends on the nature of the social risk occurred and on its development. This time is divided into separate periods so that the process of health impairment and the development of the disease may be examined and measured, and treatment of the insured person may be carried out for recovering his/her capacity for work.

369. The law establishes a specific course for watching the development of temporary incapacity for work in those cases where it lasts for a long time: for six months without interruption or for twelve months with interruption within two consecutive calendar years. In these cases, the insured person undergoes a medical examination in order to establish whether his/her temporary incapacity for work has turned into a permanent one and to check whether it is necessary for the person to be reassigned and have another job appropriate to his/her health state and his/her capacity for work, or whether the state of his/her temporary incapacity for work is still present.

However, there are certain cases where the temporary incapacity for work has its fixed duration set out by the law. These are the cases of maternity (pregnancy, childbirth and upbringing the child), these cases being equalled to the general sickness insurance risks (Articles 43–45, 50 of the SIC).

370. Depending on the degree of the incapacity for work, the temporary incapacity for work may be either complete or partial. It is complete where the capacity for work of the insured person is totally exhausted and he/she is not able to work. In these cases, the insured person is released from work, he/she is allowed a leave because of this temporary incapacity for work, and during that time he/she receives insurance indemnity (Article 42 of the SIC, *see infra*). The partial (or reduced) incapacity for work under Article 2, item 2 and Article 47 of the SIC is the temporary incapacity in which the capacity for work of the insured person is not exhausted. The person has residual capacity for work which can be used by way of his/her being reassigned to another job which is suitable for his/her residual capacity for work. This form of temporary incapacity for work is present in certain cases of realization of the risks of industrial accident, occupational disease, general sickness and maternity – for the period of pregnancy (*see infra*). The prerequisites and the procedure for carrying out the reassignment of employees to other suitable jobs are regulated in Articles 309 and 314–317 of the Labour Code.[61]

371. Temporary incapacity for work can be actual or equalled. Actual incapacity is the case where the person does not work because of the state of his/her health, as he/she has no mental or physical capability for work, or the case where if he/she continues to work, this will result in deterioration of his/her health state although

61. V. Mrachkov et al., *Komentar na Kodeksa na trouda*, 915–935.

he/she has some mental or physical powers left. Pursuant to the law in these cases, the person 'is not able to work'. The incapacity is equalled when the person, although being capable of work, has no capacity for work because of some other reasons. Pursuant to the law, in these cases the person is 'prevented from work'. The cases which belong here are the ones of quarantine, attending on a sick or quarantined member of the family, and so on (*see supra*).

372. Temporary incapacity for work is a consequence of the effect of specific causes. They are explicitly and exhaustively specified in law (the SIC). These are the insured risks, the occurrence thereof being the cause of temporary incapacity for work. However, these are not all the social risks, but only a part thereof. They can be divided into two groups. The first of them includes those insured social risks that can bring about both temporary and permanent incapacity for work. It includes the risks of general sickness, industrial accident and occupational disease. Here, in view of the hypotheses, we are interested in them as causes of temporary incapacity for work. The second group comprises the risks that can bring about temporary incapacity for work only. Such are the maternity risk (pregnancy, childbirth and upbringing of the child) and those insured risks that are equalled to general sickness – quarantine, attending on a sick or quarantined member of the family, and so on. This various 'generating energy' of the social risks causing incapacity for work is determined by their very essence. The risks, being future uncertain events, are 'charged' with different quantity and power of 'legal energy' causing a variety of incapacities for work of different natures and durations or impossibility for the insured person to perform his/her labour activities under which he/she is insured.

§2. Establishing the Temporary Incapacity for Work

373. In order for the temporary incapacity for work to become 'legally tangible' and to give rise to insurance legal consequences, it has to be established that its presence as an objective fact should be ascertained and proved. This is a specific legal-medical activity – the expertise of the incapacity for work, this expertise being carried out by expert medical bodies, which are specialized for this purpose, and in observance of a certain procedure, following a definite sequence. These bodies are regulated in Articles 103–113 of the Health Law and the Regulation on the Expertise of Incapacity for Work issued by the Council of Ministers by delegation of Article 109 of the Health Law.

374. Medical expertise is an official assessment of the insured persons' health state and the state of their capacity for work, this assessment being given by bodies and persons that are professionally prepared and empowered thereof in law. The bodies which give this assessment carry out an assessment activity and not a medical treatment or prophylaxis one. They are composed of higher-education graduates in medicine with long professional experience as physicians and dentists, because the matters on which they give conclusions in their expert decisions are grounded on medical knowledge. The organization of the activity and the management of these bodies are assigned to the Minister of Health Care and the regional healthcare centres (Article 102, paragraph 2 of the Health Law).

375. The new legal framework laid down through the Health Law of 2004 (promulgated in the OJ, No. 70 of 2004), effective since 1 January 2005, attaches great legal importance to the role of the medical expertise. Article 102 of the quoted Law provides for setting up a National Council of Medical Expertise under the Council of Ministers, this National Council being composed of: President who is a Vice President of the Council of Ministers, and members: the Minister of Health Care, the Minister of Labour and Social Policy, the Minister of Finance, the Manager of the NII, the Manager of the NHIPCDO and the Director of the NMEC. The functions of this new body are: to work out and submit to the Council of Ministers its opinion of the national health policy on those matters which are connected with medical expertise, to coordinate the state bodies' activities relating to these matters, to develop the methodology of financing and supervising the bodies of medical expertise of the incapacity for work, and so on.

376. The bodies of medical expertise of the incapacity for work are regulated in the Health Law. Their legal framework was taken out from the SIC where it used to be so far (Articles 15–17 of the SIC, repealed), and was further developed and enriched (Articles 103–113 of the Health Law).

377. The bodies of medical expertise for establishing the incapacity for work are as follows:

(a) The attending physician and other specialists of medicine who conduct the medical treatment or provide medical aid – physician's assistants, midwives in case of delivery, and other similar.
(b) *The Consultative Medical Commissions (CMCs).* They are set up and dissolved by way of an order issued by the directors of the regional healthcare centres, in medical treatment institutions for inpatients and outpatients. They are general and specialized ones – for specific types of diseases. The commission comprises at least two physicians with acknowledged speciality.
(c) *The TMECs.* They are set up and dissolved by way of an order from the regional healthcare centres in coordination with the Minister of Health Care. They form part of the medical treatment institutions under which they have been set up. They comprise: a physician-representative of the territorial department of the NII and a representative of the regional directorate for social support, and physicians with acknowledged speciality having at least ten years' length of service in the respective speciality. Panels are created therein by separate types of diseases.
(d) *The NMEC.* Its Director and members are designated by the Minister of Health Care. Specialized panels are created therein and the members of the NMEC are distributed among them. The NMEC is composed of physicians with acknowledged speciality having at least ten years' length of service in the respective speciality.

378. The temporary incapacity is established by way of a specific document called the patient's card. It is issued by the bodies of medical expertise on employment matters on the day the temporary incapacity for work is being established. The patient's card has a definite 'standard' – a unified form and requisites set out by the NII and the Ministry of Health Care. The course of issuing this document is regulated under Instruction 6500 of the Minister of Public Health of 1969. The patient's card certifies the temporary incapacity for work thereafter (Articles 1–2 of Instruction 6500).

379. The patient's card certifies the presence and duration of the temporary incapacity for work. It exempts the insured person from the obligation to perform his/her employment duties and serves as a 'title' (grounds) for the payment of insurance benefits to the insured person (*see infra*).

380. The decisions of the medical expertise bodies regarding temporary incapacity for work can be appealed against. These appeals may be lodged by the examined insured persons, the insurers, the NII and the Agency of Social Assistance. The law (Article 112, paragraph 1 of the Health Law) provides for two types of appeals: internal institutional ones and judicial ones.

381. The internal institutional appeal is made to the superior body of medical expertise. The appeals against the attending physician are lodged with the CMC, the appeals against the CMC are lodged with the TMEC, and the appeals against the latter are lodged with the NMEC. These appeals are lodged within a term of fourteen days following the day on which the appealed decision is received by the superior body of medical expertise.

382. Judicial appeal is applied after the internal institutional one, and only after the latter has been exhausted. This appeal is regulated in Article 112, paragraph 2, item 4 of the Health Law. It is applied only to the decisions of the NMEC. The decisions of the latter may be appealed to Sofia City Administrative Court in accordance with the procedure set forth in the APC. And the decisions of the latter are subject to cassation appeal to the Supreme Administrative Court. Appeals to Sofia City Administrative Court against the decisions of the NMEC may be lodged by the bodies and persons specified in Article 112, paragraph 1 of the Health Law (*see supra* paragraph 346). The background of this new and principal decision of the legislator is the fundamental understanding of the nature of the expert decisions of the NMEC as being individual administrative acts under Article 21 of the APC: they are issued by a body which is empowered thereto (the NMEC), and directly concern the insurance rights of the insured – insurance indemnities and aids (*see infra* Chapter 4, §2).

383. The renvoi to the judicial appeal of the decisions of the NMEC in accordance with the procedure set forth in the APC opens the door for the direct application of its rules to a number of problems of administrative justice: the term for filing the appeal, the procedure for its consideration, and the subsidiary application of the rules of the Civil Procedure Code to matters which are not regulated in the

APC, cassation appeal against the decisions of district administrative courts to the Supreme Administrative Court in accordance with the APC, and so on. This is an important step in the justiciability of insurance law, and the Supreme Administrative Court already has its practice in it.[62]

384. The temporary incapacity for work is connected with important consequences under social security law.

The risk of innocent non-provision of working force by the insured employee to the insurer-employer, and the non-provision of the result due by the performer to the assignor, is transferred from the insurer to the insurance body. As a result of this new distribution of the risk, the insurance body pays the insured person the insurance benefits – insurance indemnities, aid, and so on, depending on the nature of the risk incurred. These benefits replace, partially if not wholly, the missing earnings of the insured person. These insurance benefits are indemnity for the property damages sustained because of the missing earnings as a result of the temporary incapacity for work.

The time the temporary incapacity for work lasts is the period of intensive insurance relationship between the insurance body and the insured person, and it is also the time of the 'real performance' of the obligations the insurance body has to the insured person, these obligations having been in 'a latent state' before that. Prior to the occurrence of the insured risk causing the temporary incapacity for work, the insurance relationship between the insurance body and the insured person was characterized by the more active attitude on the part of the insured person by way of his/her paying the due insurance contributions to the insurance body, the insurance body having a dominant position and being the 'creditor'; now, after the risk has occurred, the situation has significantly changed and the parties 'change places': the insured person is the 'creditor' to the insurance benefits and the insurance body is his/her 'debtor'.

385. The temporary incapacity for work has important consequences relating to the position of the insured person and the legal relationship on the grounds of which he/she is insured – employment relationship, freelance one, and so on. When this relationship is an employment one, its performance is suspended. However, it continues to exist and it will 'recover' its normal existence and effect when the person restores his/her capacity for work. If this relationship is of any other type, for example, a freelance practitioner's one, the relations are settled under civil law and in compliance with what the parties have negotiated for cases of performer's innocent incapability of fulfilling his/her obligations.

62. *See* K. Sredkova, *Critical Review of the Supreme Administrative Court's Practice in Mandatory Social Insurance*, 2 Judicial World 223 (2002); 2 Judicial World 195–203 (2011); V. Mrachkov, *Social Security Law* 255–258 (Sibi Publishing House 7th ed. 2019).

Chapter 5. Temporary Incapacity Benefits

§1. Notion and Types

386. During the time the temporary incapacity for work and the loss of earnings caused thereby lasts, the insured person receives certain insurance benefits from the short-term social insurance. They constitute the good that social insurance provides to the insured persons when an insured social risk occurs, the latter causing temporary incapacity for work. These benefits replace the missing earnings of the insured persons for the time they are in the state of temporary incapacity for work. The major purpose of these benefits consists in creating economic security for the insured person who has got into temporary incapacity for work. These benefits compensate for the financial losses sustained by the person because of the missing work remuneration or other earnings he/she used to receive for his/her work. The nature of insurance benefits finds its expression here, these benefits being necessary for the maintenance of the insured person. In this sense they have the character of alimentary benefits.

387. The insurance indemnities are subjective rights of the insured regarding the insurance body. The insurance indemnity forms the main part of the content of the person's insurance relationship with the insurance body. Its nature of a subjective right means that the exercise thereof has the whole legal protection of the subjective rights, including the court claim protection. These are important juridical guarantees in the implementation of these rights.

388. The legal framework of insurance indemnities is contained in Articles 40–54 of the SIC and Articles 5–9 of the Regulation on the elements of the remuneration and incomes on which the insurance contributions are made, and the calculation of pecuniary indemnities for temporary incapacity for work, or pregnancy and maternity (promulgated in the OJ, No. 6 of 2000, amended).

389. There are various indemnities which an insured person getting into temporary incapacity for work or being granted a maternity leave receives from social insurance. Depending on the type of the insured social risk upon the occurrence of which they are due, the indemnities are divided into two groups: (1) Insurance indemnities for temporary incapacity for work resulting from general sickness, industrial accident and professional disease; (2) Insurance indemnities for maternity. They will be considered later (*see infra* §2 and §3).

§2. Insurance Indemnities for Temporary Incapacity for Work Resulting from General Sickness, Industrial Accident and Professional Disease

390. These insurance indemnities are regulated in Articles 40–47 of the SIC and Articles 5–9 of the quoted Regulation.

391. Depending on the type of the risk the occurrence of which has caused the temporary incapacity for work, the pecuniary indemnities for temporary incapacity for work are divided into two types: (1) pecuniary indemnities for temporary incapacity for work resulting from general sickness; (2) pecuniary indemnities for temporary incapacity for work resulting from industrial accident and occupational disease.

392. The insurance indemnities for temporary incapacity for work resulting from general sickness, industrial accident and occupational disease have certain common features, which shows that they belong to one and the same group. These features are as follows:

(a) They are paid from definite insurance funds. The indemnities for temporary incapacity for work resulting from general sickness are paid from the general sickness and maternity fund, while the indemnities for industrial accident and occupational disease are paid from the Industrial Accident and Occupational Disease Fund.
(b) These indemnities are paid upon the realization of a definite risk. That is why it is necessary for the person to have been insured against this specific risk, and not against another one.
(c) The insurance indemnity compensates for the lost or missing labour remuneration of the insured person. The 'compensation' means that the insurance indemnity covers the damages resulting from the absence of labour remuneration. It is the latter that the insurance indemnity restores. However, the said restoration is not complete, because the insurance indemnity does not fully replace the missing labour remuneration, and yet, does so to a degree which makes it possible for the insured person to support himself/herself. The compensation is for the missed opportunities to the profit (*lucrum cessans*) as no work remuneration is received.
(d) The insurance indemnity is an expression of transferring the risk of innocent non-provision of working force from the employer to the insurance body. This risk is assumed by the insurance body and, in the performance of the consequences of the risk transferred thereto, the insurance body makes the payments of the insurance contributions to the insured person when the risk occurs.
(e) The indemnities are paid in money.

393. The right to pecuniary indemnity for temporary incapacity for work arises if certain prerequisites are present. These prerequisites are as follows:

(a) The presence of temporary incapacity for work, either complete or partial, which has been established by the bodies of medical expertise of incapacity for work (*see supra* Chapter 3).
(b) It is necessary that either the temporary incapacity for work be caused by one of the following three risks: general sickness (including the risks equalled there to – *see supra* paragraph 392), industrial accident and professional disease, or the person be insured against them.

(c) As for the temporary incapacity for work resulting from general sickness, the minimum total length of insurance of six months is required. The sense of this requirement is to have the insured person contribute to the accumulation of financial means in the insurance funds prior to starting to consume them and use them. This requirement applies neither to the insured who have not turned 18 years of age nor to an insured person who has got into a state of temporary incapacity for work as a result of an industrial accident or occupational disease.

394. The amount of insurance indemnities is one of the most important questions determining the level of insurance protection of the insured. This amount depends on two criteria.

395. One of these criteria is the basis on which the insurance indemnity is calculated. This is the average daily gross labour remuneration or the average daily insurance income upon which the insurance contributions have been made for the last six months preceding the month in which the incapacity for work occurred. The idea is to establish a relationship of direct proportion and fairness between the amount of the insurance contributions made and the insurance indemnities paid. And the requirement regarding the six months ensues from the necessity to have an averaged value of the insurance contribution of the insured person. The amount on which the insurance indemnities are calculated may not be higher than the maximum monthly insurance income, specified in the SBL. As for 2021, the said amount was BGN 3,000 (about USD 1,784 – Article 8, paragraph 1, item 5 of the quoted Law for 2021).

396. The other criterion is the relative amount of the indemnity. It is commensurate with the missed labour income, upon which the insurance contributions were made. The indemnity the insured person receives is not the full averaged amount for the six calendar months preceding the month of occurrence of the respective insured social risk which has caused the temporary incapacity for work. The indemnity is only a part of this amount. This part is differentiated: 80% if the temporary incapacity for work has resulted from general sickness and the cases equalled thereto, and 90% if the temporary incapacity for work has resulted from industrial accident and occupational disease. The difference between 80% and 90% – between the indemnity for temporary incapacity for work resulting from general sickness, on the one hand, and the indemnity for temporary incapacity for work resulting from industrial accident and occupational disease, on the other hand – is an expression of the more favourable treatment of occupational risks in comparison with general ones (*see supra* Chapter 2, §1 and §2).

397. The next important question regarding insurance indemnities concerns the terms within which they are paid.

Pecuniary indemnities for temporary incapacity for work are paid from the first day of the occurrence thereof until it is terminated. And it is terminated upon the recovery of the insured person's full capacity for work, or upon the transition from temporary to permanent incapacity for work (disability), or upon the death of the person (Article 42 of the SIC). This does not apply to the insured risks under

Articles 43–45 of the SIC which are equalled to general sickness: they have a fixed short duration and the payment of indemnities for them is terminated upon the expiry of the fixed-term of this payment (*see supra* Chapter 1, §2).

398. There are two exceptions to this rule, which apply only to those insured persons who work under labour or service legal relationships:

(a) As for temporary incapacity for work that has occurred within thirty calendar days following the termination of the labour or service legal relationship, the pecuniary indemnity is paid until the restoration of the person's capacity for work; however, it is not paid for longer than thirty calendar days (Article 42, paragraph 2 of the SIC).
(b) As for temporary incapacity that has occurred prior to the termination of a fixed-term labour or service legal relationship, the pecuniary indemnity is also paid after the termination of the legal relationship, until the restoration of the person's capacity for work; however, it is not paid for longer than thirty calendar days (Article 42, paragraph 3 of the SIC).

399. The pecuniary indemnities for temporary incapacity for work are paid by the territorial departments of the NII.

400. According to Article 40, paragraph 5 of the SIC, the insurer pays to the insured person an indemnity for the first three working days of the temporary incapacity for work on the basis of the average daily gross remuneration for the month during which the temporary incapacity for work has occurred, this indemnity not being less than 70% of the average daily agreed remuneration. The legislative solution according to which the insurer owes insurance indemnity to the insured persons-employees for the first days of their temporary incapacity for work – this solution being introduced through the SIC which took effect on 1 January 2000 – has been the subject of frequent changes in the past years until arriving at the regulation of the late 2012 (promulgated in the OJ, No. 99 of 2012) which is currently operative. This legislative solution may not be shared. It does not comply with the essence of insurance. That is exactly what the employer-insurer pays insurance contributions for – to transfer the risk to the insurance body and to be released from the obligation to pay indemnities to the insured person in those cases where the latter gets in a state of temporary incapacity for work. Under the effect of Article 40, paragraph 5 of the SIC, the insurer pays twice: first, he/she pays insurance contributions as a price of transferring the risk to the insurance body, and second, he/she pays for the first day of the insured person's temporary incapacity for work if an insured social risk occurs, and that is not right.

401. The allotment and calculation of the pecuniary indemnities are carried out on the grounds of those data submitted by the insurers and self-insured persons to the National Revenue Agency which concern the insured persons' incomes, the risks the persons are insured against and the insurance contributions paid to the State social insurance (Article 40, paragraph 6 in relation to Article 5, paragraph 4, subparagraph 1 of the SIC). The purport of this requirement is to ensure the control over the regular payment of the insurance contributions on the part of the insurers and the insured persons under Article 4, paragraph 1 of the SIC, as well as on the part of the self-insured persons under Article 4, paragraph 3 of the SIC. The insurance indemnities are paid to the self-insured persons only if the insurance contributions due by them for the period preceding their temporary incapacity have been made.

402. The operative legislation also provides for cases in which the insurance indemnity is not paid, in spite of the occurrence of the insured person's incapacity for work. These cases are explicitly specified in detail in Article 46, paragraph 1 of the SIC. They are conditioned by the insured person's faulty and wrongful conduct, which has brought about the state of temporary incapacity for work. In this sense there is a sanctioning effect upon those insured who have got into a state of temporary incapacity for work as a result of their personal conduct.

403. These cases concern the insured who:

(a) wilfully impair their health in order to be granted leave or an insurance indemnity;
(b) fail to observe the regime prescribed to them by the health bodies;
(c) have become incapable of work either due to the consumption of alcohol, or the intake of strong intoxicants for purposes other than medical treatment ones, or due to any actions carried out under the impact of such substances;
(d) have become incapable of work due to hooligan actions or other antisocial actions which have been established in accordance with the respective procedure;
(e) have become incapable of work due to the non-observance of the rules regarding safety at work.

404. And yet, taking into account the temporary incapacity for work of these persons and the financial embarrassment which they get because of the non-payment of their insurance indemnities, the law introduces certain mitigation by way of limiting the time for which they may be deprived of receiving insurance indemnities in the cases under Article 46, paragraph 1 of the SIC.

405. This mitigation is provided for in Article 46, paragraph 2 of the SIC. In those cases where the insurance indemnities are not paid to the insured person because of his/her failure to observe the medical treatment regime prescribed by the health bodies, the non-payment applies only to the days on which he/she failed to observe the regime. And as for the cases of temporary incapacity for work resulting from the consumption of alcohol, or the intake of strong intoxicants for purposes other than medical treatment ones, or due to any hooligan actions or other antisocial actions on the part of the insured person, he/she may be deprived of insurance indemnities for a period not exceeding fifteen calendar days. As for depriving the insured person of insurance indemnities in the cases of temporary incapacity for work resulting from the non-observance of the rules regarding safety at work, the said period may not exceed three calendar days.

406. The insured person also has the right to pecuniary indemnity in the cases of Temporarily reduced capacity for work resulting from general sickness, industrial accident and occupational disease (*see supra* paragraph 370). It arises in the presence of the following prerequisites:

(a) Temporarily reduced capacity for work, which has been established by the competent expert bodies of incapacity for work (*see supra* §2).
(b) Ordered and implemented reassignment of the insured person with reduced capacity for work to another job which is suitable to his/her residual capacity for work, this being done in accordance with the procedure set forth in Article 317 of the LC.
(c) Reduction in the labour remuneration of the insured person in the new job to which he/she has been reassigned.

407. The amount of the pecuniary indemnity due in these cases is equal to the difference between the average daily labour remuneration that used to be received in the course of the last twelve calendar months preceding the month of reassignment, and the average daily labour remuneration received after the reassignment. If the person has worked less than twelve months prior to the reassignment, the indemnity amounts to the difference between the average daily labour remuneration received before and after the reassignment.

408. The indemnity for temporarily reduced capacity for work is paid for the whole time of reassignment; however, the period of receiving the indemnity may not exceed twelve calendar months, this period commencing on the day of reassignment to the new job.

409. Pecuniary compensation to an insured person is also paid where he/she has been reassigned to a new job that is suitable to his/her health status, the latter resulting from his/her temporary incapacity for work due to general sickness, an industrial accident, or an occupational disease, providing that the labour remuneration for the new job would be lower than the previous one. In practice, these are frequent cases because the new job which the insured person is reassigned to is usually easier and, consequently, the remuneration for it is usually lower than the remuneration which the person used to receive for the job he/she performed before the reassignment. In these cases, the daily pecuniary compensation paid to the reassigned person is equal to the difference between the average daily gross labour remuneration received during the eighteen calendar months preceding the month of reassignment and the one received after the reassignment; however, the compensation may not exceed the average daily gross labour remuneration received after the reassignment. Where the insured person has worked for less than eighteen calendar months prior to the reassignment, the amount of compensation is determined as the difference between the average daily gross labour remuneration received before the reassignment and the average daily gross labour remuneration received after the reassignment. In these cases, the pecuniary compensation is paid for the period of reassignment, yet for no more than six months within a calendar year.

§3. INSURANCE INDEMNITIES FOR MATERNITY

410. The right to these indemnities arises in the development of maternity risk and reflects the intensity connected with the separate stages in the development of this risk (*see supra*).

I. Indemnities for Reassignment of a Person with Reduced Capacity for Work to Another Suitable Job Due to Pregnancy and Breastfeeding (Article 48 of the SIC)

411. The prerequisites in the presence of which this indemnity arises are as follows:

(a) The woman insured against maternity has to be either pregnant or a breast feeder. This fact is established by way of an act of the health bodies.
(b) The insured woman who is either pregnant or a breast feeder should be reassigned either to another job which is suitable for her, or to the same job under relieved conditions.
(c) The average daily gross labour remuneration received by the woman in her new job to which she has been reassigned should be lower than the remuneration she used to receive prior to the reassignment.
(d) The woman who has been reassigned to another job should have at least six months' length of insurance at the time of reassignment.

412. The right to insurance indemnity is expressed in the payment of the difference between the average daily gross labour remuneration the insured woman used to receive for the twelve calendar months preceding the month of her reassignment and the average daily gross labour remuneration the insured woman receives in the job to which she has been reassigned, this payment being provided by the insurer from the general sickness and maternity fund. In those cases where the insured woman has worked less than twelve months until the day of her reassignment, the indemnity is determined as the difference between the average daily labour remuneration received before and after the reassignment.

II. Indemnities for Pregnancy and Childbirth (Articles 48'a'–50, 52 of the SIC)

413. The prerequisites in the presence of which the right to this indemnity arises are as follows:

(a) The pregnant woman should be insured against the maternity risk.
(b) The pregnancy should be in the last stage of the nine months' period of the development of the foetus and there should be forty-five calendar days left until the estimated term for the childbirth, this term being determined by the health

bodies. It is from this day onwards that the woman is granted leave due to temporary incapacity for work. The duration of the said leave is forty-five calendar days until the day of the childbirth and 365 calendar days after the childbirth, or 410 calendar days altogether.

(c) The insured woman should have at least six months' length of insurance as insured against the maternity risk.

414. The amount of the insurance indemnity is 90% of the average daily labour remuneration or the insurance income. In any case, the daily pecuniary indemnity may not be lower than the minimum daily wage for the country and higher than the average daily net remuneration for the period on the grounds of which the indemnity has been calculated.

415. This indemnity is paid for the whole period of 410 calendar days (*see supra* paragraph 414), this being the duration of the maternity and childbirth leave.

416. Where the child is stillborn, or dies immediately after it is born, or has been placed in a specialized institution for children, the mother has the right to pecuniary indemnity until the forty-second day after the childbirth. In those cases where, as a result from the childbirth, the mother's capacity for work has not been restored until the forty-second day, in the judgment of the health bodies the duration of payment of the indemnity is extended until she restores her capacity for work. In these cases, the indemnity is paid in the amounts provided for indemnity due for pregnancy and childbirth (*see supra* paragraph 385).

417. The person insured against all social risks who adopts a child has the right to indemnity in the amounts provided for pregnancy and childbirth (*see supra* paragraph 414). This indemnity is paid for the time from the day the child was placed for adoption until the expiry of the term of the due indemnity for childbirth, that is until the expiry of 365 days following the childbirth.

418. If the insurance against all insured social risks of an insured woman is terminated while she receives indemnity for pregnancy and childbirth, she continues receiving pecuniary indemnity until the expiry of the term for the pregnancy and childbirth indemnity, that is for 410 calendar days after the commencement of the pregnancy and childbirth leave (*see supra* paragraphs 413 and 414).

III. Indemnity for Raising a Young Child (Articles 52'a'–54 of the CIS)

419. The following are the prerequisites in the presence of which this indemnity is paid:

(a) The insured person has at least twelve months' length of insurance as a person insured against all social risks, or against all insured social risks except industrial accident, occupational disease and unemployment, or against all insured social risks except unemployment.

(b) The insured person has been granted leave for raising a young child, the duration thereof being the one provided for this leave: until the child becomes two years old – for the first, second and third child, or six months old – for the fourth and each consecutive child (Article 164, paragraph 1 of the LC).

420. According to Article 164, paragraph 1 of the Labour Code, after using her pregnancy and childbirth leave under Article 163 of the LC, the mother of a young child has the right to take a leave until the child attains 2 years of age. During the said leave, she receives a compensation the amount of which is laid down in the Law on the State Social Security Budget for the respective year. In recent years, the amount of the said compensation keeps increasing each year. From 1 January until 30 September 2021, the amount of this compensation is BGN 380 (about USD 226), and from 1 October until 31 December 2021, its amount is BGN 650 (about USD 387). Pursuant to Article 164, paragraph 2 of the LC, if the mother (adoptive mother) consents thereto, the leave can be taken by the father (adoptive father) or by a parent of theirs who works under an employment relationship. In those cases where the leave under Article 164, paragraph 1 is not used or the person using it suspends its use, the mother (adoptive mother) is paid a pecuniary compensation from the State social security provided that she works under an employment relationship.

421. In those cases where the insured mother (adoptive mother) does not avail herself of the leave for raising a young child, and continues working, she receives an indemnity in the amount of 50% of the indemnity under Article 53 of the SIC (*see supra* paragraph 420). The indemnity is paid if the child has not been placed in a specialized institution for children in order to be raised at the expense of the State (Article 54 of the SIC). This indemnity is aimed at supporting the insured mother in raising the child and meeting the additional expenses on the raising thereof – making a payment to another woman who assumes the care of the child for a certain period of time, and so on.

§4. Insurance Aids

I. The Notion

422. Insurance aids are a type of pecuniary social security benefit. They are paid to the insured persons from the social insurance funds on the occurrence of a social risk that the persons are insured against. Their direct purpose is to provide financial support to the insured person in the situation of serious financial embarrassment resulting from the occurrence of an insured social risk.

423. The operative legislation provides for these cases in Article 11, paragraph 1, item 2 and paragraph 2, Article 12, paragraph 1, items 2 and 4 and paragraph 2 of the SIC. They are the following ones:

(1) In the cases of disability resulting from general sickness where the insured person has no right to pension.
(2) For prophylaxis and rehabilitation.
(3) For relief devices connected with the injury.
(4) In the case of the insured person's death.

424. In principle, insurance aids have a short-term and one-time nature. They are paid either for a specified period of time, which is usually a short one, or as a lump sum on the occurrence of a strictly specified insurance case, that is on the realization of a specific risk, and not on the realization of any insured social risk. Insurance aids have the purpose of providing support to the insured person in overcoming the temporary financial embarrassment in which he/she has found himself/herself. The insurance aid is payable for the time specified by the law regardless of whether the state of severe financial embarrassment lasts longer or not. When the period for which the insurance aid is payable is over, the person starts receiving other forms of social security benefits or his/her personal work remuneration (employment remuneration or another type of remuneration). This is an important difference between the insurance aids and the social insurance indemnities, the former being due for the sole purpose of providing financial means for the maintenance of the insured person.

425. Insurance aids are incidental pecuniary benefits. They are payable either to the insured person or to his/her relatives for meeting the severe financial needs that have suddenly emerged. It is by their nature and their purpose that the insurance aids differ again from the social security indemnities, the latter having the nature of social security benefits payable, in regular periods, for the whole duration of temporary incapacity for work caused by the occurrence of an insured social risk (*see infra* paragraphs 427–435).

426. Insurance aids are a subjective right of the insured persons, these rights belonging to the category of contractual law rights. The right arises on the occurrence of specific prerequisites. They are explicitly and exhaustively specified under the effective law. These requirements are objective by nature and the right to insurance aids arises only in the case of their cumulative presence.

II. Types

427. Insurance aids are exclusive pecuniary social insurance benefits. This means they are payable in cases explicitly stipulated by the law. Besides, these cases are small in number and less rarely encountered compared to the social insurance indemnities for temporary incapacity for work.

428. Aid in case disability pension has been refused (Article 11, paragraph 1, item 2'a' of the SIC). This aid is payable to insured persons provided the following prerequisites are present:

(a) The insured has been found permanently incapacitated for work due to general sickness, and he/she belongs to one of the disability groups (*see infra*).
(b) The person has no sufficient length of service pursuant to the requirements of the SIC, so he/she can receive no disability pension for general sickness (Article 74 of the SIC).
(c) The person has not been given a job appropriate to his/her health state under Article 317 of the LC.

429. Should the prerequisites stated above be present, the insured person is given aid at the amount of the pecuniary indemnity due for temporary incapacity for work under Article 41 of the SIC. These aids are granted in the amount of sixty days' indemnity for temporary incapacity for work (Article 11, paragraph 3 of the SIC). They are paid from the general sickness and maternity insurance fund (Article 26, item 1 of the SIC).

430. Pecuniary aids for prophylaxis and rehabilitation (Article 11, paragraph 1, item 2'b' and Article 12, paragraph 1, item 2 of the SIC). The pecuniary aids for prophylaxis are granted for the implementation of measures for improving the working conditions and eliminating the harmful factors which impair the health of the insured, and may reduce their capacity for work. And the pecuniary aids for rehabilitation are granted for health promotion and complete restoration of the capacity for work of the insured.

431. These aids are granted for preventing the risks of general sickness, industrial accident and occupational disease, as well as for restoring the capacity for work of the insured, following general sickness or an occupational disease they have been through, or an industrial accident they have had. These aids are paid from the general sickness and maternity fund, and the industrial accident and occupational disease fund (Article 24, item 1 and Article 26, item 1 of the SIC), depending on the risk, among these three risks, for the prevention of the occurrence of which, or for overcoming the consequences of the occurrence of which, the respective aids have been granted.

432. Pecuniary aids for technical relief devices (Article 11, paragraph 1, item 2'c' and Article 12, paragraph 1, item 4 of the SIC). These aids are granted for the purchase of technical means connected with the injury inflicted on the health and capacity for work following the occurrence of the risks of general sickness, industrial accident and occupational disease. These relief devices are prostheses and other apparatuses and appliances which replace the absent or reduced functional capacity of the anatomic organs of the body, such as prostheses for amputated limbs, hearing apparatuses, optic apparatuses, contact lenses, orthopaedic shoes and the like. The procedure for the provision of these relief devices is set forth in Regulation No. 2 on the conditions and procedure for the provision of technical relief devices issued by the Minister of Labour and Social Policy (promulgated in the OJ, No. 20 of 1999).

433. The pecuniary aids for technical relief devices are paid from the general sickness and maternity fund, or the industrial accident and occupational disease fund, depending on the circumstances and the causes which have brought about the insured person's injury – either general sickness, or industrial accident, or occupational disease, respectively (Article 24, item 4 and Article 26, item 1 of the SIC).

434. One-time pecuniary aids in the case of death of the insured person (Article 11, paragraph 2 and Article 12, paragraph 2 of the SIC). The right to these aids arises where the insured person dies while performing his/her labour activity. The cause of the death might be the realization of the risks of general sickness, industrial accident, occupational disease, or childbirth. In these cases the right to an aid arises in favour of the closest relatives of the deceased insured person. These persons are specified in detail in the law and comprise of the following: (1) the spouse of the deceased person; (2) his/her children; (3) his/her parents where the insured person has neither a spouse nor children.

435. The total amount of the pecuniary aid is equal to two minimum monthly salaries, that is the minimum monthly salary for 2021 being BGN 650, this aid amounts to BGN 1300 (about USD 773) for the persons specified above. The aid is paid from the general sickness and maternity fund, or the industrial accident and occupational disease fund, depending on the cause and the circumstances under which the insured person's death has occurred (Article 24, item 1 and Article 26, item 1 of the SIC).

§5. Insurance Benefits in Kind

I. Medical Care

436. Medical care forms part of the benefits in the cases of temporary incapacity for work. It is the health part of insurance. It is expressed in various forms and means, characterized by their common purpose: curing the insured person and restoring his/her health and capacity for work through medical examinations made by physicians and dentists, treatment in medical treatment establishments for inpatients and outpatients, provision of medicines, sanatorium and resort treatment, prevention of diseases, diagnostics, rehabilitation, and so on.

437. The legal framework of medical care is contained in Article 52 of the Constitution and the current health legislation issued on the grounds thereof, which comprises the following: the Health Law, the HIL, the Law on Medical Treatment Institutions, the Law on Drugs and Pharmacies in Human Medicine, and so on.

438. According to the Constitution and the operative health legislation, medical care in the Republic of Bulgaria is organized and provided to the citizens in two main forms: (a) health insurance; (b) free medical services. These two forms are derived from the provision of Article 52, paragraph 1 of the Constitution, which lays down: 'Citizens have the right to medical insurance guaranteeing them accessible medical care, and the right to free medical services in accordance with conditions and procedures established by law.' It is from the content of this provision that the citizens' constitutional right to health is deduced. Although it is not explicitly worded in the Constitution in the way the other fundamental citizens' rights are – the right to life (Article 28), the right to personal freedom and privacy (Article 31, paragraph 1), the right to work (Article 48) and others, the right to health is both legally and factually known, recognized and regulated in Article 52, paragraph 1 on the basis of a common 'legal texture' – the health as a normal and natural state of human body, as Seneca said two thousand years ago: 'Man has bodily and mental health.'[63] It consists in the normal and natural state of human body, its organs and their normal functioning, and the human spirit. Health is humans' universal and supreme good, which is explicitly recognized and regulated in contemporary international humanitarian law: Article 25, paragraph 1 of the Universal Declaration of Human Rights – the United Nations of 1948 and Article 12, paragraph 1 of the International Covenant on Economic, Social and Cultural Rights of the UN of 1966 define the right to health as 'the right to the highest attainable physical and mental health'.[64] Bulgaria is a party to this Covenant, and according to Article 5, paragraph 4 of the Constitution, this Covenant forms part of the country's domestic law and has priority over those norms of domestic legislation which contravene it. Due to the differences in their content, the two constituent parts of the right to health preserve their independence and are regulated by different laws. Health insurance is regulated by the HIL of the year 1998 (promulgated in the OJ, No. 70 of 19 June 1998, amended and supplemented), while the right to free medical care is regulated by the Health Law (promulgated in the OJ, No. 70 of 10 August 2004, amended and supplemented, effective since 1 January 2005), in pursuance of the constitutional delegation for their regulation 'on conditions and in accordance with a procedure set out in law'. Although slowly, the legal construction of the constitutional 'right to health' under the operative Bulgarian law is adopted and reproduced in the practice of the Constitutional Court, thus affirming itself in the legal vocabulary and acquiring public acceptance (D. No. 8 of 4 July 2012 on c.c. No. 16 of the year 2011; D. No. 3 of 8 March 2016 on c.c. No. 6 of the year 2015, etc.).[65]

439. Health insurance has replaced the nationwide free medical care which existed in Bulgaria throughout the socialist epoch of its history – from 1947 until 1998. According to Article 52, paragraph 1 of the Constitution, health insurance

---

63. Lucius Annaeus Seneca, *Ad Lucilium Epistulae Morales* (Sofia: Riva Publishing House, 1994), 374.
64. An example of profound legal interpretation of the universal right to health under Art. 12 of the International Covenant on Economic, Social and Cultural Rights (ICESCR) on the part of the Committee for implementation of the said Covenant, and especially its part which lays down that 'Each person should have the highest attainable physical and mental health' (Observation Générale (14/2000): Le droit au meilleur état de santé susceptible d'être attaint, Conseil êconomique et social, EC, 2000/14, 11 août 2000, 4–7); M. Miccola, '*Requirement for a Comprehensive Health Care System' in: Hommage au Professeur Nikita Aliprantis* (Strasbourg: Presses Universitaires de Strasbourg, 2014), 339–440.
65. See more in V. Mrachkov, *Social Rights of Bulgarian Citizens* 347–352 (Ciela Publishing House, 2020) and the bibliography.

guarantees to the citizens 'accessible medical care'. The conditions and procedure for providing it are regulated in the HIL of 1998.

440. The 'accessible medical care' finds its expression in the presence of a sufficient number of medical treatment establishments equipped with modern medical technique and highly qualified medical personnel (physicians, dentists, nurses, midwives, laboratory assistants and the like), these establishments being: (a) physically accessible, that is situated in places close to those persons who have health insurance and need medical care; (b) economically and financially accessible, that is offering medical care at moderate prices, which can be paid by any citizen who resorts to them; (c) equally accessible to all citizens without any discrimination regarding sex, nationality, race, social or financial state, age, and so on.

441. Health insurance is implemented in two forms – mandatory and voluntary (*see supra*). Mandatory health insurance is the most widely applied. It extends to all Bulgarian citizens. It is implemented by virtue of the law (Articles 3–80 of the HIL). Voluntary insurance is implemented on the grounds of the insurance joint-stock companies licensed by type of insurance under item 2 or 1 and 2 of section II, letter A of Appendix No. 1 of the IC, which have been established for this purpose (Articles 81, 82, 83, 85 of the HIL) (*see supra*).

442. Mandatory health insurance provides medical care upon the occurrence of two health risks insured against – sickness, and pregnancy and childbirth (Article 45 of the HIL).

443. The sickness risk in health insurance is much more comprehensive than the general sickness risk as a risk insured against in social insurance. Along with the general sickness in social insurance (*see supra*), it also includes the risks of industrial accident and occupational disease. Besides, in order for medical care to be provided upon the occurrence of these three risks, it is not necessary for temporary or permanent incapacity for work to have occurred. The very fact of the disease (either general or occupational one) or the industrial accident which has caused the injury to the health is sufficient, although it has not brought about the health insured person's incapacity for work, so that medical care be due and given as a health insurance benefit. And lastly, medical care in health insurance comprises both medical and dental activities not only for treatment but also for prevention of diseases (prophylaxis), diagnostics, rehabilitation, and so on.

444. Medical care in pregnancy and childbirth includes the healthcare for the pregnancy and its normal development, periodic medical examinations of the pregnant woman, watching the development of the pregnancy, free obstetrical care in childbirth and the like.

445. Free medical care (*see supra* paragraph 438) is provided to all citizens. According to Article 82 of the Health Law, it includes: medical care in urgent cases, psychiatric care for inpatients, certain severe diseases (oncological and cardiological ones, Acquired Immune Deficiency Syndrome (AIDS) and others according to a list approved by a Regulation issued by the Minister of Health Care), provision of blood and blood products, transplantation of organs, vaccines for mandatory immunizations, and vaccines for immunizations under special indications or emergent cases, specific serums for prophylactic, anti-epidemic activities, and so on. It is worth explicitly pointing out that, in recent years, the scope and content of free medical care in terms of Article 52, paragraph 1 of the Constitution have been both widening and deepening. The 2018 amendment and supplement to the Health Law added a number of medical activities and services to the scope of those provided for free under Article 82, paragraph 1, namely: intensive treatment of people who have no health insurance; treatment with substituting and supporting programmes using methadone as well as daily mental rehabilitation programmes; provision of medical activities to patients with infectious diseases, including activities for preventing an epidemiological risk; complex dispensary (outpatient) monitoring of people suffering from skin and venereal diseases who have no health insurance, etc. (Article 82, paragraph 1, items 1a, 3a, 3b, 4, 6a, 6b, 6c, 8, 9, etc.). An important step in this direction is the new paragraph 2 of Article 82, according to which 'Apart from the medical services under para. 1, Bulgarian citizens also have the right to pay for other services related to their treatment in the country or abroad, depending on the specific disease, in the event that no mechanisms for financing with funds of the State budget or the NHIPCDO budget are explicitly provided for these services', etc. The medical activities of free medical care are financed by the State budget and the municipal ones.

II. Insurance Benefits in Kind

446. They consist of material goods granted to the insured persons. The prostheses and other relief devices are herein under classified. They are regulated under Regulation No. 7 on the terms and due course of granting prostheses, dentures and other relief devices and appliances (Regulation No. 7) issued by the Minister of Public Health in 1990 (OJ, No. 67 of 1990, amended).

447. Prostheses are artificial appliances and devices (made of wood, metal, leather, plastics, etc.) that replace an organ of the insured person's body or conceal its absence, such as amputated limbs, eyes, ears, teeth, and so on. As far as the development of science and technology makes it possible, they have the form, appearance and functions of the replaced natural anatomical part of the human body. The prostheses have an extremely wide application in orthopaedics (the bones of the upper and lower extremities, etc.). Prostheses can be temporary, permanent and cosmetic (aesthetic) ones. The medical appliances and other relief devices (contact lenses, hearing aids, spectacles and the like) have the purpose of improving, stabilizing or prolonging the residual natural functions of seeing, hearing and other similar capabilities and senses of man for his/her perception of the surrounding world, and so on. The various types of wheelchairs, devices for the blind, and so on, belong here, too.

448. The insurance benefits in kind in the form of prostheses and other aids are medical insurance benefits that constitute a supplement to and an extension to medical care. This determines their nature as insurance benefits. This nature becomes apparent through several important facts. First, they are granted to persons insured against all social risks and to persons insured only against industrial accident and occupational disease (Article 2 of the quoted Regulation No. 7). Second, expenditures on these devices and the maintenance thereof are covered by the social insurance funds (Article 7 of the quoted Regulation No. 7). Third, these devices are granted on the grounds of medical documents specifying the person's need of the device and its nature (Articles 7–18 of the quoted Regulation No. 7).

Part VII. Unemployment

Chapter 1. Unemployment in Bulgarian Social Reality

449. Unemployment is a new phenomenon in Bulgarian social reality. It appeared at the beginning of 1990 and since then it has permanently established itself in Bulgarian society. Its appearance forms part of both the transition to market economy and the profound changes in Bulgaria that began at the end of 1989.[66]

450. However, the problem is that under the conditions in Bulgaria unemployment does not develop within its optimum limits as a rehabilitation means stimulating the development of production, but it develops dramatically and acquires socially dangerous dimensions. The reason for this is the absence of a clear model of transition from the centralized planned economy, inherited from the past, to market economy. What had been created and inherited was destroyed and nothing new has been created in its place. This brought about a slump in production, which resulted in a sharp drop in the number of the employed and, thus, hundreds of thousands of employees were thrown out into the street as unemployed. The number of persons employed per 100 dropped from 49.2 in 1989 to 35.4 in 1996. The number of the unemployed increased speedily, and in 1997 it reached 540,000 people, which constitutes 14% of the active population of the country.[67] The 'peak' in the rate of unemployment was reached in March 2001, when the number of unemployed reached the menacing number of 725,000 people, which represented 21.2% of the active population of the country. As a result of the economic upsurge, a favourable tendency towards a decrease of unemployment was registered in the period 2002–2008. At the end of 2008, it dropped to 5.9% of the active population. The economic crisis, which came on the country at the beginning of 2009, brought about a new considerable growth in unemployment. In September 2013, the number of the unemployed reached 450,000, which is 12% of the active population of the country,[68] and in November 2016 the number of the unemployed reached 229,000, which is 7% of the active population of the country.[69]

451. The structure of unemployment is characterized by four basic features:

66. *The Bulgarian Challenge: Reforming Labour Market and Social Policy* 19–40 (Budapest: ILO, 1994).
67. *Human Development Report Bulgaria*, 32 (1997).
68. *Active Policy and Employment Information of the Employment Agency with the Ministry of Labour and Social Policy for 2013* 1 (Sofia: Ministry of Labour and Social Policy, September 2013).
69. *Sega* [*Now*] *Newspaper*, 5 Nov. 2021.

(a) Uneven territorial distribution. Out of all the twenty-eight regions of the country, the unemployment in the eight largest ones is at a considerably lower level – from 3% to 5%. The unemployment in the remaining regions is above the average level in the country, reaching 7% in some of them.
(b) The relative share of the permanently unemployed is large. These are people who have been unemployed for more than a year. Their part is about 40% of the unemployed in the country.
(c) The part of unemployed young people is comparatively high and represents 18% of all the unemployed in the country.[70]
(d) The unemployment among Roma and Turkish minorities is considerably higher than the average one for the country. In certain regions it reaches 20%.

70. These are data from the quoted *Active Policy and Employment Information of the Employment Agency with the Ministry of Labour and Social Policy for November 2021*, 1–2.

Chapter 2. Legal Infrastructure of Unemployment

§1. Sources of the Legal Infrastructure

452. The basis of the legal infrastructure of unemployment is contained in Article 51, paragraph 2 of the Constitution pursuant to which 'Persons that remain out of work temporarily are insured under the terms and in the due course laid down by the law.' This provision envisages unemployment as an insured social risk although it uses the euphemism of 'remaining out of work temporarily' instead of its precise appellation of 'unemployment'. This conclusion ensues from the content of the provision: social insurance is explicitly provided for those persons who have remained out of work temporarily, that is the unemployed, and the risk considered here is the unemployment risk. This conclusion is confirmed by the systematic place this provision has. It is included in Article 51 of the Constitution. Paragraph 1 of this article regulates the citizen's constitutional right to social insurance, the unemployment social insurance being a part and a manifestation thereof.

453. In performance of the delegation under Article 52, paragraph 1 of the Constitution, two laws on social insurance in unemployment have been adopted: the SIC of 1999 and the EPL of 2002.

The SIC regulates the insurance indemnities for the unemployed in the realization of the unemployment risk. These indemnities will be considered later (*see infra*).

The EPL sets forth the administrative bodies which manage the employment (Employment Agency (EA), etc.) and the measures for carrying out the so-called active policy of employment: encouraging the employers to create new workplaces and, with the assistance of the EA, to employ unemployed people for these places (Articles 1–57, 67–86). As for the specific matters of social insurance, this law contains the legal definition of 'unemployed person', which is also authoritative in social insurance and in the payment of unemployment indemnities under the SIC and regulates the vocational training of the insured (section 1, items 1–3 of the Supplementary Provisions, Articles 58–66, etc.).

§2. The Concept of Unemployment

454. Unemployment is a positive law term. It is not legally defined but the effective law contains enough provisions from which its characteristic features may be derived.

455. Unemployment is a legal term of labour law and social security law. As a 'two-branch' legal term, it is based on common legal features of the two branches. These features are as follows:

(a) The state of being out of work of persons having the capacity for work. This feature is derived from the provision of Article 51, paragraph 2 of the Constitution and §1, items 1–3 of the Supplementary Provisions of the EPL. Actually it consists of two basic constituent elements. The first of them is that the person is out of work, that is he/she does not work under any legal relationship – either an employment, especially a civil servant's one, or a freelance one (he/ she is not a freelance practitioner, a trader or the like). That is why this feature is present not only when he/she does not work under an employment contract or as a civil servant but also when he/she does not work under any other contract connected with regular and systematic performance of work for which he/she receives work remuneration. And vice versa: this feature is absent only when the person works under an employment contract, or as a civil servant, or under a freelance contract, or he/she is registered as a trader under the Commercial Law, or he/she is a freelance practitioner or similar. The second basic element in this feature is that only a person who has the capacity for work can get into this situation. This is a person who has reached a certain age (16 years, the minimum age for starting work) and has not yet reached the age for pensioning according to the category of labour under Article 68 of the SIC. In 2017 this age is 64 years for men and 61 years for women, considering the general third category of labour. The person whose age is within these age limits should have capacity for work. Only then is the requirement of the unemployed person's being capable of work present.

(b) The state of being out of work temporarily. This feature shows that the person has capacity for work in the sense considered above, he/she has worked and has remained out of work thereafter.

(c) The grounds on which the employment or civil servants' relationship has been terminated are of no importance. It does not matter whether the relationship has been terminated according to the employee's will or against it, including the termination due to his/her culpable conduct such as dismissal for breach of discipline, and so on. The objective fact suffices, this being the fact that the person, after being in a job has lost it, regardless of the legal grounds on which he/she got into this situation.

(d) Unemployment is a state in which the person wants to continue working after he/she has remained out of work due to the termination of his/her employment relationship. In this sense the person's state of being out of work is against his/ her will. The person has the will and desire to work. He/she actively seeks a job. 'A person who actively seeks a job' is the one who has not refused appointments with employers, organized by a division of the EA, and has visited employers on his/her own for being placed in a job (§1, item 3 of the Supplementary Provisions of the EPL).

(e) He/she is ready to enter a job. He/she expresses his/her constant and permanent desire and readiness to start working. However, he/she cannot find a job. This characteristic feature of unemployment pursuant to the effective law finds its expression in the will expressed by the jobless person to get registered as unemployed in the State body – the job centre, in his/her desire to seek a job relying on the assistance of the job centre in finding one, in his/her readiness to enter into an appropriate job offered to him, in his/her periodical visits (once a month) to the job centre in which he/she is registered, thus manifesting his/her state of being jobless and continuing to be a jobseeker and being available and ready to enter the appropriate job offered to him/her.[71]

§3. Unemployment as an Insured Social Risk

I. Specific Features

456. The specific features characterizing unemployment as an insured social risk should be added to these general features. These specific features are as follows:

(a) First of all, unemployment is a risk. Being a risk, unemployment is characterized by the unfavourable consequences its occurrence causes. They are expressed in the situation in which the insured has no work remuneration as he/she is out of work, all the severe financial consequences ensuing from it both for him and for his/her family being present. It is because of this situation caused by the unemployment that the latter is recognized as a social risk (*see infra*).
(b) Being a risk, unemployment is a possibility for the said unfavourable consequences to arise. This possibility has various degrees of probability. This risk never occurs in the lifetime of some insured persons and they have never been unemployed throughout their life. However, in the lifetime of other persons it does occur, even several times for some of them.
(c) Unemployment is a general insured social risk.[72] It is a risk that finds its expression in the absence of a permanent and regular job of the person (absence of 'employment') regardless of whether the question is about work performed under an employment, or a civil servants' relationship, respectively, or under another type of legal relationship, the latter being connected with performance of work. This is why no unemployment is present when the person, although not working under an employment or a civil servants' relationship, performs freelance practice, business activity, and so on or does not work at all due to his/her incapacity for work or his/her incapability of working permanently and regularly.

II. Extent of Insured Persons

457. Employees under an employment or a civil servants' relationship regardless of the grounds for the occurrence thereof.

This is the main group of persons insured against the unemployment risk, and this group should be specially considered because it includes a large number of persons.

71 K. Sredkova, *Employment and Insurance Rights of the Unemployed*, 46–68.
72. V. Mrachkov, *Social Security Law*, 208–210.

458. The persons working under a management contract as managers of commercial companies in which the State participation is prevailing. These persons are insured against all insurance cases, including unemployment.

459. The operative insurance legislation explicitly excludes certain categories of persons working under an employment legal relationship from the scope of the obligatorily insured ones. These are as follows: (1) Persons working under the programmes 'From Social Aid to Employment' and 'In Support of Maternity' (Article 4, paragraph 1, subparagraph 1, sentence 2 of the SIC); (2) Seafarers (Article 4'a' of the SIC).

460. And yet, the situation with seafarers' insurance against the risk of unemployment has certain particularities and is considerably different from the categorical inadmissibility of insuring against this risk of those persons who work under the programmes 'From Social Aid to Employment' and 'In Support of Maternity' (*see supra* paragraph 459, item 1). While the persons insured under the said programmes are categorically excluded from the scope of persons with obligatory insurance against the risk of unemployment, the solution that the law adopts as regards seafarers is more flexible. Actually, Article 4a, paragraph 1 of the SIC does not include seafarers in the scope of persons with obligatory insurance against unemployment at their own account, as it does with the other social risks insured against, which are exhaustively enumerated in Article 4a, paragraph 1 of the SIC: general sickness, old age, death, industrial accident and occupational disease. However, Article 4a, paragraph 2 of the SIC explicitly allows seafarers to get insured – at their own choosing and will, and at their own account – against unemployment as well. They have the right to do so by selecting and stating the monthly insurance income they will be insured on. The latter is in between the minimum and the maximum insurance income of self-insured persons, which is specified in the LSSSB for the respective year. According to Article 8, paragraph 1, item 2 of the said Law, the minimum insurance amount of self-insured persons is BGN 650 (about USD 387).

§4. Establishing Unemployment

461. The unemployment risk is established in a particular way. The latter corresponds to the nature of the risk and reflects its specificity as being a personal state of the insured. As for the bodies and procedure for establishing the unemployment, they are substantially different from the ones for establishing other insured social risks as well as from those for establishing a risk causing incapacity for work, in particular.

462. The unemployment risk is established by registering the person as unemployed in the job centre. The job centre is a body of the municipal administration and a territorial body of the EA with the Ministry of Labour and Social Policy. The registration is made on application by the unemployed person by the place of his/her address registration within three months after the termination of the employment or the civil servants' relationship.

463. Registration in the special State register, the person's name and vocational training, and so on being stated, constitutes the official declaration and certification of the person's state of being unemployed, that is, his/her state of being out of work against his/her will. The job centre has the obligation of registering as unemployed those persons whose employment relationship has been terminated. In these cases, the job centre acts as an insurance body as it performs a legal action that is necessary for the realization of the unemployment insurance.[73]

464. Unemployment radically changes the social state of the insured: from being a working person who used to receive work remuneration for the work personally performed by him and used to provide the maintenance of himself/herself and his/her family, he/she becomes unemployed. As a result of this, the completely new rights of the unemployed arise. They are listed under Article 17, §1, items 1–7 of the EPL and Article 54'a'–'c' of the SIC. Depending on their content and designation, these rights can be divided into two different categories.

The first category is one of the rights intended for the immediate assistance in entering a job: providing information about vacant workplaces, directing the unemployed to those places, providing information about the available forms (training courses and centres) of vocational training, providing public utility work, and so on. These rights of the unemployed in placing him/her in a job are his/her 'employment rights'. They are studied within the framework of the labour law.

The second category is the rights of the unemployed to insurance benefits. These are their insurance rights. They will be considered in the following exposition (*see infra*).

73. V. Mrachkov, *Social Security Law*, 208–211.

Chapter 3. Placement in a Job

§1. Employment Agency

465. The EA is regulated by the EPL (promulgated in the OJ, No. 112 of 29 December 2001), which took effect on 1 January 2002.

466. The EA performs three functions:

(a) *Informational one.* It consists of collecting data regarding the announced job vacancies and registered unemployed job seekers, and submitting this information both to the unemployed and to the employers.
(b) *Intermediary one.* It consists in rendering assistance and support to the job seekers and the employers seeking workforce, by way of organizing and facilitating the contacts and meetings between them.
(c) Promotion of the employment of the unemployed people.

§2. Special Encouragements

467. The law is based on the new idea of promotion of the employment of the unemployed people by way of an active policy on employment (Articles 26–46 of the EPL). It is expressed in supporting the employers in creating new workplaces, as well as in filling the job vacancies with unemployed people belonging to the 'disadvantaged groups'. These are people of lower capacity of competitiveness on the labour market, such as – young people, unemployed people of long-lasting incapacity for work, people of long-continued unemployment, unemployed women over the age of 50 and unemployed men over the age of 55, and so on. Those employers who employ people belonging to the disadvantaged groups are granted funds from the State budget for paying the labour remuneration of such people, which may not exceed twelve months (Articles 30a–40 of the EPL).

468. The year 2021 is a consecutive year in which the Council of Ministers has been developing a National Employment Plan. The latter provides that the BGN 260 million (USD 148.712 million) allotted in the 2021 State Budget shall finance the employment of 120,000 unemployed and other 60,000 unemployed who will take vocational training and retraining courses.[74]

469. The 2021 National Employment Plan focuses on encouraging and financing the employment of unemployed young people (under the age of 29) whose number in July 2021 keeps being high – 52,000 – though it has been slowly decreasing. The problem is that the portion of unemployed young people of low qualification and of no qualification whatsoever is high (about 60% of the unemployed young people), and so is the portion of the long-term unemployed (about 22%, in June

74. *Labour and Law Monthly Digest*, 9 (2013) 92.

2021 – 24%). In order to encourage and support the employment of young people, in its amendments and supplements, the EPL (promulgated in the OJ, No. 70 of 9 August 2021) provided for various forms of subsidized employment in performance of the European employment guarantee for young people in the EU. The 'European guarantee' for young people ensures that they will be offered a good job, accompanied by further education, apprenticeship and probation contracts of up to four months after leaving education or after becoming unemployed. Along with that, the period of ensuring subsidized employment for young people is extended to twelve months (one year).[75]

470. The active measures under the programme 'From Social Aid to Employment' which has been carried out since 2003 are extremely important for decreasing the unemployment. According to this programme, instead of receiving unemployment compensation, the unemployed people are employed under a labour relationship for a period of one year in 'activities for the public benefit', such as: public utility services, urbanization of settlements, protection of the environment, and the like. In 2016, the number of people employed under this Programme was 130,000.[76]

471. Encouraging the unemployed to business activities of their own (Articles 47–49 of the EPL). Those unemployed who are entitled to pecuniary indemnity for unemployment and wish to start business activities for the production of goods or provision of services, either on their own or jointly with other unemployed persons, may receive the total sum of the due indemnity after the project of the activity is approved by the respective territorial department of the EA.

---

75. E. Dimitrova, *New Measures for Youth Employment*, 8 Lab. & L. J. 48–52 (2021).
76. *Active Policy and Employment Information of the Employment Agency with the Ministry of Labour and Social Policy for 2021*, 8–11.

Chapter 4. Vocational Training

472. The organization of vocational training is one of the basic directions of the State policy for employment promotion and placement of the jobless. Its legal infrastructure is contained in Articles 58–66 of the EPL. A number of courses are conducted and training centres are set up.

473. Vocational training in the training centres and courses organized for this purpose is conducted in compliance with the State requirements. These are general requirements established and approved by the Ministries and other State bodies, these requirements concerning vocational training. On the one hand, the purpose consists of setting a sufficiently high level of requirements for vocational training or retraining. On the other hand, the purpose is to harmonize the requirements for the specific organization and training courses.

474. The State requirements apply to the organizations that conduct the training, their teaching staff, professions and specialities of the training, level of training, system of assessment, documents issued for the new training, and so on. The projects for these requirements are made by the Ministries and departments and are approved by specialized branch councils, composed of representatives of employers' and trade union organizations participating therein. They are passed by the Vocational Training National Consultative Council at the Ministry of Labour and Social Policy, this Council being expressly set up for this purpose (Article 59 of the EPL). This Council comprises representatives of the Ministry of Labour and Social Policy, the Ministry of Education and Science and members from the representative employers' and trade union organizations, and so on.

475. There are training centres and courses of various duration (three to six months, most often) depending upon the nature and complexity of the vocational training acquired. These courses are conducted by companies and organizations registered under Bulgarian legislation, training and retraining being a part of their scope of activities. They are licensed in compliance with State requirements. The terms and the due course of their organization are yet to be determined by the Council of Ministers. Vocational training may also be conducted by the vocational schools in the system of education.

The list of professions and specialities that special vocational training is required for is approved by the Vocational Training National Consultative Council at the suggestion of the Minister of Labour and Social Policy and the Minister of Education.

Vocational training ends with taking a vocational training examination or presenting a course project. Where the training has been successfully completed, a document of acquired vocational training is issued, this document being valid throughout the country.

476. The Law creates and gives special attention to a separate legal infrastructure of vocational training organized by the EA (Articles 63–66 of the EPL). Training organized by the EA is designed for the unemployed, including those who are getting ready to start business activities of their own. Training is also conducted for acquiring initial training of employees where the requirements for their vocational training have changed due to restructuring production, the number of employees in the enterprise being over fifty persons. Courses may be organized for them to acquire either additional vocational training or retraining. Employees who have been given notice of dismissal due to closing down the enterprise or a part thereof, or due to staff reduction or work reduction are also entitled to participate in these forms of vocational training. These forms of training are preceded by vocational orientation, informing and consultations. The unemployed person is obliged to choose the form and type of vocational training best suited to him/her and to the labour market demands. The training is conducted by licensed organizations and companies, training and retraining being a part of their scope of activities. These organizations are determined on the grounds of a competition. The training is conducted by the organization that has won the competition and a contract is entered into therewith. The organization that has conducted the training holds the examination of trainees at the end of the respective form of training and issues a document of acquired training.

477. The vocational training of unemployed persons and those getting ready for business activities on their own, this training being organized by the EA, is financed by the State budget. The unemployed receive a pecuniary aid from the EA for the time they attend the vocational training courses organized by the EA. This aid amounts to 60% of the indemnity due for unemployment. Thus, the participation of these persons in the training, courses and centres organized by the EA adds new forms to the classical and traditional social insurance indemnities and aids for the unemployed, these new forms giving expression to unemployment insurance as a social risk. This enriches the favourable opportunities that the insurance of the unemployed is connected with.

Chapter 5. Social Insurance Benefits

§1. Legal Infrastructure

478. The specific security law infrastructure of unemployment is contained in Article 26'a'–'b' and Article 54'a'–'h' of the SIC. It comprises two basic questions: (a) the legal status of the unemployment insurance fund; (b) the insurance indemnities due to the unemployed for unemployment.

479. The legal status of the unemployment insurance fund was considered in the preceding exposition (*see supra*). The exposition below deals with the insurance indemnities due for unemployment (*see infra* §2).

§2. Social Insurance Indemnities

480. The unemployed have the right to social insurance benefits. These persons possess two legal qualities that characterize them:

(1) These are persons insured against unemployment risk, that is persons within the extent of those insured against this risk (*see supra*).
(2) Persons within the extent of those insured against unemployment for whom the risk of unemployment has occurred. This quality is additional to the preceding one. This means the following:
   (a) The person should not be employed; that is, he/she should not work on any of a certain range of specified grounds and legal forms. There are two of these forms. First, he/she should not work under an employment relationship, including part-time work under Article 138 of the LC, regardless of the length of working time or under a management contract or be a member of Producers' Cooperative or a farmer. He/she should not perform activities on the grounds of a registration under the Commercial Law or in some other way. Second, he/she should not perform work as a self-employed person. This is the activity the person performs when working at his/her own expense either alone or in partnership with other persons. The general idea this requirement ensues from is that the person should not perform permanent and regular work, deriving his/her work remuneration therefrom.
   (b) The person should have acquired neither the right to a pension for length of service and old age nor the right to professional pension for early pensioning. The idea is that persons receiving these pensions have the minimum financial means for their maintenance and they are recognized as totally incapacitated for work.
   (c) The insurance contributions due for the insured person should have been made. The 'making' of the insurance contributions means that the insurance contributions due for the person have been remitted to the National Revenue Agency. That is to say: as for the insured persons working under employment legal relationships, the insurance contributions should have

been remitted – both the part due by the insurer and the part due by the insured person in the ratio of 60:40 – and as for the civil servants, the appointment body should have remitted the amount due. 'Due' insurance contributions are those which the insurers and the insured persons owe in law; however, as at the time the insured person becomes unemployed, these contributions have not been paid up yet.

481. The subjective right to social security indemnities for unemployment arises where the following prerequisites are present:

(a) The unemployed person has worked and has been insured or was subject to being insured for at least nine months within the last fifteen months (Article 54'a', paragraph 1 of the SIC). The requirement that the person should have worked and should have been insured includes work under an employment or civil servants' relationship regardless of the grounds under which it has arisen. The reason for this requirement is to establish the length and constancy of the employment of the insured and to establish the payment of unemployment insurance contributions so that he/she is entitled to receive indemnities and aid while he/she remains out of work.
(b) The requirement that the insured person should have worked for a certain period of time before getting jobless poses two further questions. The first question is that these persons used to work before becoming unemployed and were insured against unemployment. In other words, pursuant to the effective legal provisions, the prerequisite for the person's right to insurance benefits is that he/she should have worked under an employment or civil servants' relationship. The effective legal provisions do not allow for 'initial unemployment', that is, the state where the person is out of work at the beginning of his/her employment life (young persons who have just finished their secondary or higher education or their compulsory military service and other similar). This is a serious restriction the new legal infrastructure has imposed on insurance protection in unemployment. The second question is that pursuant to the effective legal regulations the grounds on which the employment, or the civil servants' relationship, respectively, has been terminated are of no importance, this termination being the one that has resulted in the person's state of being unemployed. This termination might have taken place on the initiative of the employer (dismissal with or without giving notice) or on the initiative of the employee or by their mutual consent. What is important and sufficient is that the employment, or the civil servants' relationship, respectively, has been terminated and the person has remained out of a job. This is a fair solution that extends the insurance protection in cases of unemployment.
(c) The insured person should have been registered as an unemployed person with the respective territorial job centre. This means that after the insured person is discharged from employment and his/her employment or service legal relationship is terminated, the insured person has to make his/her appearance in the job centre and to file an application, enclosing the Discharge Ordinance and his/ her Labour or Service Record, which has the Discharge Ordinance entered therein.

The latest amendments to Article 54‘a’, paragraphs 4, 5 and 6 of the SIC (promulgated in the OJ, No. 100 of 2010) have provided for substantial changes in the submission of applications and the registration of unemployed persons. The application should be submitted within three months following the insured person’s discharge from employment, while the registration of the person as an unemployed one should be performed within seven days following his/her discharge. If the insured person fails either to submit an application or to get registered within the terms laid down in law without having a reasonable excuse for it, the pecuniary indemnity shall be paid to him/her from the date of submitting the application, respectively, from the date of his/her registration as an unemployed person.

482. The judgment about the presence of the prerequisites needed for the right to indemnity for unemployment to arise is made by the official who is in charge of the unemployment indemnities in the territorial department of the NII (Article 54‘j’, paragraph 1 of the SIC).

483. Pecuniary indemnities of different amounts are granted in the case of unemployment. Their minimum and maximum limits are specified under Article 54‘b’, paragraph 1 of the SIC. The amount of the insurance indemnity is 60% of the average monthly insurance income upon which the insurance contributions are either paid or payable for the twenty-four months preceding the person’s discharge from work, the person having mandatory insurance against unemployment for that time. The adoption of this method of determining the amount of indemnity due has the purpose of taking account of the labour remuneration the person has received for the last nine months, proportioning the indemnity to this remuneration and ‘keeping it at a certain distance’ from this remuneration because the person does not work during that time. This method also takes account of the insurance contributions paid to UF, which highlights the contributory nature of insurance indemnities for unemployment. Apart from that, the limits are set for the range of insurance indemnity due. In order to track and react to the dynamic changes in the economic and social situation in the country in the conditions of the current Covid-19 pandemic, the minimum and maximum amounts of daily unemployment benefit are monitored, and each year they are set out in the LSSSB. According to Article 11 of the said Law, the minimum amount of this daily compensation in the year 2021 is BGN 12 (about USD 7.14) and the maximum amount is BGN 74.29 (about USD 44.20).

484. The insurance indemnities of these amounts are payable for a fixed period of time. This period varies from four to twelve months, and it differs depending on the length of service of the unemployed person. The principle is as follows: the longer the time of service of the unemployed, the longer the period for which he/she receives insurance indemnity. In view of this criterion, the unemployed are divided into seven groups, the time of service of each subsequent group being longer and the period for which unemployment indemnity is payable being longer also: first group – length of service up to three years – the indemnity is payable for up to four months; second group – length of service from three to five years – for up to six months; third group – length of service from five to ten years – for up to eight months; fourth group – length of service from ten to fifteen years – for up to nine months; fifth group – length of service from fifteen to twenty years – for up to ten months; sixth group – length of service from twenty to twenty-five years – for up to eleven months and seventh group – length of service over twenty-five years – for up to twelve months. The duration for which insurance indemnity is payable is 'up to four months', 'up to six months', 'up to eight months', and so on, which means: for the whole time of unemployment of the person, but not exceeding four months, six months, eight months, and so on.

485. It is again this minimum of four months for which pecuniary indemnity according to Article 54'b', paragraph 3 of the SIC is payable to the unemployed where the employment relationship has been terminated:

(a) on his/her initiative. These are the cases of: termination of the employment contract by mutual consent (Article 325, paragraph 1, item 1 of the LC); cases where, after being unlawfully dismissed and reinstated in his/her previous job by the court, the employee fails to appear in order to take it (Article 325, paragraph 1, item 2 of the LC) or where the employment contract has been terminated at the will of the employee upon prior written notice (Article 326 of the LC);
(b) where, due to his/her culpable conduct, the employee was dismissed without prior notice. These cases are regulated in Article 330 of the LC and include: dismissal of an employee because of his/her being sentenced to imprisonment for a crime he/she has committed and is detained for serving the sentence; disciplinary dismissal for committing a grave disciplinary offence; cases where the employee – a doctor, a dentist, a pharmacist, a healthcare specialist has been struck off the register of the respective professional organization he/she is a member of, due to committing a grave disciplinary offence in the course of performing their official duties, etc.

Those unemployed persons who have acquired the right to a pecuniary benefit under Article 54a of the SIC (*see supra*) before the expiry of a three years' term following a previous exercise of the right to an unemployment benefit are entitled to receive the minimum amount of the benefit for a term of four months (Article 54b, paragraph 4 of the SIC).

486. If the unemployed has been working part-time before unemployment occurred, the pecuniary indemnity payable to him is determined in proportion to the work remuneration he/she used to receive for his/her part-time work (Article 54'b', paragraph 5 of the quoted SIC). This idea is the logical continuation of the general requirement for determining the amount of pecuniary indemnity on the grounds of the average monthly gross work remuneration. The work remuneration is proportionate to the shorter working time of the part-time work. The amount of insurance contributions to UF is determined on the grounds thereof as well.

487. Insurance indemnities are paid by the territorial department of the NII at which the unemployed is registered. In this case, the latter acts as an insurance body that performs obligations relating to the insurance relationship with the unemployed by way of paying him/her insurance indemnities. The payment of insurance indemnities continues for the whole period for which insurance indemnities are due under Article 54‘c’ of the SIC, this article specifying the different periods of time.

488. Payment of insurance indemnity can be suspended pursuant to Article 54‘d’ of the quoted SIC where the person receives an indemnity for temporary incapacity for work (caused by general sickness, pregnancy and childbirth, etc.). In these cases, the unemployed person is obliged to state this fact before the respective territorial body of the NII. The payment of the indemnity is resumed when the grounds for the remainder of the period have ceased to exist, the unemployed person being obliged to notify thereof the territorial body of the NII.

489. Payment of unemployment indemnity is terminated where certain grounds are present, the latter being specified in detail under Article 54‘e’ of the quoted SIC.

Circumstances under which payment is terminated are those showing that a prerequisite for the right to indemnity to arise has definitively ceased to exist. And these circumstances are connected with the conduct of the unemployed person and they concern the cases where he/she:

(a) starts labour activity for which he/she is subject to mandatory insurance under Article 4 of the SIC. In those cases where the activity started by the unemployed person continues for less than nine months, the payment of the indemnity is resumed for the remainder of the period as at the date of the termination of the activity;
(b) has his/her registration in the EA terminated;
(c) acquires the right to insurance length of service and old age, or professional pension for early pensioning;
(d) dies.

490. The pecuniary indemnities for unemployment are granted, changed, refused, suspended, terminated, resumed and restored by way of a ruling of the official who is in charge of the unemployment indemnities in the respective territorial body of the NII.

491. Each month the EA and the NII have the obligation to provide each other with information regarding the indemnities that have been granted and paid, and regarding those amounts which have been granted and paid for the promotion of employment (Article 54‘h’ of the SIC).

Part VIII. Pensions

Chapter 1. Legal Infrastructure and Types of Pensions

492. The legal infrastructure of pensions is contained in Part I, Chapter 6, Part II, Chapters 9–11 of the SIC of 1999. The effective legal infrastructure of pension insurance is codified therein.

493. The operative pension insurance contained in the SIC of 1999 creates the so-called three-pillar structure of pension insurance:

(1) State social insurance.
(2) Additional mandatory pension insurance.
(3) Additional voluntary pension insurance.

This is the sequence in which they will be considered in the following exposition.

Chapter 2. State Social Insurance Pensions

§1. Legal Infrastructure and Types of Pensions

494. The legal infrastructure of the State social insurance pensions is contained in Part I, Chapter 6, Articles 68–106 of the SIC and the Regulation on Pensions and Insurance Length of Service (promulgated in the OJ, No. 21 of 2000, amended), and the Regulation on the Categorization of Labour upon Pensioning (promulgated in the OJ, No. 123 of 1998), governing the application of the SIC.

495. The following pensions are set out under the State social insurance:

(1) Insurance length of service and old-age pensions.
(2) Disability pensions.
(3) Social pensions.
(4) Personal pensions.
(5) Survivors' Pensions.[77]

They will be considered in the following exposition (*see infra*).

496. The State social insurance pensions are the basic form of pension insurance in Bulgaria. This means they concern all Bulgarian citizens and, both currently and in the near future, these pensions are the ones mostly relied upon. They are the most common form of pension insurance used by the insured.

§2. Insurance Length of Service and Old-Age Pensions

497. Legal infrastructure. The insurance length of service and old-age pensions are regulated under Articles 68–70'a' of the SIC and Articles 1–21 of the Rules on its application.

498. The insurance length of service and old-age pensions are the most common type of personal pensions: about 70% of all State social insurance pensions. This is due to the large extent of persons insured for this type of pensions, and to the constant tendency towards the ageing of the population. By the way, this tendency is characteristic of the whole of Europe.

---

77. Until the end of 2012, there used to exist one more type of pension, which was regulated in Art. 91 of the SIC: the special merits pension. This type of pension has had its long tradition (since 1883) in Bulgarian legislation and was known as 'State pension'. The late 2012 amendments to the Social Insurance Code (promulgated in the OJ, No. 89 of 13 Nov. 2012) repealed Art. 91 of the SIC as from 1 Jan. 2013. Thus, the grounds for granting these pensions ceased to exist. A new Law was adopted – the Law on Awarding People for Special Merits, effective since 1 Jan. 2013, which regulates the conditions and procedure for granting State pecuniary award for special merits to the Bulgarian State and nation. This award is called 'State pecuniary award for special merits' and does not form part of the subject matter of social security law, so it is not dealt with in the exposition hereinafter.

499. The insured social risk for the realization of which these pensions are granted is old age (*see supra*). In pension law, the 'old age' as an insured social risk is the age limit determined as a relatively high number of years of age the person has attained.

500. The subjects of the right to insurance length of service and old-age pensions are those individuals who belong to the extent of the insured for the old age risk. They were specified in the preceding exposition to which we are making a renvoi (*see supra* Part II, Chapter 2, paragraphs 94–98).

501. The subjective right to insurance length of service and old-age pension arises in the presence of certain prerequisites set forth in law. They are specified in Article 68, paragraph 1 of the SIC and are two in number: (1) the attainment of certain age; (2) the acquisition of a certain insurance length of service.

502. As for the age of pensioning, the operative Bulgarian legislation has two particular features. The first one is that the age of pensioning for men and women differs – the age of pensioning for women is three years lower than the age of pensioning for men. And the second feature is that, by virtue of the SIC, from 2000 until 2009 the pension age was dynamic, and not a constant one. It is a variable which changes and increases its value. The adoption of this legislative solution was necessitated by the low pension age for both sexes which used to exist for years on end until that time, and also by the presence of a considerable difference between the age of pensioning of men and women, this difference not complying with the modern requirements and needs of the country. This age used to be 60 years of age for men and 55 for women. It was necessary that the pension age existing at the time the SIC took effect be increased.

503. The increase of the pension age could have been made in two ways: either sharply and abruptly or smoothly and gradually. The legislator has adopted the second approach, which was the reasonable one in my opinion. Thus, a gradual increase of the pension age by six months per a calendar year was adopted for the next ten years: in 2000 – 60 years and 6 months for men, and 55 years and 6 months for women; in 2001 – 61 years for men, and 56 years for women; in 2002 – 61 years and 6 months for men, and 56 years and 6 months for women; in 2003 – 62 years for men, and 57 years for women; in 2004 – 62 years and 6 months for men, and 57 years and 6 months for women; in 2005 – 63 years for men, and 58 years for women.

Since 2006 the increase of the pension age for men has stopped, while the pension age for women has kept increasing in order to have the difference between their pension age decreased, as follows: in 2006 it was 58 years and 6 months, in 2007 – 59 years, in 2008 – 59 years and 6 months, and in 2009 – 60 years.

504. Since 2005 the men's pension age has been 63, while the women's pension age has been raised by six months yearly from 2006 onwards, as follows: 2006 – 58 years and 6 months, 2007 – 59 years, 2008 – 59 years and 6 months and 2009 – 60 years, and so on.

505. According to the late 2015 amendments to Article 68, paragraph 1 of the SIC (promulgated in the OJ, No. 61 of 2015), the right to pension for insurance length of service and old age is acquired upon attaining the age of 60 years and 10 months and the length of service of 35 years and 2 months for women, and the age of 63 years and 10 months and the length of service of 38 years and 2 months for men.

506. According to the same legal provision, as from 31 December 2016 the age is raised. Until 31 December 2029 the retirement age and length of service of men and women is gradually increased from the first day of each calendar year, as specified in No. 42, letter 'd' above. The slow and gradual upgrading of the requirements regarding age and contributory length of service is still going on and will be on in the years to come. For instance, in 2020 the requirements were: women – age 61 years and 6 months, and men – 64 years and 3 months, and contributory length of service as follows: women – 35 years and 10 months, and men – 38 years and 10 months; in the year 2021 the requirements are: women – 61 years and 8 months, and men – 64 years and 4 months, and contributory length of service as follows: women – 36 years and men – 39 years; in the year 2022 the requirements will be: women – age 61 years and 8 months, and men – 64 years and 5 months; and contributory length of service as follows: women – 36 years and 2 months, and men – 39 years and 2 months, etc.

507. Along with it, the operative legislation also provides for the right to insurance length of service and old-age pension of a reduced amount. The legal framework thereof is contained in Article 68, paragraph 3 of the SIC. The right to the pension of a reduced amount arises in the presence of two prerequisites:

(a) Age for both men and women – 65 years of age attained.
(b) Total insurance length of service for both men and women – 15 years of real service. This means the actual time during which the insured person was really exercising labour activity and insurance contributions were made upon his/her insurance income. As of 31 December 2011 the age was raised by four months from the first day of each calendar year until reaching 67 for both women and men (Article 68, paragraph 3, sentences 1 and 2 of the SIC).
(c) A separate type of pension – the one of a reduced amount – introduced through the amendments made to the Social Security Code in the year 2015, is the pension under Article 68a, paragraph 1 of which lays down: 'Those persons who have the contributory length of service required under Art. 68, para. 2, are entitled, if they so wish, to retire up to one year before attaining the age under Art. 68, para. 1.' This pension is granted from the date on which the application is filed and is paid 'in its reduced amount for life' (promulgated in the OJ, No. 61 of the year 2015). During the first year of its being granted, this pension is paid with a reduction of 0.4% for each month in shortage, until the person attains the age under Article 68, paragraph 1, which makes a total reduction of 4.8% for the year. In the year 2021, when the retirement age for women is 61 years and 8 months, and 64 years and 4 months for men (*see supra* No. 507), the age at which the pension under Article 68a, paragraph 1 of the SIC is granted

is: 60 years and 8 months for women and 63 years and 4 months for men (*see supra* No. 507). When recalculating the reduced amount of the pension under Article 68a, paragraph 1, sentence 2 of the SIC, the percentage of reduction does not change, remaining the same for the pensioner's lifetime. The constitutionality of the provision of Article 68a, paragraph 1, sentence 2 of the SIC in its part concerning 'for the lifetime' of the pensioner was challenged by the national ombudsman on the grounds of Article 150, paragraph 3 and Article 149, paragraph 2 of the Constitution and it was required that the said provision should be declared unconstitutional because it contravenes the principle of justice and does not comply with the social State under indents 3 and 5 of the Constitution and the citizens' constitutional right to social security under Article 51, paragraph 1, sentence 1 of the Constitution. The Constitutional Court has not rendered its decision thus far.

508. The operative insurance legislation lays down the minimum of the full amount and the reduced amount of the insurance length of service and old-age pension (Article 70, paragraph 7 of the SIC). As for the full pension, this amount is 115% of the old age social pension, while for the reduced pension this amount is 105% of the old age social pension.

509. The 2016 amendments to the SIC specified above (*see supra* paragraphs 506 and 507) introduced changes and additions to the retirement conditions for certain categories of persons who perform particular types of work under particular conditions and, because of that, specific requirements are laid down for them to acquire the right to pension based on their length of service and old age. The foregoing is applicable to the military staff, the civil servants in the State bodies of public order and security, ballet dancers, as well as other dancers working under severe conditions (I and II category of work) and teachers (*see infra* paragraphs 510–513).

510. It is through the amendments made to the SIC in August 2016 (promulgated in the OJ. No. 61 of 2016) that the military staff acquired the right to pension under the Law on Defence and Armed Forces of the Republic of Bulgaria. They need to attain the age of 52 years and 10 months and the insurance length of service of 27 years and 10 months, two-thirds thereof, i.e., 18 years, being actual length of service as military staff. According to § 1, item 12 of the Supplementary Provisions to the SIC, in order for the length of service under an employment relationship or a service relationship to be actual length of service as military staff, the person must have worked or served as a military person. The same retirement conditions apply to the civil servants under the Law on the Ministry of the Interior, the Law on the State Agency for National Security, the Law on the Execution of Penalties and Detention as well as to those civil servants who carry out activities of safeguarding the judiciary (Article 69, paragraph 2 of the SIC).

511. Specific retirement conditions are laid down for ballet dancers as well as for the other dancers. In 2016 this category of insured persons retires when having an insurance length of service of 25 years and an age of 42. Starting from 1 January

2017, the retirement age will increase by 2 months from the first day of each calendar year until it reaches 45 years of age (Article 69a of the SIC).

512. The insured persons of categories I and II carry out their work under severe conditions. The scope of insured persons included in these categories of work are explicitly and exhaustively listed in the 1998 Regulation on the Categorization of Labour upon Pensioning, which is approved by the Council of Ministers on the grounds of Article 104 of the SIC and has been effective since 1 January 2000. For instance, the category I of work includes workers and engineers who work underground, or in nuclear power plants, etc., while category II of work includes engine drivers, tram drivers, trolley bus drivers and other drivers. Pursuant to Article 69b of the SIC, the persons working under category I are pensioned as follows: women – upon attainment of the age of 47 years and 8 months, and an aggregate of 94 of the insurance length of service and the age, and men – upon attainment of the age of 52 years and 8 months, and an aggregate of 100. Commencing on 1 January 2017, from the first day of each calendar year the retirement age will increase by 4 months for women and 2 months for men until reaching 60 years of age (Article 69a of the SIC).

513. By a century-old tradition dating back to 1883, teachers have been retiring on specific conditions that are favourable to them. This is due to the great social significance attached to the teacher's profession and the specific stress connected with exercising it (Article 69c of the SIC). From 1 January 2017 women retire upon attainment of the age of 57 years and 10 months and teacher's length of service of 25 years and 8 months, while men retire upon attainment of the age of 60 and teacher's length of service of 30 years and 8 months. According to Article 19, paragraph 1 of 2000, adopted by the Council of Ministers (promulgated in the OJ, No. 21 of 2000, amended), the teacher's length of service is determined as his/her length of service acquired while holding the position of a teacher or an educator in a school or an educational establishment. The insurance length of service of directors or deputy directors of schools or educational establishments is also recognized as teacher's length of service if they completely fulfil the norms regarding the mandatory hours of teaching. From 31 December 2017 onwards there is a gradual annual increase in the retirement age by 2 months for women and 1 month for men until the age reaches 62.

§3. Disability Pensions

I. General Questions and Types of Disability Pensions

514. The legal infrastructure of disability pensions is contained in Articles 71–79 and 85–88 of the SIC as well as in Articles 22–30 of the Rules on Pensions.

515. These pensions are granted if disability has occurred. Disability is constant or permanent incapacity for work. Article 71 of the SIC defines disability as 'total or partial loss of the capacity for work, this loss being forever or for a long time':

(a) The essential element of this definition is the loss of capacity for work, this loss being expressed in the absence of physical or mental power for the person to work. What is new in this element of disability as grounds for granting disability pension is that disability is present where the capacity for work is 50% or more, this specification being introduced through Article 72 of the SIC. Therefore, since 1 January 2000 onwards not any loss of capacity for work, but only the loss in this comparatively high degree turns it into disability, the latter being relevant grounds for disability pension.
(b) The other elements of this definition – the degrees of loss of capacity for work (total or partial) and the duration of time this loss of capacity for work lasts for specifying certain aspects of disability. Thus, what is essential for disability is that it is a premature constant incapacity for work where the lost capacity for work is 50% or more.

516. Disability is related to the work the insured person performs. It is the incapability of the person to perform this very work and not his/her incapability of performing any other work. In this sense, it is incapacity for work concerning specific professional activity – the one the person used to perform and to provide his/her own and his/her family's maintenance with the earnings from it.

517. Disability is a general term in disability pensions; that is, it is used for all types of pensions regardless of the risk whose occurrence has caused it. The incapability of work is one and the same regardless of whether it has been caused by general sickness or industrial accident or occupational disease or impairments of civil or paramilitary persons' health. The way it is established is the same and so are the bodies that establish it (the bodies of the medical expert examination on employment matters), the due course, and so on. And it always brings about incapability of the person to work and his/her incapability 'working his/her earnings' and, because of that and in compensation for it, he/she is granted the disability pension.

518. Depending on the degree of the loss of capacity for work, there are three degrees. The disability degree is determined by the CMC on Employment Matters.

519. According to Article 75, paragraph 2 of the SIC, the degrees of lost capacity for work are:

(a) over 90%;
(b) from 71% to 90%;
(c) from 50% to 70.99%.

520. The first disability degree is the one of persons who have totally lost their capacity for any type of work and persons with heavy, irremediable and progressive impairments. The list of these impairments is approved by the Minister of Health Care (amputation of extremities, total or practically definitive blindness, etc.).

The second disability degree is of persons who, owing to their health state, have lost their capacity for work concerning both their own profession and any other profession, but they can adapt to work under conditions specially created for them. It is here that persons with heavy impairments (amputation of humerus, gonycampsis, etc.) under a list approved by the Minister of Public Health belong as well.

The third disability degree is of persons who, owing to their health state, have changed or have to change the working conditions of their profession and persons with heavy, irremediable and progressive impairments (amputation of four fingers of the same hand, amputation of the arm up to the elbow, etc.) under a list approved by the Minister of Health Care.

521. The SIC sets out the following four types of disability pensions:

(1) Disability pensions, the disability being caused by general sickness.
(2) Disability pensions, the disability being caused by an industrial accident or occupational disease.
(3) Disability pensions of civil persons.
(4) Disability pensions of military persons.

II. Disability Pensions, the Disability Being Caused by General Sickness

522. Persons insured for disability pension, the disability being caused by general sickness are all the employees, civil servants, the members of Producers' Cooperatives and self-employed persons such as freelance practitioners and traders insured at their own expense. This large extent of persons insured for disability pension, the disability being caused by general sickness, ensues from the nature of general sickness risk and its being widespread.

523. Prerequisites. The rights to disability pension, the disability being caused by general sickness, arises in the presence of two basic prerequisites:

(a) Established disability resulting from general sickness, this disability belonging to a certain disability degree. This prerequisite is established through the expert conclusion of the Expert CMC on Employment Matters (the National Expert CMC on Employment Matters), which determines the disability degree and the general sickness that has brought it about.
(b) Minimum total insurance length of service. It is the same for all disability degrees; however, it differs depending on the person's age. The idea is: the older the person the greater his/her possibility to have worked, the longer his/her length of service, the longer the time he/she has participated in forming the insurance funds through his/her insurance contributions thereto.

524. No insurance length of service is required for disabled persons younger than 20, neither is it required for persons born blind nor for persons who have become blind before entering a job, regardless of their insurance length of service. However, for persons over 20 years of age, the required length of service gradually increases as follows: the required insurance length of service is one year for persons up to the age of 25, and three years for persons up to the age of 30, and seven years for persons over the age of 30 (Article 74 of the SIC). According to the new paragraph 2 of Article 74 of the SIC of December 2014 (promulgated in the OJ, No. 107 of 2014), one-third of the insurance length of service under Article 74, paragraph 1, items 2–4 of the SIC that is necessary for acquiring the right to pension for disability caused by general sickness must be actual length of service within the meaning of § 1, item 12 of the Supplementary Provisions to of the SIC. As for the term 'actual insurance length of service' *see supra* paragraph 510. This new regulation is aimed at ensuring the participation – though a minimum one – of persons aged over 20 in exercising work activity prior to being granted a pension for disability caused by general sickness.

Those people who were born disabled, as well as those who have become disabled prior to entering a job, acquire the right to disability pension if they have at least one year's insurance length of service (Article 74, paragraph 2 of the SIC).

525. The right to disability pension arises upon the date of occurrence of disability and is granted for the term of disability. And the disability pensions of those persons who have attained the pension age for acquiring the right to insurance length of service and old age are granted for life. As for those persons who were born blind, and those who have become blind prior to entering a job the right to a pension arises on the date of filing an application for having a pension granted (Article 73 of the SIC).

526. The amount of the disability pensions, this disability being caused by general sickness, is determined according to two basic criteria established under Article 75 of the SIC. These are:

(a) The income upon which the insurance contributions of the insured person have been made.
(b) The duration of the insurance length of service of the person prior to his/her becoming disabled.

527. In those cases where as at the date of becoming disabled the insured person's age is lower than the pension age, the difference between his/her age and the pension age is recognized as insurance length of service by multiplying it by the coefficient provided for in Article 75, paragraph 2 of the SIC as follows:

(a) For persons who have lost over 90% of their capacity for work – 0.9.
(b) For persons who have lost from 71% to 90% of their capacity for work – 0.7.
(c) For persons who have lost from 50% to 70.99% of their capacity for work – 0.5.

528. In the early 1960s minimum amounts were established for disability pensions, the disability being caused by general sickness. These minimum amounts depend on the disability degree (Article 75, paragraph 4 of the SIC). Pursuant to the effective legislation they are differentiated as follows: for the disability degree over 90%–140% of the old age social pension, for the disability degree from 71% to 90%

– 130% of the old age social pension, and for the disability degree from 50% to 70.99% – 105% of the old age social pension. No disability pension, the disability being caused by general sickness, may be below this lowest limit.

III. Disability Pensions, the Disability Being Caused by an Industrial Accident or Occupational Disease

529. Disability caused by industrial accident or occupational disease is treated more favourably than disability caused by general sickness. This is explained by the occupational nature of the risks of industrial accident and occupational disease.

530. The extent of persons insured for disability pension, the disability being caused by an industrial accident or occupational disease, is the same as the extent of those insured against these two risks (*see supra*) as it is only the occurrence thereof that brings about the disability forming the grounds for granting the pension. These are only persons working under an employment or civil servants' relationship, freelance practitioners being excluded as not working under an employment or civil servants' relationship.

531. The prerequisite that is necessary in order for the right to this disability pension to arise is one: the presence of disability of the person established by the CMC on Employment Matters or the National Medical Consultative Commission on Employment Matters. Here again, disability denotes a loss of 50% or more of the capacity for work. There is no requirement concerning the length of service here (Article 78 of the SIC). This legislative solution has been adopted because of the occupational nature of the risks.

532. The amount of the pension is determined according to two criteria laid down under Article 79 of the SIC:

(a) The degree of disability. Here again the principle is as follows: the higher the degree of loss of capacity for work, that is the higher the disability degree, the higher the amount of the pension.
(b) The average monthly gross work remuneration for the twelve months preceding the occurrence of the industrial accident or the occupational disease or the disability caused thereby.

533. Minimum amounts are established for the disability pensions, this disability being caused by industrial accident or occupational disease. These amounts are based on the social pension and differ depending on the disability degree: for the disability degree over 90%–150% of the old age social pension, for the disability degree from 71% to 90% – 140% of the old age social pension, and for the disability degree from 50% to 70.99% – 115% of the old age social pension (Article 79, paragraph 2 of the SIC).

IV. Disability Pensions of Civilians

534. The extent of persons insured for disability pensions of civilians is determined under Articles 87–88 of the SIC.

As for their nature, these pensions are non-contributory ones. They are paid from funds granted to the NII by the State budget, and the insured do not make insurance contributions for them.

535. The prerequisites for the right to disability pension of civilians to arise are as follows: the persons should have been injured under specific circumstances.

'The persons should have been injured' means they should have suffered an impairment that finds its expression in disability (i.e., when the partial or total permanent loss of capacity for work is 50% or more). The latter is established in compliance with all the rules and requirements by the expert examination by physicians on employment matters that are competent thereof – the CMC on Employment Matters and the National CMC on Employment Matters.

536. The circumstances under which these persons have been injured are different in each specific case. These are the following persons:

(a) Those who have been injured while performing a civil or public duty. These are the cases where the persons have sustained an injury during rescue operations in disasters such as earthquakes, a flood, a storm, and so on, in saving human life, public property, and so on.
(b) Those who have been accidentally injured by the authority bodies while the latter were performing their official duties. The authority bodies envisaged here are the following: the police, other bodies of public order and security, the army, and so on in performing the 'official duties' assigned thereto by the law. Citizens may also suffer an injury while criminals are being chased or during a police action against criminals, and so on. What is needed here is that the citizens should have been injured 'accidentally', that is out of negligence by the authority bodies and not while being 'chased' for crimes committed by them.

537. The operative legislation lays down the minimum amounts of the disability pensions of civilians (Article 88, paragraph 1 of the SIC). The amount of these pensions may not be lower than the amount of the old-age social pension, as follows:

(a) For persons who have lost over 90% of their capacity for work – 150%.
(b) For persons who have lost from 71% to 90% of their capacity for work – 140%.
(c) For persons who have lost from 50% to 70.99% of their capacity for work – 115%.

538. As for those civilians who have been insured either against all social risks or only against industrial accident and occupational disease, their disability pension is calculated in accordance with the procedure laid down for the disability pensions where the disability has been caused by an industrial accident or an occupational disease if that is more favourable to the person.

V. Disability Pensions of Military Persons

539. The disability pensions of military persons are non-contributory ones as well. They are also paid from funds granted by the State budget, which are transferred to the NII.

540. The legal framework of the disability pensions of military persons is contained in Articles 85–86 of the SIC.

541. The extent of persons insured for this pension is outlined under Article 85 of the SIC. It comprises persons who have lost their capacity for work either because they have become ill or have been injured during or on the occasion of:

(a) performing their duties in the course of doing their national service in the army;
(b) performing their duties in the course of their military service on the reserve or in refresher courses;
(c) rendering assistance to the Armed Forces, or have perished or are missing.

542. The prerequisites for the right to disability pension of military persons to arise are as follows:

(a) The persons within the extent of the insured ones for disability pension of military persons should have been injured. This circumstance is expressed in the fact of their disability having been established in the due course and the degree of disability being determined.
(b) They should have sustained the injury during their military service or while rendering assistance to the Armed Forces.

543. The amounts of the disability pensions of military persons are determined with respect to the military rank of the injured and the disability degree in proportion with (as percentage of) the old age social pension as follows for privates and sergeants: (a) disability degree over 90%–150% of the old age social pension; (b) disability degree from 71% to 90% – 140% of the old age social pension; (c) disability degree from 50% to 70.99% – 115% of the old age social pension. As for the officers, the respective amounts are as follows: for ‘a’ – 160% of the old age social pension; for ‘b’ – 150% of the old age social pension; for ‘c’ – 120% of the old age social pension.

§4. Social Pensions

I. Legal Infrastructure, Notion and Types

544. Social pensions are a relatively new legal phenomenon in pension legislation. They were introduced in 1973 through the new Part IV ‘Social Pensions’ of the 1957 Pensions Law (repealed). Later the legal infrastructure thereof has been enlarged and in the eve of adopting the SIC in December 1999, their number reached six different types of social pensions. This sizable infrastructure of social pensions reflected the large-scale impoverishment of large strata of the population and the aim of the legislator to react to the severe social problems which society was facing. This legal infrastructure continued existing until the end of 1999, and on 1 January 2000 it was repealed by the SIC.

545. The operative legal infrastructure of social pensions is contained in Articles 89–90 of the SIC and Article 6 of the Regulation on Pensions. It has considerably diminished the types of social pensions (*see supra* paragraph 498).[78]

546. The notion. The social pension is an insurance pension benefit for the poorest part (the paupers) of Bulgarian society. This benefit is granted in cases where the persons are not entitled to any other pension under the SIC. In this sense, the social pensions are the *ultima ratio* of pension law applied by the State by using State budget means for providing the maintenance of the poor. These pensions also belong to the category of 'non-contributory pensions'.

547. The types. The effective social security law establishes the following two types of social pensions:

(a) Social pensions for elderly persons.
(b) Social pensions for persons born disabled.

548. In the period from the end of 2010 until the end of 2012, the legislative regulation of social pensions underwent a rapid and contradictory development. Surprisingly, the legal regulation of social pensions, which has existed for decades, was totally repealed at the end of 2010 (promulgated in the OJ, No. 100 of 2010). The officially stated motives thereof invoked the non-contributory nature of these pensions (*see supra* paragraph 546), although the SIC preserved some other non-contributory pensions (military and civil disability ones) under Articles 85–88 of the SIC (*see supra* paragraphs 510–519) and did not repeal their regulation. It has been provided that after the legal regulation of social pensions in the SIC is repealed, their regulation will be set out in the Law on Social Support. The repeal of the legal regulation of social pensions of December 2010 was to take effect on 1 January 2013. However, as surprisingly and without sound legal grounds was the regulation of social pensions in Articles 89 and 90 of the SIC repealed in December 2010, so surprisingly was 'the repeal of the said texts repealed' in December 2012 (promulgated in the OJ, No. 99 of 2012), in the eve of coming into force of the repeal of these texts, and they were restored *in extenso*. They were literally restored in the 'newly created' Articles 89a and 90a of the SIC and took effect on 1 January 2013, i.e., on the same day on which their repeal was to come into force as provided two years before. Thus, the legal regulation of social pensions under the 1999 SIC has

78. Part of the social pensions provided for in the repealed Pensions Law of 1957 has been introduced as personal pensions under Art. 92 of the SIC and Art. 7 of the Regulation on Pensions (*see infra* §6).

actually continued being operative without interruption. The restored 'new old regulation' thereof is their legal regulation which is operative even now (*see supra* paragraph 521). These abrupt changes in social pension's regulation under the same parliamentary majority disclose the absence of elementary understanding of the essence of social pensions and their role in the State's social policy, especially in the conditions of the severe economic crisis the country continues to be under.

II. Social Pensions for Elderly Persons (Article 89a of the SIC)

549. Advanced age is the insured social risk for this pension. The law establishes the age of 70 and labels those persons as 'elderly persons'. As at 1 June 2021 the number of persons who receive social pensions as elderly persons is 3,936.[79]

The prerequisites, the simultaneous (cumulative) presence thereof being required for the right to this pension to arise are as follows:

(a) The person should have turned 70. The age of 70 applies for both men and women.
(b) The annual income of a family member should be less than one-half of the sum of the guaranteed minimum income established for the country for the last twelve months. Within the meaning of Article 89 of the SIC, 'family members' are: the husband, the wife and the children younger than 18, as well as the children over this age if they are incapacitated for work and are single. The guaranteed minimum income for 2021 was BGN 75 (about EUR 44.61) per month (Article 1 of Decree of the Council of Ministers No. 9 of 2020, promulgated in the OJ No. 18 of 2020).

550. The amount of the social pension for elderly persons is determined by the Council of Ministers at the suggestion of the Minister of Labour and Social Policy and the NII (Article 89a, paragraph 2 of the SIC). Since 1 July 2021 the amount of this pension has been BGN 141.63 (about EUR 85.42).

III. Social Pension for Disability (Article 90a of the SIC)

551. The insured social risk for this pension is the general sickness, the occurrence thereof having caused severe disability in early age. At the end of June 2021 the number of persons who receive social pensions for disability is 52,348.[80]

552. The right to this social pension arises in the cumulative presence of the following prerequisites:

(a) The person should be disabled of 71% or more. This means that a Territorial CMC should have established the disability and it should have determined that

79. *Statistical Bulletin NII, Sofia,* 2021, 8.
80. *Ibid.*, p. 6.

the person belongs to this degree of disability. The type of disease and the circumstances under which it has occurred are of no importance. The disability could have resulted from severe disease from birth, mental or physical impairment or it might have resulted thereafter or be the result of an accident sustained, etc.

(b) The person should have turned 16 years of age. The age of 16 is fixed as this is the minimum age for acquisition of general employment capacity under our labour legislation (Article 301 of the LC). The idea of the law is as follows: if the person had been capable of work, he/she could have started working from this age onwards; however, his/her high-degree incapacity for work does not allow him/her to do so.

553. The amount of the social pension for disability is determined on the grounds of the amount of the social pension. For those persons who have lost from 71% to 90% of their capacity for work, the social pension for disability amounts to 110% of the social pension for elderly persons, and for those who have lost over 90% of their capacity for work, it amounts to 120% of the social pension for elderly persons (Article 90a, paragraph 2 of the SIC) (*See supra* paragraph 555).

554. The consideration of the degree of reduced capacity for work in determining the amount of the social pension for disability is a new point in national pension law, as it did not exist until the end of 1999. It is more fair, as it takes into account the extremely severe situation of these persons and deserves being supported.

§5. Personal Pensions

I. Legal Infrastructure, Notion and Types

555. Personal pensions are regulated in Article 92 of the SIC and Article 7 of the Regulation on pensions and insurance length of service. According to Article 92 of the SIC 'Under certain conditions and in accordance with a procedure determined for it, in exceptional cases the Council of Ministers is entitled to grant pensions to persons regarding which certain requirements of this Code are not met.' And Article 7 of the quoted Regulation explicitly specifies in detail these 'exceptional cases'. At the end of June 2016 the number of persons who receive personal pensions is 3014.[81]

556. Personal pensions are those in which a prerequisite for granting a personal pension among those above is not present: a pension for insurance length of service, a disability pension, a special merits pension or a social pension (*see supra* §§2–5); however, the person has no other means of support. And in order to make it possible for these persons to overcome the financial deadlock they are in, the legislator has delegated to the Council of Ministers the right to grant personal pensions to such people in exceptional cases, in accordance with the procedure determined

81. *Ibid.*, p. 6.

by the Council of Ministers and specified in Article 7 of the quoted Regulation, in performance of the delegation provided thereto by law.

557. On the grounds of the delegation under Article 92 of the SIC, in Article 7 of the quoted Regulation the Council of Ministers provides for three types of personal pensions:

(1) Personal pensions for children.
(2) Personal pensions for mothers of numerous children.
(3) Personal pensions for nursing a disabled family member.

558. The Personal pensions are non-contributory ones. No insurance contributions are made for them. They are paid from financial means provided for in the State budget. They are a subjective right of the categories of persons specified in the quoted Regulation, this right arising in those cases where the prerequisites provided for in Article 7 thereof are present. Therefore, the refusal of the Council of Ministers to grant them may be appealed on general grounds in accordance with the procedure set forth in Article 132, paragraph 2 of the APC. And this is an important judicial guarantee for the protection of the right to personal pensions.

II. Personal Pensions for Children (Article 7, Paragraph 2, Item 1 of the Quoted Regulation)

559. The prerequisites for granting personal pensions for children are as under:

(a) The person to whom the pension is granted should be a child. Within the meaning of Article 7, paragraph 2, item 1 of the quoted Regulation, 'a child' is a person aged below 18, or below 26 if he/she is a student, who has the right to receive survivor's pension under Article 82 of the SIC (see infra §7).
(b) The child's parent (the mother and/or the father) should have died.
(c) The child should not be entitled to survivor's pension according to Article 82 of the SIC. These are the cases of a deceased parent who has been receiving a survivor's pension which may not be inherited, or a parent who has been receiving another type of pension which may not be inherited, or, generally speaking, a parent who has died before having acquired the right to disability pension under Article 74 of the SIC, and so on.

560. This pension replaces the survivor's pension of the child from his/her deceased parent, which the child may not receive because the legal prerequisites for it are not present (*see infra* §7).

III. Personal Pension for Mothers of Numerous Children (Article 7, Paragraph 2, Item 2 of the Quoted Regulation)

561. Advanced age is the insured social risk for granting this pension.

562. The prerequisites the presence thereof giving rise to the right to this pension are the following ones:

(a) The mother should have given birth to five or more children and should have raised them until they reached 18 years of age.
(b) The mother should not have been deprived of parental rights, and her parental rights should not have been restricted under Articles 74–75 of the Family Code.
(c) The children should not have been placed in a public institution for being raised there for a period of time longer than a year unless this has been done for medical reasons (for treatment, examination and other similar).
(d) The mother should have turned 65.
(e) The annual income per member of the mother's family should be less than half of the sum of the guaranteed minimum income for the last twelve months preceding the filing of the application for granting the pension.
(f) The mother should have at least three years' insurance length of service.

IV. Personal Pensions for Nursing a Disabled Family Member (Article 7, Paragraph 2, Item 3 of the Quoted Regulation)

563. It is advanced age again that is the insured social risk for this pension.

564. The prerequisites for the cumulative presence thereof giving rise to the right to this pension are as follows:

(a) The person who has been nursing the disabled person should have attained the age under Article 68, paragraph 3 of the SIC, i.e., 66 years and 6 months in 2021. From 31 December 2021 onwards the age will increase by 2 months from the first day of each calendar year until reaching 67 years of age.
(b) The person should have taken care of a disabled person who is in need of constant attendance and is a member of the family. Members of the family are the husband, the wife, as well as their lineal ascendants and descendants. These are persons of a disability degree of more than 90%.
(c) The attendance (the nursing) should have lasted for more than ten years.
(d) The annual income per member of the disabled person's family should be less than half of the sum of the guaranteed minimum income for the last twelve months preceding the filing of the application for the pension.
(e) The person who has taken care of a disabled member of the family should have at least three years' insurance length of service.

V. Procedure for Granting Personal Pensions and Amounts Thereof

565. The procedure for granting personal pensions in accordance with the legal delegation under Article 92 of the SIC is laid down by the Council of Ministers. The legal regulation of this procedure is contained in Article 7, paragraphs 1 and 4 of the quoted Regulation. It includes the following:

(a) An application on behalf of the person. It is filed with the NII through the respective territorial department thereof by the permanent address of the applicant. This application shows the grounds for granting the personal pension under Article 92 of the SIC.
(b) An order of the official of the territorial department of the NII showing that the person is not entitled to any other pension under the SIC.
(c) A proposal to the Minister of Labour and Social Policy for granting the pension. This proposal is made by the municipal council of the region where the place of permanent residence of the person is.
(d) It is on the grounds of the said proposal and the examination of its being well founded that the Minister of Labour and Social Policy and the Minister of Finance make a report to the Council of Ministers.

566. It is on the grounds of the said proposal that the Council of Ministers makes a decision concerning the granting of the personal pension. The decision of the Council of Ministers is the juridical act on the grounds of which the pension is granted. The said decision specifies the date on which the personal pension is granted and the payment thereof begins.

567. The amount of the personal pensions is specified in Article 7, paragraph 5 of the quoted Regulation. This amount is equal to 90% of the social pensions for elderly persons (*see supra* §4).

§6. Survivors' Pensions

568. The legal infrastructure of the survivors' pensions is contained in Articles 80–84 of the SIC, Articles 31–36 of the quoted Regulation.

569. The basic particularity of the survivors' pensions is the insured social risk at the occurrence of which they are granted. Death is this risk.

Under the effective SIC, the extent of persons insured against death is a large one. It comprises all the employees, members of Producers' Cooperatives, freelance practitioners and traders, managers and controllers of commercial companies.

570. The right to survivors' pension arises at the presence of two prerequisites:

(a) The occurrence of the insured person's death, this person having his/her dependants as specified under the law. It is the dependants that the law envisages as the 'family members' maintained by the deceased person under Article 80, paragraph 2 of the SIC.
(b) The deceased person should have provided during his/her lifetime the maintenance of some persons among those specified in detail under Article 80, paragraph 2 of the SIC. These are his/her relatives. They are called 'members of his/her family'. There is a family legal relation – relation by origin – between these persons and the insured deceased one – lineal relationship (parents and children) or conjugal relationship. This prerequisite poses two important questions

concerning the extent of these persons and the content of the legal requirement for their being the deceased person's dependants.

571. The first question concerns the extent of the dependants. The following categories of the insured deceased person's relatives are included here:

(a) His/her children (natural, adopted and stepchildren). The extent of children entitled to survivors' pension includes the children up to the age of 18, or if they are students in educational institutions – up to the age of 26 as well as above this age if disability has occurred prior to the attainment of the age of 18 or 26, respectively.
(b) The parents of the insured deceased person when reaching the age for acquiring the right to full pension for insurance length of service and old age (*see supra* §2) or even before that age in case of their incapacity for work, that is if they have been found to belong to a certain degree of disability – 50% or more of their capacity for work being lost.
(c) The spouse of the insured deceased person has the right to survivors' pension five years earlier than the age of acquiring the right to full pension for insurance length of service and old age under Article 68, paragraph 1 of the SIC, or even before that date if he/she is incapacitated for work.

572. The second question is: what does dependants mean? What it means is that these persons have regularly and constantly received their maintenance or the largest part thereof from the deceased person. The surviving spouse (over the age indicated in *supra* paragraph 549 'a') and the children (under the age indicated in *supra* paragraph 549 'b') are regarded as the deceased person's dependants although they might have been working. This is an irrefutable presumption with regard to the maintenance of the insured deceased person for these categories of his/her relatives.

573. The amount of the survivors' pensions is determined as a part (percentage) of the personal pension of the deceased insured person depending on the number of heirs as follows: in case of one heir – 50% of the personal pension of the deceased person, in case of two heirs – 75%, in case of three or more heirs – 100% of the personal pension of the deceased insured person (Article 81, paragraph 1 of the SIC). All heirs are entitled to receive an equal share of the personal pension of the legator (Article 81, paragraph 2 of the SIC).

574. The effective pension legislation also establishes the minimum amount of the survivors' pension for the separate heir. The amount of this pension may not be less than 90% of the social old-age pension (Article 81, paragraph 2 of the SIC). Therefore, in case the share of the survivors' pension due to a heir is below this amount it is payable at the amount of 90% of the social old-age pension. This is the minimum survivors' pension payable to each separate heir.

575. The separate heirs depending on the family legal relations thereof with the legator receive the survivors' pension for a specific duration.

The children receive the survivors' pension until they come of age, and if they are students – until they finish their training, but not after they reach 26 years of age, and if they lose their capacity for work – until they recover it.

The surviving spouse receives survivors' pension for life unless he/she marries again. In this case, the survivors' pension is suspended (Article 96, paragraph 1, item 3 of the SIC).

Pursuant to Article 82, paragraph 3 of the SIC, the parents receive survivors' pension for their deceased children for life.

576. Since 1 September 2011 the pensioner has had the right to an additional sum in the amount of 26.5% of the pension which the deceased spouse used to receive. This additional sum may not be received together with the survivors' pension from the same legator (Article 84, paragraph 3 of the SIC).

Chapter 3. Pension Proceedings

§1. Legal Infrastructure, Notion and Stages in Pension Proceedings

577. The legal provisions on pension proceedings are contained in Articles 94–106, 117–120 of the SIC and Articles 1–49'a' of the quoted Regulation.

578. Pension proceedings establish the procedure through which the subjective right to pension is exercised as a part of the citizens' constitutional right to social insurance under Article 51, paragraph 1 of the Constitution. Pension proceedings provide certainty in the implementation of pension insurance.

579. Pension proceedings consist of two stages: administrative and judicial. They develop consecutively: the administrative stage takes place first, and then the judicial one. While the administrative stage of pension proceedings is obligatory and inevitable in exercising the right to pension, the judicial one is possible and supplementary. It is applied only where the persons concerned appeal against the administrative acts regarding the granting, changing, updating, suspending and terminating of the pension. However, this does not at all mean that judicial pension proceedings are of minor importance. On the contrary. They are extremely important because it is through these proceedings that judicial supervision is exercised over the lawfulness of the individual administrative acts in the field of the citizens' pension rights, and it is through these proceedings again that judicial protection of the citizens' constitutional right to social insurance is provided.

§2. Administrative Pension Proceedings

580. The administrative pension proceedings are conducted before the administrative bodies. These are the territorial departments of the NII, and more specifically, the pension insurance officials and the Head thereof.

I. Granting the Pensions

581. The granting of the pension sets the starting point of the pension relationship within the framework of the general insurance legal relationship. It comprises four basic points:

(a) The competent State body's official recognition that the right to the pension and the prerequisites thereof for exercising this right are present.
(b) Determining the monthly amount of the pension in Bulgarian currency rounded off in lv.
(c) The liability of the insurance body for the pension and for the payment thereof in cash.
(d) Specifying the date from which the pension is payable onwards. Pensions are payable from the date the right to the pension arises if the application and the

required documents thereto have been filed with the territorial department of the NII within six months after the date the right to the pension has arisen. However, if the application and the required documents thereto have been filed after this date, the commencement date of the pension granted is the date of filing the application.

582. The pension is granted by order of the official who has been assigned the management of the pension insurance within the territorial department of the NII.

II. Changes in the Pensions

583. Changes in the pensions are regulated under Articles 98 and 99 of the SIC. This regulation concerns the pension of the individual, and it shows the development of the pension after it has been granted. The change concerns the amount of the pension. This change is made by the body which has granted the pension, at the request of the person concerned. The change in the pension is made where:

(a) the insured person submits new evidence relating to the insurance length of service, the insurance income, the civil status and other circumstances which influence the amount of the pension. The change is made from the date of submitting the new evidence;
(b) upon its being granted, the amount of the pension was higher or lower. In this case the change is aimed at bringing the amount of the pension in line with the legal criteria and requirements regarding this amount. The change may also be made on office grounds by the insurance body. It is made from the date of granting the pension;
(c) a manifest factual mistake is involved in the order for granting it, in determining the individual coefficient of the pensioner, in calculating its amount and the like. In this case, the change in the pension is effective since the day it was granted.

III. Updating the Pensions

584. The most topical problems that have the greatest legal and social significance are those set by the so-called updating of the pensions. The problem has acquired extreme importance in recent years.

'Updating' the pensions means bringing the amount thereof in line with the changes that have occurred in the socio-economic conditions in the country. It is applied to all types of pensions and is carried out on the grounds of two basic criteria: (a) economic one – the increase of the average insurance income for the country; (b) social one – changes in the prices of consumer goods in the preceding calendar year. Of course, this criterion refers to the past as it concerns the preceding year, and the price level of the current year can never be 'caught up' with this criterion. In spite of these shortcomings, updating is an achievement of our pension legislation. It has been carried out since 2001.

585. According to Article 100 of the SIC, each year an updating of the pensions granted prior to 31 December of the preceding year is made, this updating commencing on 1 July of the current calendar year. The updating is made by decision of the Supervisory Board of the NII. This decision also determines the amount of the updating. It ranges between 5% and 6% of the average amount of pensions.

586. Unfortunately, the economic crisis, which hit the country in the second half of 2009, has made it impossible for the pensions' regular updating – provided for in Article 100 of the SIC – to be carried out in 2010, 2011 and 2012. That was a gross violation of Article 100 of the SIC. The 'freezing' of all pensions in the last more than three years – the amount thereof was miserably low even before the crisis – is one of the most severe social consequences, which affects the pensioners, who are doomed to indecent existence, and turns them into one of the most vulnerable groups in society.
'''

IV. Suspension of Pensions

587. Suspension of the pension is the temporary discontinuance of the payment of the person's pension.

588. The basic legal provisions on the suspension of pensions are contained in Article 95 of the SIC. In may be ordered on certain grounds. These grounds are as follows.

589. A demand (an application) by the pensioner. The motives for the application are of no importance. There are neither requirements for these motives being stated nor restrictions as to the reasons for demanding the suspension of the pensioner's pension. These reasons could be the following: receiving another type of pension of a higher amount, the person opting for it instead of the old-age pension he/she used to receive, the second pension being incompatible with the first. These grounds ensue from the nature of the subjective right to this pension.

590. When the pension is not payable. These are the cases provided for under Article 101 of the SIC where the person may not receive the pension granted to him/her along with another pension although he/she is entitled to it as well (for instance an old-age pension along with a personal or survivors' disability pension in the case of general sickness or along with a survivors' old-age pension, etc.). The suspension of the old-age pension in these cases is in pursuance of the legal prohibition on receiving it along with another type of pension.

591. In cases where the pension has not been received by the person for six consecutive months (Article 21, paragraph 1, subparagraph 'd' of the quoted Regulation). The grounds thereof proceed from the assumption that since the pensioner has not received his/her pension for a long time (for six months or more) and does not show any interest in it this means he/she does not want to receive it.

592. Non-performance of the pensioner's obligations to the insurance body. It concerns the case where a pensioner called on office grounds for re-examination fails to appear without any reasonable excuse. The re-examination is necessary when the state of incapacity for work requires that the development of the incapacity (its improvement or deterioration) for work be regularly examined and that the disability degree, the amount of the pension, and so on be specified on the grounds thereof.

V. Termination of Pensions

A. General Grounds

593. The pension is not an insurance payment forever. In spite of being a long-term one, some day it is terminated. The termination of the pension means that the pension legal relation between the insurance body and the pensioner does not exist anymore and the payment of the pension is terminated definitively. However, this termination is done in the specified due course and in the presence of specific grounds. These are new legal facts that arise after the pension has been granted.

594. The grounds for the termination of the pension laid down under Article 96 of the SIC can be divided into four groups regarding their nature and field of application.

595. The pensioner's death. The pension is an insurance benefit for a specifically defined individual. Because of that the pension is terminated on his/her death. However, in cases where the pensioner, through his/her pension, has been providing for maintenance of persons under Article 80, paragraph 2 of the SIC, his/her personal pension turns into a survivors' pension for his/her dependants.

596. When the children reach the age up to which they are entitled to receive a survivors' pension (*see* Chapter 2, §7). These grounds ensue from the very nature of the survivors' pensions, their purpose and the prerequisites for granting thereof. These grounds emerge for each separate heir when he/she reaches the respective age and they do not affect the right to the survivors' pension of the other heirs to the legator.

597. When the surviving spouse contracts a new marriage. The considerations relating to this solution are of moral nature. It is assumed, with regard to the respect for the deceased legator's memory, that, as the surviving spouse has married again, it is immoral that a pension be received and rights be derived based on the legator's death and the conjugal cohabitation with him. On the other hand, it is presumed that the surviving spouse has found the normal conjugal help and maintenance by way of contracting this new marriage.

598. The grounds for receiving the respective pension are over. This applies to those pensions regarding which that is possible: for instance, the pensioner has recovered his/her capacity for work, and because of that his/her disability no more forms grounds for receiving a disability pension; the personal incomes of a person receiving a social pension as an elderly person have augmented, and therefore, he/she meets no more the requirements for receiving such a pension, and so on.

599. The pensions are granted, changed, updated, suspended and terminated by way of an order of the official who is in charge of the management of pension insurance in the territorial department of the NII (Article 98, paragraph 1 of the SIC). This is the Head of the Pension Section of the respective regional department of the NII by the permanent address of the pensioner. As for their legal nature, these orders are individual administrative acts within the meaning of Article 2 of the Administrative Proceedings Law.

600. The orders of the Head of the Pension Section of the regional department of the NII may be appealed against by the persons concerned to the Head of the territorial department of the NII within three months following their receipt. The Head of the territorial department considers the appeal within one month after receiving it and renders his/her decision on it. Through this decision he/she may confirm, reverse or change the appealed decision of the Head of the Pension Section. The decision is communicated to the appellant within seven days following the day it has been rendered. As for its legal nature, the decision of the Head of the territorial department of the NII is an individual administrative act. And the appeal thereto, and the proceedings in which the appeal is considered and the decision is rendered, constitute an administrative appeal against an individual administrative act to a superior administrative body in accordance with Article 81 of the APC. The rendering of the decision of the Head of the territorial department of the NII on the appeal against the order of the Head of the Pensions Section puts an end to the administrative pension proceedings.

§3. Judicial Pension Proceedings

601. Judicial pension proceedings are regulated under Articles 118–120 of the SIC. Through these proceedings the lawfulness of individual administrative acts is challenged, these being the acts of the territorial departments of the NII either rejecting the granting of a pension, or determining the amount thereof, or changing, updating, suspending or terminating the pension.

602. Judicial pension proceedings are two-instance ones: before the administrative court and before the Supreme Administrative Court.

603. The proceedings before the administrative court start upon a motivated appeal of a person concerned – the insured person or the insurer – against the order of the Head of the territorial department of the NII.

The appeal is lodged with the administrative court in writing within fourteen days following the day the person concerned has received the order. The appeal should substantiate the alleged unlawfulness of the order of the Head of the territorial department of the NII, and should contain supporting evidence.

604. The administrative court considers the appeal in a panel of one judge with the participation of a public prosecutor. The proceedings are conducted in accordance with the rules set forth in the APC, the following persons being subpoenaed: the Head of the territorial department of the NII who has issued the order, the appellant and the other persons concerned. The court hears them out and also collects other evidence admissible under the APC (Articles 145–178).

605. On the grounds of the collected evidence, the court judges the lawfulness of the appealed order and renders its decision on the appeal. Where the appeal is fully upheld, it reverses the order of the Head of the territorial department of the NII and renders its own decision. Where the court partially upholds the appeal, it renders its own decision on the reversed part of the decision, and confirms the other part. And lastly, where the court totally disallows the appeal, it confirms the lawfulness of the challenged order.

606. The second stage of judicial proceedings is conducted before the Supreme Administrative Court. It starts upon the written motivated cassation appeal against the decision of the administrative court, this appeal being lodged by the dissatisfied party. That might be the territorial department of the NII, or the insured person, or the insurer. The appeal is lodged within fourteen days following the announcement of the decision of the district court.

607. The cassation appeal is considered by a panel of three supreme judges in accordance with the cassation procedure set forth in Articles 208–228 of the APC.

608. The Supreme Administrative Court is entitled to preserve the validity of the appealed decision, either in full or in part, or to reverse it. Where the court reverses it because of serious violations of the rules of procedure, it refers the case back to the district court in order to be reconsidered by a new panel of judges. Where the decision is reversed on other grounds (improper application of substantive law or groundlessness) the Supreme Administrative Court renders its decision on the merits.

609. The decision of the Supreme Administrative Court is final and is not subject to appeal.

Chapter 4. Additional Mandatory Pension Insurance

§1. Legal Infrastructure and Notion

610. Additional mandatory pension insurance is a novelty in Bulgarian social security legislation. It was regulated for the first time in the SIC of 1999. Its provisions have been applied since 1 January 2000.

611. The legal framework of additional mandatory pension insurance is contained in Articles 120‘a’–208 of the SIC.

612. Additional mandatory pension insurance is implemented through the participation of the insured in universal and professional pension funds, which are established and managed by pension insurance companies licensed under the SIC. The pensions the insured receive through this insurance are complementary to the basic mandatory State pension insurance (*see supra* Chapter 3).

613. Additional mandatory pension insurance is the second ‘pillar’ of the national pension insurance system. It provides the insured with the opportunity to acquire an additional life pension for old age and a fixed-term pension for early pensioning (*see infra* §4).

§2. Basic Organizational Elements of Additional Mandatory Pension Insurance

614. The basic organizational elements of additional mandatory pension insurance are the pension insurance companies and the universal and professional pension funds created in accordance with the procedure set forth in the SIC.

I. Pension Insurance Companies

615. The pension insurance companies are joint-stock companies, which are established, registered and managed according to the Commercial Law (Article 121, paragraph 1 of the SIC). They have a specific scope of activities: exclusive participation in additional mandatory pension insurance with a minimum capital of BGN 5 million (about USD 3.55 million), which should have been deposited in cash prior to the establishment of the company.

616. The pension insurance companies are licensed by a specialized State body – the FSC – for carrying out activities of additional mandatory pension insurance. They are licensed in accordance with the procedure for special administrative proceedings, in the course of which the following is examined: the financial, organizational and managerial aptitude of the company for carrying out activities of additional mandatory pension insurance (Articles 13–18 of the Law on the FSC for 2003 as amended). The pension insurance companies, being joint-stock companies with a specific scope of activities – additional pension insurance – are subject, on general grounds, to an entry into the commercial register of the Registry Agency. They are entered in the said register after submitting their pension licence issued by the FSC. They are also subject to a parallel entry in the FSC (Article 122d and Article 122e of the SIC). The said parallel entry is aimed at giving more transparency and reliability to the legal existence of the pension insurance companies and to the activity they perform.

617. In 2021 there were nine licensed pension insurance companies in Bulgaria: 'Doverie', 'Saglasie', 'Rodina', 'Allianz-Bulgaria', ING, 'CKB-Sila', 'Badeshte', 'Toplina' and 'Pensionnoosiguritelen institut'.

618. The pension insurance companies carry out their activity in accordance with the SIC and the functions the latter assigns to them, and in compliance with the statutes adopted by the general assembly of the company's shareholders, the rules on the organization and activity of the two pension funds for additional pension insurance that are managed by the company, and the other internal acts of the company adopted by the bodies managing its activity (Article 121, paragraph 6 of the SIC).

II. Pension Insurance Funds

619. Pension insurance funds are differentiated property, which consists of the contributions made therein by the insured. They are separate legal entities, differentiated by pension insurance companies.

620. The SIC establishes two pension insurance funds: universal and professional. The universal pension fund is the one in which all persons born after 1 January 1960 have mandatory insurance, while the professional insurance fund is the one in which the persons working under I or II category of work have mandatory insurance, regardless of their date of birth or age.[82]

621. Pension insurance funds are managed by the pension insurance companies. A pension insurance company is entitled to manage only one universal and one professional pension insurance fund (Article 133, paragraphs 1 and 4 of the SIC).

622. The amendments to the SIC of December 2010 (promulgated in the OJ, No. 100 of 21 December 2010) introduced changes into the additional State social insurance. According to §4'a' of the Interim and Concluding Provisions of the SIC:

82. As at 30 Nov. 2021 the number of people who had mandatory pension insurance in the universal pension fund was 2,824 thousand, and the number of those who had mandatory pension insurance in the professional pension fund was 184 thousand ('Social Security Yearbook 2021 (Sofia: Labour and Law Publishing House 2021)).

> The pecuniary resources available as at 1 January 2011 in the individual lots of those women born between 1 January 1955 and 31 December 1959 inclusive, and in the individual lots of those men born between 1 January 1952 and 31 December 1959 inclusive who have been insured in a professional pension fund until 31 December 2010 shall be transferred to the Pension Fund of the State social insurance.

This alteration changes the management of the resources of these funds – private property – and the disposition thereof on the part of the insured persons and the pension insurance companies, which used to manage the resources of these funds, and transfers them – through the said legal provision – for their being managed and disposed of by the NII as a public State body. The constitutionality of this provision has been challenged before the Constitutional Court by a group of deputies as being in conflict with Article 17 of the Constitution relating to the inviolability and protection of private property. A constitutional case was instituted and the Constitutional Court is expected to rule upon this matter in the forthcoming months.

§3. Insured Social Risks and Insurance Contributions

623. The insured social risks in additional mandatory pension insurance are: old age, disability and death (Article 1, item 2'a', Article 139 and Article 142 of the SIC). The content and occurrence of these risks is determined by the provisions regarding their essence and procedure for establishing them, these provisions forming part of the legal infrastructure of State social insurance.

624. The insurance contributions in additional mandatory pension insurance are regulated in Articles 157–159 of the SIC. Their amount is determined in Article 157, paragraph 1 of the SIC. It is differentiated for the two funds, depending on the severity and harmfulness of working conditions: as for those insured in the professional pension fund, this amount is 12% of the gross labour remuneration of the persons working under the conditions of the I category of work, and 7% for those working under the conditions of the II category of work. These contributions are paid in full by the insurers. As for the persons insured in the universal pension fund, the insurance contributions are: for 2005 – 3%, for 2006 – 4%, and since 2007 – 5%. Since 2007 they have been distributed between the insurers and the insured in the ratio specified in Article 6, paragraph 3 of the SIC – 2,80% for the insurers and 2,20% for the insured, respectively. As for the contributions in professional funds, they are entirely paid by the insurers (Article 157, paragraph 2 of the SIC).

625. The insurance contributions for additional mandatory pension insurance are collected by the NII along with the insurance contributions for State social insurance. They are remitted to the specialized account specified by the pension insurance company which manages the respective pension fund. The relationships between the NII and the pension insurance companies relating to the collection of insurance contributions are settled by way of a contract (Article 159 of the SIC).

§4. Rights of the Insured

626. The rights of the insured in additional mandatory pension insurance are regulated in Articles 163–174 of the SIC. They are differentiated depending on the type of the pension fund in which the persons are insured.

627. The persons insured in a universal pension fund receive an old-age pension for life upon acquiring the right to pension for insurance length of service and old age (*see supra* Chapter 3, §2). The right to this pension arises concurrently with the right to pension for insurance length of service and old age under State social insurance. The amount of the pension is determined in accordance with Article 169, paragraph 1 of the SIC and depends on the amount accumulated in the individual lot of the insured person and the biometric tables approved by the Deputy Chairman of the FSC who heads the department which is in charge of the insurance supervision.

628. The persons insured in a professional pension fund receive the so-called professional pension for early pensioning (Article 168, paragraph 1 of the SIC). The right to this pension arises in the presence of the following prerequisites:

(a) The insured persons should have worked either under the conditions of I category of work for at least ten years, or under the conditions of the II category of work for at least fifteen years.
(b) The insured persons should have attained a certain age. As for those who have worked under the conditions of the I category of work this age is eight years lower than the age for acquiring the right to pension for insurance length of service and old age, and for those who have worked under the conditions of the II category of work this age is three years lower than the age for acquiring the right to pension for insurance length of service and old age. This means that in 2021, when the age of acquiring the right to pension for insurance length of service and old age is 52 years for men and 50 years and 8 months for women, the men working under the conditions of the I category of work will start receiving this pension at the age of 55, and the women – at the age of 53 years and 8 months, while the men working under the conditions of the II category of work will start receiving this pension at the age of 61, and the women – at the age of 57 and 8 months (Article 69b of the SIC).

629. The insured have certain rights relating to their participation in additional mandatory insurance:

(a) to receive free information from the insurance company about the state of their individual lot (Article 173 of the SIC);
(b) to transfer the amounts accumulated in their individual lot from the universal or professional fund of an insurance company into another such fund, once in a year, after the expiry of two years following the start of their participation in the respective pension fund (Article 137 and Article 140 of the SIC);

(c) to draw the whole amount accumulated in the individual lot upon the occurrence of the right to pension for insurance length of service and old age under State social insurance (Article 172 of the SIC).

630. A considerable change in the insured persons' rights was affected in 2014 and 2015. It consists in establishing the new right of the insured having additional mandatory pension insurance in a universal pension fund to change this insurance, at their own choosing, into insurance in the Pension Fund or the 'Pensions under Article 69' Fund of the State social insurance at the NII; and the new right of the insured having additional mandatory pension insurance in a professional pension fund to change it into insurance in the Pension Fund of the State social insurance (*see infra* paragraphs 631 and 632).

631. According to Article 4b of the SIC, the persons who have additional mandatory pension insurance in a universal pension fund are granted the right to change it into insurance in the Pension Fund of the State social insurance or the 'Pensions under Article 69' Fund, respectively, the latter being the Fund in which the following persons are insured: military staff and civil servants employed at the Ministry of the Interior or other State security bodies (*see supra* 510). The change is effected through increasing the insurance contribution for the universal pension fund, not later than 5 years before the insured person attains the age of retirement under Article 68, paragraph 1 of the SIC, which is 61 years of age for women and 64 years of age for men (*see supra* paragraph 513) in 2017. Along with that, those insured persons who change their insurance, transfer the pecuniary amounts accumulated in their personal lots from the universal insurance fund into the Pension Fund of the State social insurance. The insured are entitled to exercise this right upon the expiry of one year after they make their choice under Article 4b of the SIC. The insurance takes effect on the first day of the month following the month in which the choice of changing the insurance was made.

632. Article 4c of the SIC provides the persons having additional mandatory pension insurance in a professional pension fund to change it into insurance in the Pension Fund of the State social insurance with an increased insurance contribution. According to Article 157, paragraph 1, item 2 of the SIC, this contribution is 12% for the insured persons working under the conditions of the I category of work and 7% for those under the II category of work. Along with that, the insured persons transfer the pecuniary amounts accumulated in their personal lots from the professional insurance fund into the Pension Fund of the State social insurance.

The procedure for making the choice of changing the insurance from a universal fund (*see supra* paragraph 631) or a professional fund into additional mandatory pension insurance in the funds of the State social insurance and the way of collecting and distributing the increased amounts of insurance contributions in these cases are set forth in the Ordinance on Distribution of Insurance Contributions, which is issued by the Council of Ministers under Article 179, paragraph 3 of the Tax and Social Security Procedure Code (promulgated in the OJ, No. 1 of 2006).

Chapter 5. Additional Voluntary Pension Insurance

§1. Legal Infrastructure and Functions

633. Additional voluntary pension insurance is a novelty in Bulgarian pension insurance. In practice, it sprang up in the mid-1990s of the last century on the grounds of the principle of freedom of contracting under Article 9 of the Law on Obligations and Contracts, and the provisions relating to joint-stock companies in Articles 158–252 of the Commercial Law. Later on it received the sizeable legal infrastructure of its own.

634. In 1999 additional voluntary pension insurance was regulated in a separate law – the Law on Voluntary Pension Insurance (promulgated in the OJ, No. 65 of 1999, amended), which was repealed in 2003 (promulgated in the OJ, No. 67 of 29 July 2003), and its legal infrastructure became a part of the SIC.

635. The operative legal infrastructure of additional voluntary pension insurance is contained in Articles 120a–123i and Articles 209–259 of the SIC.

636. The basic functions of additional voluntary pension insurance are as follows:

(a) To provide additional financial means for the maintenance of the insured.
(b) To encourage the insurance economy of the insured.
(c) To promote the social initiative of the employers for the voluntary insurance of their employees.

637. The legal infrastructure of additional voluntary pension insurance shows certain closeness to additional mandatory pension insurance (*see supra* Chapter 3). What this closeness consists in is that both of them are forms of insurance which are additional to the basic State pension insurance, and both of them use the same legal mechanisms – pension insurance funds and companies. However, they differ considerably. The differences between them ensue from the voluntary nature of the additional pension insurance considered above, which has its impact upon both its nature and legal infrastructure (*see infra* §§2–4).

§2. Pension Insurance Companies and Funds

638. The pension insurance companies for voluntary pension insurance are regulated under Articles 120‘a’–123‘i’ of the SIC. The legal infrastructure is the same regarding the pension insurance companies for additional mandatory pension insurance and those for additional voluntary pension insurance (*see supra* Chapter 4, §2).

639. Pension insurance companies are the insurance body for the insured and the insurers in voluntary pension insurance. All the ten licensed pension insurance companies, which carry out additional mandatory pension insurance (*see supra* Chapter

4, §2), carry out additional voluntary pension insurance as well. For the insured persons and the insurers they are what the insurance companies are in additional mandatory pension insurance (*see supra* §2) and what the NII is for the State social insurance (*see supra* Part I, Chapter 2).

640. As for the pension insurance funds for additional voluntary pension insurance, their legal regulation is specific. The participation of the insured therein is voluntary and is grounded on the insurance contracts concluded between the company which manages the fund and the insured persons.

641. The new regulation of 2006 (Articles 214–229 of the SIC) has provided for the setup of two funds in the additional voluntary pension insurance: a general fund for additional voluntary pension insurance and a fund for additional voluntary pension insurance under professional schemes.

642. As for the general fund for additional voluntary pension insurance, anybody who has attained the age of 16 can be insured therein, regardless of whether he/she is employed or not.

As for the fund for additional voluntary pension insurance under professional schemes, the insurance is carried out under the rules stipulated in the collective labour contract or the collective agreement between the enterprise-insurer and the insured person under Article 4, paragraph 1 of the SIC. The collective labour contract or the collective agreement is concluded in accordance with the procedure set forth in Articles 50–60 of the LC.[83] The insurance under professional schemes is applied to insured persons of permanent employment. These are mainly employees working under employment legal relationships and civil servants working under service legal relationships.

643. The decision regarding the management of the voluntary pension fund by the pension insurance company is granted and revoked by the Deputy Chairman of the FSC who exercises supervision of social insurance. The granted permit is entered in the register of the district court and from that time on the pension insurance company has the quality of a legal entity.

644. The pension insurance company is entitled to manage only one voluntary pension fund (Article 214, paragraph 3 of the SIC). This makes it possible for the pension insurance companies to concentrate their efforts upon the effective management of the fund.

83. V. Mrachkov, *Labour Law – Bulgaria, International Encyclopaedia of Laws,* 226–243.

§3. Insured Persons, Insured Social Risks, Insurance Contracts and Insurance Contributions

645. All persons who have attained the age of 16 are entitled to insurance in voluntary pension funds. This insurance is personal (Article 210, paragraph 2 of the SIC). In 2021 the number of insured persons is 14,384.[84]

646. In voluntary pension insurance the insured social risks are: old age, disability and death (Article 1, item 2'b' of the SIC). The content of these risks in additional voluntary pension insurance is the same as their content in State social insurance (*see supra* Chapter 2, §§2, 3 and 7).

647. Insurance contracts are concluded between the pension insurance company and the insured person. Where the insured person is an employee or a civil servant, the insurance contract may also be concluded by the employer, or by the body which has appointed the person, respectively, in favour of the insured person – as a contract in favour of a third person. An insurance contract in favour of a third person may also be concluded by a spouse or a parent, who insures his/her spouse, child, and so on (Article 235 of the SIC).

648. The insurance contract specifies the risks against which the person is insured, the amount of the insurance contributions, the terms for their payment, as well as the conditions regarding the termination of the contract.

649. Insurance contributions are regulated under Articles 230–234 of the SIC. They are paid monthly and are reported in the personal lot of the insured person. They are paid by the insured person, or, if that is explicitly agreed, or by the employers and those persons and bodies which assign the performance of the respective work or service (*see supra* paragraph 647). The amount of the insurance contributions is specified in the insurance contract.

§4. Rights of the Insured

650. The rights of the insured are regulated under Articles 243–248 of the SIC. They are of the following two types: (1) Pension rights; (2) Other rights connected with the participation of the persons insured in additional voluntary pension insurance funds.

651. The pension rights are:

(a) Right to an additional personal pension as an elderly person. It is granted to the insured who have attained the age of acquiring the pension for insurance length of service and old age under Article 68 of the SIC.

84. L. Yazadzhieva, '*Additional Pension Insurance' in Social Security* 872–884 (Labour and Law Publishing House 2021).

(b) Right to an additional personal disability pension. It is granted to the insured upon the occurrence of disability. Here again, disability is a state of permanent incapacity for work, ascertained by the medical expertise bodies dealing with determining the capacity for work in relation to disability pensions under State pension insurance.
(c) Survivors' pension. It is granted, upon the insured person's death, to his/her relatives specified in the rules of the fund as well as in the insurance contract concluded with the insured person.

652. According to Article 13, paragraph 1, item 7 of the Law on Taxation of Individuals' Income (promulgated in the OJ, No. 95 of 2006 as amended), the income received from additional pension insurance after acquiring the right to an additional pension is not subject to taxation. This tax treatment of the income received from additional voluntary pension insurance, introduced in 2007 (§1, item 12 of the Supplementary Provisions of the said Law) applies in 2013 as well. This treatment is more favourable than the tax treatment which used to be operative in the preceding years and provided for pension taxation according to the standard procedure in cases where tax relief has been enjoyed in connection with the instalments under the voluntary pension insurance contract. This treatment also applies to additional voluntary pension insurance income received from a pension fund which carries out additional voluntary pension insurance activity under the legislation of a EU Member State or a country which is a party to the Agreement on the European Economic Area. The operative tax treatment favours the insured persons and promotes the expansion of additional voluntary pension insurance.[85]

653. The other rights of the insured having an additional voluntary pension insurance are as under:

(a) The right to transfer to his/her name the financial amounts accumulated in his/her individual lot from one voluntary pension fund into another, the latter being managed by another pension insurance company.
(b) The right to transfer the financial amounts accumulated in his/her personal lot, or a part thereof, to a spouse, children, parents, and vice versa.
(c) To draw at any time the financial amounts accumulated in his/her personal lot as well as to dispose thereof in his/her own discretion.

85. L. Yazadzhieva, '*Additional Pension Insurance*', *supra*, 874–881.

Part IX. Handicapped Persons

Chapter 1. State Policy Concerning the Disabled

654. The State pursues a policy of increased protection of the disabled. The bases of this policy are contained in Article 51, paragraph 3 of the Constitution, pursuant to which 'The persons with physical or mental impairments are under the special protection of the State and society.'

655. In 2004 a new Law on the Integration of People with Impairments (promulgated in the OJ, No. 81 of 2004 as amended) was adopted, which took effect on 1 January 2005, as a further development of this constitutional idea. This Law regulates the rights to integration of the disabled and the obligations of the State bodies, economic and public organizations in the implementation thereof. The Council of Ministers has adopted the Rules on its application (promulgated in the OJ, No. 115 of 2004 as amended).

656. The State policy concerning the disabled is implemented by the Council of Ministers. For this purpose a National Council on Integration of the Disabled (Article 5 of the quoted Law) was set up by the Council of Ministers. The said National Council has consultative functions and it consists of representatives of the government, the national representative organizations of the disabled (the blind, the profoundly deaf and persons with other physical disabilities), the organizations of employers and employees, and the National Association of Municipalities.

657. For the implementation of the State policy on the integration of people with impairments, an Agency for People with Impairments was created with the Minister of Labour and Social Policy. Its functions are as follows: to permit the manufacture, import, sale and maintenance of relief devices for people with impairments; to exercise control over the observance of the criteria regarding the use of these devices; to keep a register of the specialized enterprises and cooperative societies employing people with impairments, to take part in developing the bills of normative acts and to give opinion thereof, these being normative acts concerning the protection of people with impairments, and so on (Articles 7–9 of the quoted law).

658. The protection of people with impairments concerns two categories of people: (1) people with impairments; (2) people with permanent impairments.

659. People with impairments are those with any loss or disturbance in the anatomic structure, physiology or psychics of the individual (§1, item 1 of the Supplementary Provisions of the quoted law).

660. People with permanent impairments are those who, as a result of an anatomical, physiological or mental impairment, have a permanently reduced capacity for carrying out activities in a way and degree which are possible for a healthy person. The bodies of medical expertise of capacity for work should have established that the capacity of the person for social adaptation is reduced by 50% or more. These are disabled persons within the meaning of the SIC (*see supra*).

661. The Law on the Integration of People with Impairments lays down various degrees of legal protection of persons with impairments. It is stronger for people with permanent impairments and weaker for the others.

662. The integration of people with impairments is carried out by way of the following: (1) Prophylaxis and rehabilitation of impairments; (2) Education and professional training; (3) Work activities; (4) Creating conditions for an accessible living environment; (5) Socio-economic protection. They will be considered in Chapters 2–5.

663. The assessment of the impairments is performed by way of a medical expertise and social assessment (Article 10 of the quoted law).

664. The medical expertise is performed by the bodies of expertise of the capacity for work: the territorial expert medical commissions and the National Expert Medical Commission (*see supra*).

665. The social assessment is carried out on the grounds of medical expertise. It determines the need for rehabilitation. The assessment is carried out by a consultative commission of the Social Support Directorate of the Agency of Social Assistance.

Chapter 2. Fields of Integration of People with Impairments

§1. Prophylaxis and Rehabilitation of Impairments

I. Prophylaxis of Impairments

666. The prophylaxis of impairments is carried out through the provision of knowledge regarding health and environment for the purpose of limiting the risk factors connected with the way of life and the environment, as well as through health prophylaxis and provision of healthy and safe working conditions in the enterprises and cooperative societies employing people with impairments.

667. The prophylaxis of impairments is carried out under programmes adopted by the Council of Ministers, at the suggestion of the Ministry of Health Care. Assistance in the implementation of these programmes is provided by the bodies of local self-government, the representative organizations of people with impairments, and the representative organizations of employers and trade unions.

II. Medical and Social Rehabilitation

668. Medical rehabilitation of the persons with impairments is regulated under Article 15, paragraphs 2–3 of the quoted Law. It finds its expression in supporting the persons with impairments to achieve the optimum level of their physical, intellectual and mental powers and capacities, preserving them and increasing the level of these persons' own independence. This results in preserving and increasing their standard of living and the quality thereof.

669. Medical rehabilitation is a complex activity. It comprises occupational therapy and, depending on the impaired organ or the impaired functions thereof, it might also comprise the following: hearing therapy, speech therapy, sight therapy as well as therapy of mobility, communicative skills, psychotherapy and the like (Article 15, paragraph 2 of the quoted Law).

670. Medical rehabilitation is carried out at special medical institutions. Their specialization and the activities performed there are determined by the Minister of Health Care.

671. The persons with impairments are entitled to life-saving and life-supporting medicines free of charge. The type thereof as well as the due course of receiving them is specified by the Minister of Health Care in coordination with the Minister of Finance (Article 15 of the quoted Law).

672. Along with the medical rehabilitation activities, the prevention and prophylaxis activity of disability is conducted as well. This activity is carried out by the Ministry of Education and Science, the Ministry of Health Care, the Ministry of Labour and Social Policy, the municipal councils and employers. This activity finds its expression in the medical and ecological instruction, assistance in providing healthy and safe working conditions and other similar. And the Council of Ministers approves a Prophylaxis Programme specifying the priorities, measures and resources for overcoming disability and the aggravation thereof (Articles 6–7 of the quoted Law).

673. Social rehabilitation consists in creating skills for independent life by way of restoring the sight, hearing and speech, the possibility of movements, provision of social services and other similar activities.

§2. Education and Vocational Training

674. The Ministry of Education and Science is assigned the task to develop specialized training programmes for persons with impairments and to provide them with free school appliances, appropriate modern technical means for the training and with school aids until they finish their secondary school education. The persons with impairments are entitled to specialized vocational training and specialized preparation for their work activity.

675. Vocational training and retraining of persons with impairments is organized and carried out by the employers for the employed persons with impairments, by the job centres – for the unemployed persons with impairments, by the national organizations of the disabled and the specialized enterprises and cooperatives – for the disabled working therein. Training of the disabled is carried out by licensed legal entities and individuals at the working places of the disabled.

676. Higher schools provide supportive environment, special devices, appropriate training materials and additional teaching assistance in the process of training and assessing the persons with impairments.

677. The Ministry of Labour and Social Policy and the municipal councils set up and finance vocational training centres for the initial vocational training and retraining of the disabled in certain professions. These centres perform vocational training, probation practice and daily attendance of the disabled.

§3. Employment

678. There is a special legal infrastructure for regulating the employment of the disabled under Articles 314–321 of the LC and Articles 22–31 of the quoted Law, as well as under Article 52 of the EPL.

679. The employment of persons with impairments is encouraged and supported by the State through national programmes and measures, which are developed by the Ministry of Labour and Social Policy and the Agency for Persons with Impairments. Financial means are provided therein for stimulating those employers which employ persons with impairments. They are entitled to apply, by way of projects, to the EA in order to receive financial means granted under these programmes for ensuring access to the working places, and the adaptation thereof, and for the provision of devices for persons with permanent impairments. Where a project is approved, a contract is concluded between the Agency and the employer. This contract specifies the financial means granted for the implementation of the respective programme, as well as the financial means from the national budget for covering 30% of the insurance contributions due by the employer for State social insurance, mandatory health insurance and additional mandatory pension insurance of the employed persons with permanent impairments (Articles 22–26 of the quoted law).

680. The disabled are placed in workplaces that are appropriate for their reduced capacity for work. Employers are obliged to allot 4%–10% of the total number of workplaces in the enterprise to disabled. Once a year, these workplaces are publicized in the job centres of the municipal administration.

681. The placement of the disabled in workplaces specified for them is encouraged by the Agency for Persons with Impairments: the minimum salary for the country is paid for the first twelve months for each disabled person reassigned to a suitable job, this disabled person having been sent by the job centre in excess of the specified percentage (Article 52, paragraph 1 of the EPL). The persons with reduced capacity for work enjoy stronger protection. Those persons whose capacity for work has been reduced while working under an employment relationship, regardless of the reason for occurrence of the reduction (general sickness, industrial or household accident, occupational disease, etc.), have their stronger protection regulated in Articles 314–320 of the Labour Code. These people need the said protection because their reduced capacity for work makes them helpless and threatened with the risk of the employer suspending the employment relationship with all the resulting unfavourable consequences as regards their subsistence and their way of life. Depending on the nature and extent of the reduction of their capacity for work, the Code of Labour offers these people two opportunities and two rights: a) their placement in an appropriate job in the enterprise. For the realization thereof, the Code of Labour imposes a specific obligation on the employer if the enterprise has more than fifty workers and employees: each year the employer has to identify 4 up to 10 percent of the total number of workplaces as being appropriate for job placement of persons with reduced capacity for work, depending on the nature of the activity of the enterprise (Article 315 of the LC). Ordinance No. RD -07-1 of the year 2012 of the Minister of Labour and Social Policy specifies the percentage – '4 up to 10' – of the workplaces for persons with reduced capacity for work in the various sectors. The principle is: the easier the activity in view of human efforts and safe working conditions (e.g., 'advertising activity', 'human healthcare', etc.), the higher the percentage (10%) of the total number of workplaces for people with reduced capacity for work. And vice versa – the more difficult the working conditions are (coal mining, production of oil, gas and the like), the lower this percentage is (4%); b) transfer to a job of alleviated conditions, for instance, a working day of four hours instead of eight, or working on certain days of the week only (e.g., on Monday, Wednesday and Friday) and the like (Article 317 of the LC). In each separate case, the choice between the two possibilities of job placement is determined by the instruction of the competent medical body – the attending physician, Medical Consultation Commission, Medical Expert Commission on Employment Matters. The medical judgment is binding on the employer, the worker and the employee. Depending on the nature of impairment, the extent of reduction of the capacity for work and the prospects for its development, the placement in a certain job of the person with reduced capacity for work may either be permanent or last for a certain period of time.

682. For each new temporary, seasonal or hourly job in which persons with permanent impairments sent by the EA are employed, the employer is granted certain sums for labour remuneration, additional labour remuneration of minimum amount, basic paid annual leave and contributions due at the employer's expense for the Pension Fund, the Industrial Accident and Occupational Disease Fund, and the General Sickness and Maternity Fund for the period of time during which the said persons were employed, however, for no more than six months (Article 52, paragraph 2 of the EPL).

683. State and municipal enterprises and cooperatives and workshops are set up for disabled to be reassigned to suitable jobs. Favourable and facilitated working conditions with medical rehabilitation and social integration of the disabled are provided there. The Council of Ministers makes a list of the goods and services manufactured and provided in these enterprises and fixes the quotas of products, imported and exported raw stuff and materials, equipment, and so on. These enterprises enjoy tax relief. They may not be privatized.

684. Employees belonging to a disability group are entitled to an extended paid annual leave of at least twenty-six working days (Article 319 of the LC).

685. The disabled who have been reassigned to a suitable job may be dismissed only where the employer demands and receives advance permission from the regional labour inspection at the address of the employer's registered office (Article 333 of the LC).

§4. Proper Living Environment

686. The Ministry of Regional Development and Public Works and the municipal councils are obliged to create appropriate conditions for the unimpeded movement of the disabled on all floors of the housing buildings, office buildings and other places for public use, car parks, and so on. For this purpose, the means of public transport are to be adapted to the needs and capabilities of the disabled and there should be special light, sound and other signal installations for persons of impaired sight, hearing, and so on.

687. The Law on Persons with Impairments also assigns specific obligations to other Ministries, within their competence, for creating an accessible living environment: the Ministry of Transport is assigned the implementation of technical devices in public transport for facilitating the transportation of persons with impairments; the Ministry of Labour and Social Policy is assigned the import, sale and maintenance of relief devices; the Ministry of Culture is assigned the support and development of talents and the encouragement of the creative achievements of persons with impairments; the Ministry of Youth and Sports is assigned the support to the participation of persons with impairments in sports training and competitions, and so on. And the municipalities are obliged to create accessible architectural environment in kindergartens and schools, access for persons with impairments, accompanied by guide dogs to places used by the public, and so on (Articles 34–38 of the quoted law).

688. As to the cultural affiliation of the disabled, the Law assigns special tasks to the Bulgarian National Television, Bulgarian National Radio and Bulgarian News Agency. They are obliged to provide the disabled of impaired sight and hearing with specialized information free of charge. The Law provides for specialized devices in entertainment, cultural, sports and tourist undertakings for creating conditions so that the disabled can use cultural and sports facilities – by providing the appropriate video and audio translation of cultural, sports and other programmes and materials for the disabled, by preserving 5% of the seats of the cultural and sports undertakings for the disabled either free of charge or at 50% discount of the ticket price, and so on. Lastly, municipal councils and administrations are obliged to provide the premises – clubs, halls, and so on needed for the social contacts of the disabled (Article 39 of the quoted law).

§5. Social and Economic Protection

689. The disabled enjoy an increased social and economic protection. It finds its expression in the following: (a) special regime of their pensioning; (b) additions for their social integration; (c) aids and relief for specific purposes.

690. The special regime of their pensioning finds its expression in the due course and the terms under which the disability pensions and disability social pensions are granted (*see supra* Part VII, Chapter 1, §2 and §4).

691. The disabled are entitled to a special monthly addition for social integration:

(a) When receiving labour remuneration under Article 41 of the quoted law they enjoy tax relief. It is expressed in a reduction of 50% of the taxes due by them on labour remuneration (Article 29, paragraphs 3 and 4 of the Law on Taxation of Individuals).

(b) They receive monthly additional sums for social integration – for transport services, diet, medicines (Article 42 of the quoted law and §§2 and 3 of the Rules on the application thereof).
(c) Monthly additional sum at the amount of 70% of the minimum salary, which is BGN 650 (about USD 387) since 1 January 2021, for children with permanent impairments aged below 18 until they graduate from secondary school, but not after they turn 20. This additional sum is paid to those parents who raise children with permanent impairments, as well as to the families of relatives and foster families with which children with permanent impairments have been placed (Article 43 of the quoted law).
(d) Right to sums allotted for specific purposes – purchase and adaptation of a personal motor vehicle and a parking place, for reorganizing a housing accommodation, for persons accompanying children of poor eyesight or difficulties in movement, or interpreters for children of poor hearing (Article 44 of the quoted law).

692. The monthly additional sums for persons with permanent impairments under Articles 42–44 of the quoted law (*see supra* paragraph 681) are exempt from taxes and fees (Article 45 of the quoted law).

693. The territorial departments of social welfare provide the disabled with daily care by way of nursing them at their homes, home social patronage, public refectories and dietetic canteens, day centres, specialized shops, everyday services, and so on.

Chapter 3. Financing the Activities of Protection, Social Integration and Rehabilitation of the Disabled

694. The financial means are spent on prophylaxis, medical rehabilitation, education, vocational orientation and training, promoting the employment of the disabled, subsidies for specialized enterprises, cooperatives, production enterprises and workshops for disabled, as well as on providing the appropriate living environment, social support to disabled, and so on (*see* Chapter 1 *supra*).

695. The activities under the Law on the Integration of Persons with Impairments are financed by financial means from the State budget and municipal budgets, national and international programmes, donations, and so on.

696. The administrator of the financial means for financing the activities under the Law on Persons with Impairments is the Agency for Persons with Impairments with the Minister of Labour and Social Policy (*see supra* Chapter 1).

Part X. Minimum Income Benefit

Chapter 1. Introduction

697. Social assistance has attained great importance since 1990. Until recently it used to be State activity of limited application while in the last years it had its intensive development, covered a large number of people and turned into one of the principal manifestations of the social State. The reason for it is the large-scale and drastic impoverishment of a large part of the population that hardly manages to subsist 'on the verge of survival'.

698. Social assistance also received its considerable legal infrastructure. It is developing rapidly and is undergoing frequent changes in order to keep pace with the newly emerging problems in the social situation in the country. Until recently, most of the legal provisions on social support were contained in sublegal normative acts, mostly in the Social Assistance Rules issued by the Council of Ministers. In May 1998, the Social Assistance Law, the first one of this type, was adopted, this Law having been effective since 23 May 1998 (promulgated in the OJ, No. 56 of 1998). The Council of Ministers has also adopted the Rules on its application (promulgated in the OJ, No. 133 of 1998), which took effect on 1 November 1998.

699. The most important in the legal development of social assistance in the last years is expressed in two basic points. The first one is that pursuant to Article 51, paragraph 1 of the Constitution, the right to social assistance has been recognized as a fundamental right of the citizens. The second point is that in the development of the current legal infrastructure, social assistance became a subjective right of the citizens, this right being exercised in the presence of certain prerequisites specified under the law. This is a manifestation of the increased legal protection and the great legal and social significance that the law attaches to social assistance.

Chapter 2. Institutions

700. State policy in the field of social assistance is determined by the Council of Ministers. Its specialized body is the Ministry of Labour and Social Policy. The latter pursues, administers, coordinates and controls State activities in the field of social assistance. The Ministry of Labour and Social Policy performs its functions in concert with the municipal economic organizations and the non-profit making ones that work for charitable or other humane purposes (Article 4, paragraphs 1–3 of the quoted Law).

701. The National Social Assistance Council was set up (Article 4, paragraph 4 of the quoted Law) at the Ministry of Labour and Social Policy in order for collaboration in the field of social assistance to be achieved. This Council is a consultative body. It comprises representatives of the Ministry of Labour and Social Policy, the Ministry of Finance, the Ministry of Health Care, the Ministry of Science and Education, the Ministry of Regional Development and Public Works, the National Association of the Municipalities, representatives of the representative employers' and trade union organizations, and representatives of charity organizations and organizations for other humane purposes dealing with social assistance.

702. The Agency of Social Assistance is the standing administrative body of the Ministry of Labour and Social Policy that directly carries out State activities in the field of social assistance. This Agency makes and proposes to the competent State bodies draft projects for normative acts in the field of social assistance. Besides, it administers and controls the activity of the regional and municipal social assistance offices, provides the licences for performing social services, and so on (Articles 5–6 of the quoted Law).

703. The Agency of Social Assistance also has its local bodies. These are the regional and municipal social assistance offices. The regional social assistance offices perform methodological guidance of the social assistance municipal offices. They submit information to the Agency of Social Assistance, this being information about their activities and those of the municipal offices. The municipal offices search for persons in need of social assistance, register them, examine the truthfulness of the circumstances declared by the persons and families that have filed applications for social assistance, summarize the needs of social assistance, perform social assistance activities on the territory of the municipality, provide consultations on the issues of social assistance, and so on.

Social assistance regional and municipal offices work in close collaboration with non-profit organizations, the purpose thereof being either charity or another humane purpose, and encourage their activity in the field of social assistance.

Chapter 3. Who Can Benefit?

704. Two major groups of subjects of law have the right to social assistance: (a) Bulgarian citizens; (b) Foreigners.

705. According to Article 2, paragraph 3 of the quoted law, Bulgarian citizens, for their part, are divided into three categories of subjects of law: (a) Separate individuals; (b) Families; (c) Cohabitants. Each of them has its particularities (*see infra*).

706. Bulgarian citizens as individuals form the basic and most numerous group of subjects of the right to social assistance. The subjects of the right to social assistance are those persons who are Bulgarian citizens pursuant to the Constitution (Article 25) and the Bulgarian Citizenship Law of 1998 (Articles 8–19) by birth or by naturalization. The individual may also have foreign citizenship (a person of double citizenship, triple citizenship, etc.). However, in order for the person to have the right to social assistance, he should have Bulgarian citizenship as well.

No requirement concerning the duration of the Bulgarian citizen's residence in the country is set in order for the person to have the right to social assistance. What is important and sufficient is that the Bulgarian citizens should be residents in the country and should have their address registered in the respective town at the time of filing the application for being granted the social aid (*see infra* §5).

707. The family has the right to social assistance in case it consists of Bulgarian citizens. Within the meaning of the Social Assistance Law, a family denotes the spouses and their minor children or their adult children, where they are incapable of work and live within the same household.

708. Cohabitants are those persons who share the same home, and are connected either by relationship, such as brothers and sisters, or without any relationship, such as persons living together like spouses without being married to each other. Besides, cohabitants should be registered at the same address.

709. According to Article 2, paragraph 4 of the quoted law, foreigners, as being subjects of social assistance, include the following groups:

(a) Foreigners having a permit for permanent residence in the country in accordance with Article 23 of the Law on Foreigners in Bulgaria (promulgated in the OJ, No. 153 of 1998, amended).
(b) Foreigners who have been granted the right to asylum in accordance with Article 27 of the Constitution and Article 7 of the Law on Asylum and Refugees (promulgated in the OJ, No. 54 of 2002, amended).
(c) Foreigners who have been granted the status of refugees under Article 8 of the quoted Law on Asylum and Refugees.
(d) Foreigners who have been granted the humanitarian status under Article 9 of the quoted Law on Asylum and Refugees.

(e) Foreigners for whom that has been provided for in an international treaty, Bulgaria being a party thereto.

710. The right to social assistance of the specified subjects of law arises in the presence of certain prerequisites:

(1) Persons who have the right to social assistance should have found themselves in a situation of serious financial embarrassment. This situation finds its expression in their incapability to maintain themselves and to meet the bare necessities of life either on their own or with the help of those persons who are legally obliged to support them.
(2) They might have got into this situation for various reasons – age, health, family, social ones and others. These reasons are objective ones; that is, they are beyond the person's control.
(3) They should be in a situation of serious financial embarrassment. Incomes per person should be below the specified threshold of poverty. This means they should be receiving less than a specified minimum income. This is the so-called basic minimum income. It is a national generally established sum of money, which covers the most essential bare necessities of life. They include enough food, clothing and dwelling for the survival of the person depending on the social and economic development of the country (§1, item 1 of the quoted Law). The amount of the basic minimum income is determined by the Council of Ministers. It is periodically updated depending on the general economic state of the country: the price level, inflation and the like. Under the terms of the Currency Board in the country, it also depends on the arrangements periodically arrived at in the negotiations with the International Monetary Fund. As at 30 October 2021 the amount of the basic minimum income was BGN 75, that is about USD 48 (Article 1, paragraph 1, item 2 of Ordinance No. 30 of 29 March 2018, promulgated in the OJ, No. 24 of 2018). This amount is extremely insufficient.

    It is through Decree of the Council of Ministers No. 241 dated 24 September 2019 (promulgated in the OJ, No. 76 of 27 September 2019) that a new methodology was adopted for determining the poverty line per household member in the country. This methodology is used for designing the State policy in the field of incomes and standard of living, as well as for determining the social protection measures. Poverty line is used as a basis for specifying the State's financial support for the poor and for people with impairments. It is calculated each year on the grounds of a study entitled 'Statistics of Incomes and Living Conditions' carried out by the National Statistical Institute under the methodology of Eurostat. In the year 2020, the poverty line per household member is BGN 363 (promulgated in the OJ, No. 94 of the year 2019); in the year 2021, it was BGN 369 (promulgated in the OJ, No. 70 of the year 2021), and BGN 413 for the year 2022 (promulgated in the OJ, No. 69 of the year 2021). This amount is extremely insufficient.

Chapter 4. Benefits

711. Social assistance finds its expression in providing two basic types of benefits: (1) Social aids; (2) Social services (Article 2, paragraph 1 of the quoted Law). They have the common purpose of providing support to people in serious financial embarrassment in order to satisfy their most common necessities of life when it is impossible for them to do so through their personal earnings, personal property or with the help of the persons who are legally bound to support them. These two forms of social assistance have their important particularities concerning both their content (*see infra* I and II) and the procedure of granting them (*see infra* §§3–5).

§1. Social Aids

712. Social aid is benefit in money or in kind. There are three types:

(1) *Monthly ones.* They are payable monthly for the time the conditions are present for the supported persons, the head of the municipal social assistance office having determined the amount of the aid. The aid is equal to the difference between the actual income of the supported person and the basic minimum income specified under Ordinance No. 6 of 15 January 2009 (promulgated in the OJ, No. 7 of 29 March 2018). As of 1 March 2018 the basic minimum income is BGN 75 (*see supra* paragraph 710).
(2) *Aid for specific purposes.* This is granted for specific purposes to the persons in need thereof: to children of the family, who are pupils, at the beginning of the school year for buying textbooks, paying school fees and the like; in winter – for heating, and so on. This aid may also be granted in kind: coal supplies for heating, clothes and textbooks for pupils at the beginning of the school year, and so on. Aid for specific purposes may not be granted more than three times within a calendar year (Article 12, paragraph 1, item 2 of the quoted Law).
(3) *Lump sum aid.* This is granted for needs arising as a result of disease – for treatment, medicines and other similar (Article 12, paragraph 1, item 3 of the quoted Law).

713. The amount of the aid is determined depending on the need and purpose it is destined for and the available financial means for social assistance (*see infra*).

714. Social aid is payable from the State budget or the municipal one and also from the Social Assistance Fund at the Ministry of Labour and Social Policy. This fund is raised from subsidies of the State budget, donations, wills, fees for social service licences issued, and so on (Article 11 and Articles 24–30 of the quoted Law).

§2. Social Services

715. Social services consist of conducting certain activities, such as: preparing and delivering food at home for persons in need of social assistance (disabled, elderly people, etc.), feeding disabled and sick persons at their home, cleaning such persons' dwelling, washing and the like.

716. Social services are rendered by the municipal offices and by private legal entities and individuals in the due course stipulated under a regulation issued by the Minister of Labour and Social Policy. Legal entities and individuals entitled to perform this activity are licensed by the National Social Assistance Office at the Ministry of Labour and Social Policy (Articles 18–19 of the quoted Law).

717. Social services are rendered in return for payment of fees by the persons using them. The amount of the fees is determined by the Ministry of Labour and Social Policy. These fees are either paid in full by the persons using the services or paid partially by them, the other part being paid by the municipal social assistance offices, or paid in full by the municipal social assistance office, this being applied when the persons using the services are financially embarrassed and meet the requirements for receiving social assistance (Article 17 of the quoted Law).

Chapter 5. Conditions

718. The right to monthly social aid is enjoyed by the persons, families and cohabitants whose income for the preceding month is equal, higher or lower than the so-called differentiated minimum income (Article 9, paragraph 1 of the quoted Rules).

719. The differentiated minimum income is a derivative value of the basic minimum income that has already been considered (*see supra* §2). Its amount is determined by a coefficient versus the amount of the basic minimum income. This coefficient is differentiated; that is, it is specified in relation to the basic minimum income depending on the family status of the person or persons that the aid is granted to, as follows: for a person living alone – 1.0; for a disabled person who has had his/her capacity for work reduced by 50% or more – 1.2; for an orphan child or children – up to 1.2; for a person over the age of 75 living alone – 2.0; for spouses living together – 1.8; for a child younger than 18 – 0.9; for a cohabitant – 0.9 (Article 9 of the quoted Law). It is because of this differentiation of the minimum income of the separate person or separate persons versus the nationally established general basic minimum income that it is called differentiated minimum monthly income.

720. Apart from their income being below the differentiated minimum income as specified above, the separate categories of persons should meet several more requirements in order to be entitled to receive monthly aid:

(a) The dwelling the person lives in should be the only one he has.
(b) The person should not have registered a company under the Commercial Law.
(c) The person should not have receivables, deposits or securities exceeding BGN 500 per member of the family.
(d) The person should not be the owner of real or personal property that incomes can be derived from, for example, by letting it out, and so on (Article 10 of the quoted Rules).
(e) If the person is unemployed before reaching retirement age (61 years and 8 months in 2021 for women and 64 years and 4 months for men), he/she should have been registered at the job centre for at least six months before filing the application for social aid, and he/she should not have refused an appropriate job that has been offered him/her by the job centre. These requirements have the purpose of establishing that the person does not have personal incomes that would allow him to meet his/her bare necessities of life, his/her physical (biological) survival being endangered without these incomes.

721. Monthly aid is specified for the time the conditions are present for granting the financial aid. Yet, the unemployed persons who have not reached the retirement age may receive financial aid for a period not exceeding three years. It is supposed that, however long the unemployment might be, the person capable of work would find a job within three years' time. The right to monthly financial social assistance to unemployed persons is restored when a year expires after the suspension of this right. Monthly financial social assistance is resumed in the due course and under the terms provided for the initial granting of the aid.

722. Monthly financial social assistance is suspended if the grounds for granting it are removed.

Chapter 6. Procedure

723. Social aid is granted on the application for aid made by a mature person. This application is of a standard form and it should contain certain requisites. This brings about unification of the way the aid is applied for and of the data for judging about the presence of the required conditions.

The application is addressed to the head of the social assistance municipal office. Documents should be enclosed to the application concerning the financial, health and family status of the person applying for social aid (Article 26 of the quoted Rules).

724. Within twenty days after the application has been filed, the social assistance municipal office makes a so-called social enquiry. It consists in studying the documents filed and examining the truthfulness of the data thereof relating to the presence of the conditions for granting the social aid (*see supra* §4). On the grounds of this enquiry and the results thereof, the official of the social assistance office makes a proposal to the head of the social assistance municipal office suggesting either granting the social aid of a specified amount to the applicant or refusing it. On the grounds of this proposal and the data contained in the application the head of the Office takes the definitive decision. Through this decision, he either grants the social aid and specifies its amount, if the conditions thereof are present, or refuses granting thereof, if the conditions required under the law are not present (Articles 27–28 of the quoted Rules).

725. The decision of the head of the social assistance municipal office may be appealed by the person concerned to the Director of the Social Assistance Regional Directorate within fourteen days after the decision is announced (Article 13 of the quoted Law). If the person concerned is dissatisfied with the decision of the Director of the Social Assistance Regional Directorate, he/she may appeal against it within fourteen days to the administrative court. And the adjudication of the district court is subject to cassation appeal to the Supreme Administrative Court within fourteen days after the administrative court's adjudication is announced (Articles 145–178 and Articles 208–228 of the APC). The adjudication of the Supreme Administrative Court is a definitive one.

Part XI. Claims and Adjudication

Chapter 1. Claims

726. The social security benefits under Bulgarian social security law are not granted to the beneficiaries '*d'office*' on the initiative of the respective insurance institutions, but only on demand by the persons concerned. This demand is expressed by way of the written application filed by the person concerned with the respective insurance institution or with the body, to which the law has assigned the task of providing the social security benefits on behalf of the insurance body. The required documents should be enclosed to the application, these documents depending on the type of social security benefit and certifying the right and the amount of the due social security benefit as well as the length of time for which it should be due.

727. The course of filing the application, the required documents and the way of approaching the respective insurance body or another competent body depend on the nature of the insurance benefit – monthly children's allowances, indemnities and aid in cases of unemployment, indemnities in case of temporary incapacity for work or permanent incapacity for work pension, and so on. It is important to underline that the application and the required documents enclosed thereto are filed with the insurance body that has been empowered by the law to provide the respective insurance benefits. The body the application has been filed with examines whether the grounds are present according to the legal prerequisites in each specific case (depending on the nature and type of the respective insurance benefit). On the grounds thereof, the request is either complied with or declined. The insurance body is obliged to specify the amount of indemnity for each insured person in each specific case of occurrence of the insured risk.

728. The right to pension is not lost by limitation. Once the right to the respective type of pension has occurred, the legal prerequisites thereof being present, the beneficiary is entitled to exercise this right whenever he/she wishes to do so. For this purpose, he/she should file an application with the insurance body, the required documents being enclosed therein. If the person files the application within six months after the occurrence of his/her right to pension, the latter is granted from the date the right to pension has occurred. If the application is filed later than six months from the date of occurrence of the right to pension, the pension is granted from the date of filing the application (Article 94, paragraph 1 of the SIC).

729. The activities connected with the requests of the insured persons concerning insurance benefits, specifying the amount thereof, refusing to comply with the request, that is declining to comply with the request, constitute jurisdictional activity carried out by administrative bodies: by the territorial bodies of the NII – for the pensions and for indemnities against temporary incapacity for work. This activity is carried out by the territorial bodies of the NII. This activity is jurisdictional because it consists of examining the presence of the insured persons' subjective insurance rights and complying therewith where the prerequisites provided for by the law are present, or declining it where these prerequisites are absent. Legal disputes arise in this activity. The procedure of consideration thereof is regulated under Chapter 8 'Disputes' of the SIC (Articles 117–120).

730. Written documents are enclosed with the application. These are documents supporting the demand of the concerned person or challenging the refusal of the competent body or its decision concerning the determination or change in the amount of the respective insurance benefit or proving its being unlawful. The type of these documents and the nature thereof depends on the disputed right to the respective type of insurance benefit. It is important to stress that the evidence may only be in writing and the proceedings for considering the complaint are closed ones. This means that the complaint is considered without announcing a session of the body the complaint is addressed to – the social security regional department, in this case, and without calling the claimant to present his/her case and without interrogation of witnesses and assessors or considering other evidence, and so on.

731. Upon the request of the person concerned, and depending on the type of insurance payment and the insurance for which the payment is due (unemployment indemnity, or temporary incapacity for work indemnity, pension, etc.), the respective competent official of the territorial department of the NII who is in charge of the specific type of insurance renders his/her decision. This official is designated by the Head of the department. The act through which the said official renders his/her decision is called 'an order'. The order is made known to the person concerned.

732. The persons concerned are entitled to appeal against decisions declining the request or ones of improper calculation of the amount of pensions, or ones changing the amount of pensions, pecuniary indemnities, aid, or other insurance payments. These complaints are addressed to the head of the respective territorial department of the NII – the respective social security regional department – within fourteen days following the receipt thereof, or within three months if a pension order is concerned (Article 117, paragraph 2 of the SIC).

733. The decision on the complaint is taken by the head of the territorial department of the NII. He/she takes this decision after studying the complaint and considering the arguments it contains and the written evidence enclosed to the complaint in support thereof. Through this decision, the head of the territorial department of the NII may totally or partially set aside or change the appealed order concerning its grounds and the amount of the insurance benefits. In both these cases, he/she decides on the merits of the case. The head of the social security regional department is obliged to rule upon the complaint within one month after it has been filed. The decision is announced to the person concerned within seven days after it has been rendered (Article 117, paragraph 3 of the quoted Code).

734. As for the disputes arising in connection with the implementation of mandatory health insurance, they have already been considered in the preceding exposition, to which we are making a renvoi (*see supra* Part III, Chapter 5, §3).

Chapter 2. Adjudication

735. The decision of the head of the territorial department of the NII (*see supra* Chapter 1) may be appealed to the district court within fourteen days after it has been announced to the person concerned (Article 118 of the quoted Code). The appeal is filed through the head of the territorial department of the NII. He/she is obliged to send it to the court within seven days. The district court hears the case in the due course laid down under the APC.

736. The appeal against the decisions of the head of the territorial department of the NII does not suspend the execution thereof. The court may suspend only the execution of the collection of amounts under records of deficit (Article 117, paragraph 1, item 2'c' of the SIC) where the request for suspension has been made concurrently with filing the appeal, and the court has rendered its decision thereupon within seven days. The refusal of the court to suspend the execution is not subject to appeal (Article 118'a', paragraphs 2 and 3 of the SIC).

737. The adjudication of the district court is subject to cassation appeal in the due course under the APC (Article 119 of the SIC). The complaint is lodged with the district court, and its adjudication may be appealed within fourteen days of the date it is announced that the adjudication of the district court and the motives thereto have been made out. The case is heard at an open session by a jury consisting of three judges and with the involvement of the public prosecutor.

738. The Supreme Administrative Court may wholly or partially set aside the repealed adjudication or may change it. When it wholly or partially sets aside the adjudication of the district court because of incongruity with the law or because of lack of grounds, it decides on the merits of the case. And when it sets aside the adjudication because of substantial breach of procedural rules, it sends the case to be reviewed by another jury of the same court. The Supreme Administrative Court acts in the same way when setting aside the adjudication of the district court that has already been appealed against twice.

739. All papers and documents that are filed, issued or made in connection with insurance benefits and the payment thereof are exempt from taxation (Article 120, paragraph 1 of the SIC).

If the appeal is upheld, the appellant is entitled to receive the expenses he/she has made and the attorney fee he/she has paid in proportion to the upheld part (Article 120, paragraph 2 of the SIC).

740. The pecuniary benefits payable from social security as indemnities and aid for temporary incapacity for work, pensions for permanent incapacity for work and other similar are exempt from taxation, postage and other fees (Article 12, paragraph 1, item 4 of the Law on Taxation of Individuals). The beneficiaries receive these benefits in their full amount as determined under the law on the respective insurance benefit.

741. The payment of insurance benefits is under special protection. The purpose thereof is to guarantee their being paid at an amount, which is as close as possible to their nominal amount determined by the insurance body pursuant to the requirements of the law. This protection is based, on the one hand, on the attitude of the legislator according to which the insurance benefit is paid to the insured persons for the time they are in a vulnerable state (in a state of temporary or permanent incapacity for work, accompanied by an increase in their expenses or in a state of being unemployed, etc.), and on the other hand, on the fact that insurance benefit is often the only source of financial means for the insured person's and his/her family members' means of livelihood. That is why no distress may be levied on an insurance benefit (pension, etc.) whose amount is below the minimum monthly wage except for alimony or for overpaid pension or liabilities resulting from crimes, injuries or unauthorized financial expenditures. Should the amount of the insurance benefit exceed the amount of the minimum monthly wage established in the country, distress may be levied according to the general rules for compulsory execution set out under Article 341 of the Civil Procedure Code – depending on the amount of the pensions and the other insurance benefits and on the family status of the beneficiary and the members of the family who are his/her dependants.

742. The total amount of deductions from insured person's benefit may not exceed the limits established in Article 446 of the Civil Procedure Code. These limits are the following:

(a) if the insured person receives a monthly remuneration of an amount between the minimum monthly salary (BGN 650) and the double amount of the minimum monthly salary, the limit is one-third if he/she has no children, or one-fourth if he/she has children and provides them with means of subsistence;
(b) if the insured person receives a monthly remuneration of an amount between the double amount of the minimum monthly salary and the fourfold amount of the minimum monthly salary, the limit is one-half if he/she has no children, or one-third if he/she has children and provides them with means of subsistence;
(c) if the insured person receives a monthly remuneration exceeding the fourfold amount of the minimum monthly salary, the limit is the amount exceeding the double amount of the minimum monthly salary if he/she has no children, or the amount exceeding two and a half times the amount of the minimum monthly salary if he/she has children and provides them with means of subsistence.
The limitations specified above take into consideration the presence or absence of children that the insured person provides with means of subsistence. However, these limitations do not concern the obligations regarding the subsistence itself. In these cases, the subsistence is adjudged in its full amount.

743. The main concern of the legislation has been to secure a current monthly income for the insured person, which does not substantially differ from his/her normal income. The permitted maximum extent of deductions has been established by using two criteria which have a major social significance. The limit is lower for a debtor who is married or is a widower (widow) with children, and higher for a debtor who is unmarried (Article 446, paragraph 1(a)–(c) of the Civil Procedure

Code). The ruling of Article 446, paragraph 1 of the Civil Procedure Code is imperative and a debtor's renunciation of the protection given by it is null and void (Article 447 of the Civil Procedure Code). In this way, the law takes the defence of the insured person's benefit into its own hands, and, taking into account the high social interest of its actual receipt by the insured person, does not even allow the latter the subjective right to renounce it.[86]

744. Those disputes connected with the performance of the contracts between the NHIPCDO, the RHIPCDO and the providers of healthcare under mandatory health insurance, which cannot be settled through arbitration (*see supra* Part III, Chapter 5, §3) are settled in accordance with the general court procedure (Article 80 of the HIL).

86. Zh. Stalev, Bulgarsko grajdansko prozessualno pravo [*Bulgarian Civil Procedure Law*] 1023–1026 (Ciela Publishing House 9th ed. 2012).

Selected Bibliography

§1. Legislation

Social Insurance Code, 24th edition, Pocket edition series. Sofia: Sibi Publishing House, 2016.

Health Insurance Law, 17th edition, Pocket edition series. Sofia: Sibi Publishing House, 2016.

Sozialno ossigouriavane 2021. *Avtorski kolektiv* [*Social Security 2016*]. Sofia: Labour and Law Publishing House, 2021.

§2. Judicial Decisions

Spisanie. *Administrativno pravossadie* [*Administrative Justice Review*]. Sofia: Supreme Administrative Court of the Republic of Bulgaria, since 1998.

Spisanie. *Juridicheski Sviat* [*Juridical World Review*]. Sofia: Sibi Publishing House, since 1999.

§3. Specialized Monographs

Guenova, Y. *Ossigurenite litsa v Darjavnoto obshtestveno ossiguriavane* [*Persons Insured in State Social Insurance*]. Sofia: Ciela Publishing House, 2010.

Guevrenova, N. *Specialna zakrila na rabotnicite i slujitelite s namalena rabotospossobnost* [*Special Protection of Workers and Employees with Reduced Capacity for Work*]. Sofia: Sibi Publishing House, 2013.

Ianoulov, I. *Obshtestveno ossigouriavane pri kapitalizma i socializma* [*Social Security under Capitalism and Socialism*]. Sofia: Publishing House of the Bulgarian Academy of Sciences, 1964.

Kazarov, I. *Obshtestveno ossigouriavane na rabotnizite i sloujitelite* [*Social Security of the Employees*]. Sofia: Science and Art Publishing House, 1957.

Mingov, E. *Obezshtetenia za vremenna nerabotospossobnost* [*Indemnities on Temporary Incapacity for Work*]. Sofia: Sibi Publishing House, 2003.

Mrachkov, V. *Balgarskoto troudovo zakonodatelstvo i mejdounarodnite troudovi konvencii i preporaki* [*Bulgarian Labour Legislation and International Labour Conventions and Recommendations*]. Sofia: Science and Art Publishing House, 1978.

Mrachkov, V. 'Mejdounarodni pravni normi v oblastta na obshtestvenoto ossigouriavane i balgarskoto ossigouritelno zakonodatelstvo' ['International Standards in the Field of Social Security and the Bulgarian Social Security

Legislation']. In *Studies on International Law*, vol. IV. Sofia: Publishing House of the Bulgarian Academy of Sciences, 1989.
Mrachkov, V. *Labour Law –Bulgaria,* Suppl. … … .., *International Encyclopaedia of Laws*. The Hague: Kluwer Law International, February 2017.
Mrachkov, V. et al. *Comments on the Code of Mandatory Social Security*. Sofia: Labour and Law Publishing House, 2000.
Mrachkov, V. *Mejdounarodno troudovo pravo* [*International Labour Law*]. Sofia: Sibi Publishing House, 2000.
Mrachkov, V. *Ossigouritelno pravo* [*Social Security Law*]. 7th edn. Sofia: Sibi Publishing House, 2019.
Mrachkov, V. *Sotsialni prava na balgarskite grajdani* [*Social Rights of Bulgarian Citizens*]. Sofia: Ciela Publishing House, 2020.
Radoilski, L. *Troudovo pravo na Narodna Republika Bulgaria* [*Labour Law of the People's Republic of Bulgaria*]. Sofia: Science and Art Publishing House, 1957.
La sécurité sociale et la primauté du droit, BIT, Genève, 2011
Sredkova, Kr. *Ossigouritelno pravo* [*Social Security Law*]. 5th edn. Sofia: Sibi Publishing House, 2016.
Vassilev, A. *Obezshtetenia po troudovoto pravootnoshenie* [*Employment Relationship Indemnities*]. Sofia: Sibi Publishing House, 1997.

Index

The numbers here refer to paragraph numbers.

Index

www.ingramcontent.com/pod-product-compliance
Ingram Content Group UK Ltd.
Pitfield, Milton Keynes, MK11 3LW, UK
UKHW020138290926
15471UKWH00003B/571

9 789403 507569